AF498880

Harold Spender

The Prime Minister

e-artnow 2024

Harold Spender

The Prime Minister

e-artnow, 2024
Contact: eartnow.info@gmail.com

ISBN: 978-80-273-8836-3

Contents

CHAPTER I

CHILDHOOD

"When that I was and a little tiny boy,
With hey, ho, the wind and the rain."
Shakespeare's Twelfth Night, Act v, Sc. i.

Every school-child is familiar with that striking shape taken by North Wales on the map of Britain, so like to a human being pointing with outstretched arm down St. George's Channel towards the Atlantic. In that shape Anglesey is the head, and Carnarvonshire is the pointed arm. On the lower side of the arm, towards the hollow of the armpit, there lie a village and two small towns. Naming from west to east they are Llanystumdwy, Criccieth, and Portmadoc.

In these three places and in the country around them the childhood and youth of David Lloyd George was entirely spent. It was there that he was trained and educated, and there that his mind first formed vivid impressions of the universe-there, on the sea-limits of Wales between the mountains and the ocean.

It is a fertile country, watered by streams from the mountains and showers from the Irish Channel, a country of deep grasses and rich woods right up to the foot of the mountains and down to the verge of the sea. From every raised point you obtain wide-stretching views. Facing you along the south-eastern horizon are the hills of Merionethshire, often shrouded in sea-mist, but on good days clear to the utmost detail of field and hedgerow. Still farther away, in the very best weather, can sometimes be seen even the outline of St. David's Head and of the Pembrokeshire hills. Nearer home, the great stretch of Cardigan Bay sweeps round to the east in many a bend and fold of the coast. From above Criccieth you can see the famous castle of Harlech and the golden glitter of the sands at Barmouth, though you cannot hear the "moaning of the bar." Taking it all in all, there are few finer prospects along the immense and varied sea-board of these islands.

Turn from the sea and look northwards; and you will gain glorious glimpses of the great piled mountains of the Snowdon group, sometimes hidden in cloud, sometimes clear to every wrinkle of their rugged outlines. These are "Eyri" —the "Eagle Rocks" —black in storm, blue and green in the sunshine, purple and crimson in the sunset. There is no mere prettiness in these mighty views, no soft luxury of Italian backgrounds, and yet no barren terrors of arctic solitudes. On all sides there is majesty and power-the power of the height and the storm, the majesty of the winds and the deeps.

Of these three places in which Mr. Lloyd George spent his childhood and youth, Portmadoc is the business town, Criccieth is the pleasure resort, and Llanystumdwy is the village. Portmadoc, with its straight-set streets of little grey houses, speaks of money and affairs; Criccieth is a little watering-place of lodging-houses and villas prettily placed in the innermost bend of Cardigan Bay; Llanystumdwy is just a little Welsh village drawn back from the sea and cosily hidden away in the woods, astride a little mountain river which hurries down to the sea with many a rippling murmur and many a gleam of white foam on its brown waters.

It was to this little village of Llanystumdwy-Welsh of the Welsh in name, situation, and tradition-that David Lloyd George was brought at the age of a year and a half.

Up to that time, indeed, life had not gone very well with the young child. For his father, William George, had just died in the prime of his life, at forty-four years of age. Mrs. William George, with David and his elder sister Mary, had been left but scantily provided to face an unsmiling world.

David's father, William George, was an able, earnest man, very sociable, full of fun and humour, and very happy in his home life. Brought up on a prosperous farm in South Wales, he could easily have followed smoothly and serenely in the steps of his thriving forefathers. For there, on that fertile coast, his father and grandfather had farmed well and fared sumptuously, holding their heads high.[1]

But William George was not content with farming. Early in life he fell in love with books and the things of the mind; and through his short life he wandered —a true "scholar-gipsy" —from school to school, trying to kindle the youth of Wales to the passion for knowledge in those early difficult days before the Education Acts had come to make the schoolmaster a power in the land. He taught in London and Liverpool; he opened a grammar-school of his own in Haverfordwest; he served the Free Churches and the Unitarians-any and all who felt the fire of knowledge and shared his passion to extend its power. He became the friend of that great, pure spirit, Henry Martineau[2] —a fact alone sufficient to prove his high quality.

The fire of the schoolmaster's zeal burnt him up. He was never a strong man; and a life of excessive labour had exhausted him before his time. He resolved to lay down his ferule and return to the land of his forefathers. As his last teaching task, he took a temporary headmastership at Manchester and lodged in a little house in York Place, off Oxford Road. A few years before, when teaching at Pwllheli, he had loved and wedded Elizabeth, the daughter of a Baptist minister, David Lloyd, who preached and ministered in Criccieth and the village of Llanystumdwy.

With fair skin and a wealth of dark hair, Mrs. William George was in youth and early womanhood a comely and fascinating woman. I saw her only in later life; and, though sorrows and trials had told on her frail frame, her troubles had only added to the fine charm and spirituality of her character. "Happy he with such a mother!" She proved to William George a capital housewife, and helped him to save enough to leave to her a small property even out of their hard-earned savings.

To this couple had already been born the daughter Mary. Now, on January 17th, 1863, a son was born also and named David, after his two grandfathers-David George and David Lloyd. His admiring father recorded at the time that the little David was a "sturdy, healthy little fellow" with curly hair. At any rate, his father thought so; and thus, as a last flash of happiness to his dying father, little David came into the world.

By such a chance twist of events, Manchester can claim to be the birthplace of David Lloyd George.

Before he went to Manchester, William George had already decided to give up schoolmastering; and soon after David's birth, towards the end of 1863, he left Manchester and entered into occupation of a small farm named Bwlford, about four miles from Haverfordwest in Pembrokeshire.

It was close to the home of his fathers.

But this change came too late to save his life. He was already a tired man, and he was not equal to the strain of outdoor labour. On June 7th, 1864, he died of pneumonia, due to a chill caught in gardening.

Thus little David was left fatherless before he had lived eighteen months on the earth; and on the threshold of life he was robbed of the influence which ought to be the strongest prop and stay of a young boy's life. His father left him before the age of memory. Yet memory is a strange thing; for when Mr. Lloyd George revisited the home of his infancy some few years ago, he recalled instantly, with surprising accuracy, some features of his father's farm.[3]

The sudden death of William George left David's mother with two small children on her hands, and another on the way to this vale of tears. The family inheritance ought to have left her in comparative security to bring up this family well. But William George, with that large-hearted generosity which had always characterised him, had allowed the family patrimony which devolved on him as heir-at-law to be enjoyed by others whom he thought to be in greater need than himself. Such savings as they had put together from a schoolmaster's salary could not suffice to bring up a family in comfort or security. Thus to the grief of her husband's death there was added for Mrs. William George a grave and acute anxiety for the upbringing of her children. It looked as if that little family would be driven into that wilderness of poverty which is no easy dwelling-place in these islands.

But far away up in Carnarvonshire, in that little Welsh village which was her birthplace, Mrs. William George had a brother named Richard Lloyd.[4] He was not at all like the wealthy godfather of the storybooks. He was not by any means rich or prosperous. He was just the village bootmaker at a time when boots were still made in villages. True, he was also, like his father before him, a preacher and a minister. But he possessed no rich living or easy sinecure; on the contrary, like Paul the tent-maker, he received no penny of pay for either his preaching or his ministry. He belonged to a religious community classed with the Baptists and called the "Disciples of Christ," who held a belief, unpopular in ecclesiastical circles, that a man ought to preach the Gospel of Christ and feed His flock without pay or reward.[5]

In that simple faith he then preached and taught in the plain, grey little chapel above Criccieth and baptized in the little green basin of fresh spring water ever renewed by the running stream.

Yet this preaching bootmaker did not seem to have suffered seriously in his Christianity by this strange and rare distaste for endowment. If it be still, as an Apostle once thought, "true religion and undefiled" to "visit the widow and the fatherless," Richard Lloyd went straight to the mark. For on receiving his sister's tragic news he put down his tools, left his workshop, and started out to help his bereaved relations. There was no railway from Criccieth to Carnarvon in those days; so for some twenty miles he journeyed on foot. Then from Carnarvon he took the train to Haverfordwest, and joined his widowed sister on her farm, a true friend and comforter. He stayed for some months helping her with the sale of her farm-lease and her stock. Then he took back the mother and the two children, Mary and David, to his own little home at Llanystumdwy. That is a plain record of a simple and heroic act.

There, in that little Welsh mountain village, without any show or fuss, the sister and her children became part of Richard Lloyd's home. A few months later the third child was born posthumously—a second boy, William George. The little stranger was welcomed in that simple, hospitable home.

So for the next twelve years the little family lived and throve in the bootmaker's cottage at Llanystumdwy; and there, in those village surroundings, little David grew from infancy to manhood.

Let us see what the surroundings were.

The little cottage stands to-day for all the world to visit-two-storied, four-roomed, creepered, slate-roofed; then called "Highgate," now "Rose Cottage"—a sweet-smelling name. The front door opens on to the living-room—a warm, cosy chamber with a raftered ceiling, a big fireplace, and a floor of worn slate-slabs. It was in this room that the family had their meals and gathered in the evenings when the uncle read and talked to them. It was there that he cheered and rebuked those growing boys.

You step round a low screen into a smaller room, once a storeroom for leather, but in those years used as the boys' study. Here the boys were "interned" during the daily hours of home work; for Uncle Lloyd was as strict as he was kind.

Between the two rooms a small cottage staircase mounts to the bedrooms-now three, in those days two. The boys slept in the little front room looking over the street.

Descend again and pass through the back door. You pass into a fair-sized cottage garden, with several fruit-trees—apple, plum, and gooseberry. Every inch of the soil is filled with vegetables. There are traces of an old pigsty that once stood against the cottage wall. Move a few steps to your left, and you can enter a little stone building that gives the impression of having been a single-roomed cottage. It is now like a capacious cave. This was Richard Lloyd's workshop. There is a large fireplace in the corner near the garden. On the side nearer the road is a space where the benches of Richard Lloyd's workmen ran along the wall by the small window. There by the door is the little hole in the wall where Richard Lloyd kept his papers and into which the boys pushed their books. It looks like an old spy-hole, now blocked at the farther end.

This place was not merely a workshop. It was known as "the village Parliament." Here the "village Hampdens" poured out their grievances; hither the evicted farmers and underpaid labourers came to consult the village oracle. On wet days the place was crowded. For bootmakers are notorious storm-centres both in town and country; and this bootmaker was a prophet and priest as well.

It was always both the refuge and the guard-room of the village children. There, against the corner, looking into the sad grey wall, stood the children who had misbehaved, waiting for Richard Lloyd's kindly word of release. Good boys would often bring bad boys to be punished; and the good boys did not always get off without a clearance of soul. Who could tell whether "Uncle Lloyd" was going to be stern or soft? It was always a fascinating mystery for children-that workshop; in any case, there were always the bootmakers' tools to finger and handle if you were lucky. The children knew that Uncle Lloyd found it very hard to refuse a thread; and what more fascinating than beeswax? Sticky, black, and smelly! But put out your hand for the knife-then ten to one he would see you-and instantly the stern look would come into his grey eyes, his eyebrows would contract, and he would cry in the voice which thrilled you —"No! No! Not that! Not that!"

Pass out of this little crumbling old building, with the slates now sagging down as if the whole thing might collapse, but for the one upright beam which now supports the roof, and take a few steps still to your left along the stone footpath. There you find the garden divided from the street only by a low wall of rubble. Over that wall, David-like that other David, the sweet-singing psalmist of Israel[6] would often leap, and head across the village on some boyish adventure.

In these buildings the Lloyds had lived for several generations. There is still (1920) living in the village of Llanystumdwy an old tailor of ninety-five years of age whose chief pride it is that he made the first pair of trousers for the Prime Minister of England. The old man can remember David Lloyd, the grandfather of the Prime Minister, cutting leather in the little room on the right of the entrance door of the cottage. He can remember this friend and neighbour, who was also a minister and preacher, breaking forth into singing verse when moved, as those bardic preachers of Wales are still wont to do.[7] Bobby Jones, the son of this old tailor, was one of David's intimate comrades of boybood; and they two carved their names together on the trees in the woods and on the village bridge.

Many legends have already grown round Richard Lloyd's cottage and the life lived in it. There is no need to exaggerate the poverty of that home. Richard Lloyd was a master bootmaker and always employed at least two hands. He must have earned a good weekly sum. His chief fault was that he could not collect his money. It was somewhat distressing to Mrs. William George to hear her brother serenely say to customers: "I can wait-any time will do." She, being a woman, well knew that in the matter of collecting debts there is no time like the present.

At any rate, all that he had was theirs. They were fed on simple fare-more oats and barley, as Mr. Lloyd George has since told us, than wheat-but they were well fed. Eggs were cheap in the village, and the garden was full of vegetables. There were doubtless hard times. There was little meat-perhaps they were none the worse for that. But these children were nevertheless always held up in school as models of neatness and cleanliness. There was little to spare for pleasure. There was no easy flow of "pocket-money" for these boys. But they possessed the heart of the whole matter. They loved one another, and they were happy. "It was a little paradise," says one who stayed there often,[8] and when asked to explain she adds: "there was such high talk."

"Plain living and high thinking," was the note of that little home. Here, indeed, was —

"Fearful innocence,

And pure religion, breathing household laws."

There was also much kindness and humanity. Richard Lloyd could not for long be a stern uncle. The pictures handed down to us are Goldsmithian in their quaint and simple charm-the little David sitting on one of his uncle's knees and punctuating his infant periods by beating his fist on the other; or, in later years, wheedling his uncle with some clever boyish defence of an indefensible prank; or listening for long hours, with open mouth and eyes, to the "deep sighing of the poor," as the farmers and labourers from all the district round poured their tales of woe into the ears of the gentle village seer.

I saw much of Richard Lloyd at a later time. He was a man who always lived on the heights of thought and feeling; he was one of nature's great men to whom goodness was a delight: he was one of God's crusaders. Tall and bearded, but with a clean-shaven mouth and dark eyebrows, he was a man of singular dignity and strength both in bearing and expression. It is difficult to describe the impression of mingled strength and tenderness which he gave. His face had some of the vigour of the eagle; and yet with it all his voice had some of the softness of the dove. He loved children with all the strength of his large, warm heart; and yet he was never weak with them, but sometimes very stern, with the strength of those who can be "cruel only to be kind."

"He was the most selfless man I ever knew," is the deliberate verdict of one of his foster children to-day. "Even in illness he never spoke of himself. It was painful to him even to think of himself."

Such was the high influence that filled that little cottage and made it a fit nursery for a ruler of men. From the moment that Richard Lloyd took over the guardianship of his sister's bereaved family he gave to the task all his resources of money, love, and wisdom. He was not one of those who know limits to giving —

"Give all thou canst; high Heaven rejects the lore

Of nicely calculated less or more."

He laboured for these children as if they had been his own. If money was spared it was only to save it for their better training in later years.

The only available school at that time in Llandystumdwy was the National School provided by the Established Church of England and Wales; and to that school the children had to go. Many years afterwards, when the House of Commons was in the midst of one of its chronic wrangles over religious education, Mr. Lloyd George startled the High Churchmen by putting himself forward as a specimen of their chosen education. He was well within the letter of the fact; but I doubt whether the Llanystumdwy Voluntary School at that time could be called an average Church School; for the head master of the school —a Welshman named David Evans-was more than an average schoolmaster.[9] He was a good "scholar" and mathematician, and he taught well. He gave the young boys that thorough grounding in the elements of knowledge which is really a better gift for the young than all the frills of a more dainty schooling. Richard Lloyd, at any rate, showed his confidenec in this teaching by keeping the boys on at school for two years beyond the ordinary limited time. From twelve to fourteen years of age David Lloyd George worked with a small group of boys also still remaining on at school in what would now be called an "Ex VIIth" standard. These boys carried their mathematics on as far as trigonometry, learned the elements of Latin, and were encouraged to read widely. David Evans kept a close eye on these studies, and Richard Lloyd found the fees well worth his while.

I have talked to one of the boys[10] who stayed on at school with David Lloyd George, and his impressions of that time are still very vivid. His recollection is that David Lloyd George was the quickest boy of this little group. David could do twice as much work as any other boy in the same time. He still remembers the envy and annoyance which this habit used to cause among David's companions. But little David was especially quick at higher mathematics. "He was through trigonometry," says this witness, "by the time we started." He was very rapid at mental arithmetic.

But perhaps the most active part of his growth came outside his school life. Most of the other boys of their age had left school and gone out to work, and those few picked ones that remained were a small company and hardly numerous enough for games on a large scale. Thus it was that they took to walking instead of play; and during these walks David began to develop that habit of keen discussion which he has loved throughout his life. His favourite subjects in those days were Baptism and Tithe. Among the little company were two pupil-teachers who were a little older than the boys themselves. Both of these teachers were destined for the

Church; one of them became a rector and another became a canon of St. David's.[11] We can imagine the debates that took place within this little company of keen, honest, ardent youths!

Thus, in this varied life of work and play, the young David grew from infancy to youth, there in that distant little Welsh village, between the mountains and the sea.

---

[1] Here is his pedigree on the paternal side:
William George (farmer) and his wife (lived to 80 and 90 years respectively)
|
David George (farmer, died at 33)
|
William George (schoolmaster, died at 44)
|
David Lloyd George.

[2] A large engraving of Dr. Henry Martineau, signed by himself and set in a massive oak frame, is one of the treasured family heirlooms to-day.

[3] He noticed that a passage had been widened, and he asked after a green gate which was found to have been removed. He can still remember his sister putting stones under the gate to prevent the men from coming to take away his father's goods.

[4] At this time thirty years of age. Born in July 1834.

[5] The movement had its origin in one of those great efforts after a return to simple Christianity which have from time to time stirred the surface of the Welsh Churches. This was led by Mr. J. R. Jones of Ramoth, who died in 1822. David Lloyd became one of its elders, and was largely influenced by the writings of the Campbells. The Campbellites in the United States still number some 2,000,000.

[6] See Psalm xviii. verse 29.

[7] He was ordained on May 20th, 1828, in the Baptist chapel at Criccieth and died in 1839. This singing habit it known as "hwyl."

[8] Miss Jones, a niece of Richard Lloyd.

[9] See Mr. Lloyd George's charming sketch of the schoolmaster in his speech at Llanystumdwy on September 8th, 1917: "He had a genius for teaching."

[10] Mr. William Williams, who occupies a farm near Llanystumdwy.

[11] The Rev. Owen Owens and Canon Camber-Williams of St. David's.

MR. WILLIAM GEORGE,
THE FATHER OF DAVID LLOYD GEORGE.

"HIGHGATE" NOW "BOSE COTTAGE" —THE COTTAGE AT
LLANYSTUMDWY WHERE MR. LLOYD GEORGE
WAS BROUGHT UP AS A BOY.

CHAPTER II

SCHOOL DAYS

"Ye Presences of Nature in the sky
    And on the earth! Ye visions of the hills
    And Souls of lonely places! can I think
    A vulgar hope was yours when ye employed
    Such ministry?"
Wordsworth's Prelude.

The training of a little Welsh Nonconformist child in a village Church School must lead either to submission or to revolt. In most cases it leads to submission. In this case it led to revolt. That is what makes the story of David Lloyd George worth telling.

To subject children of one faith to the religious discipline of another in a school subsidised by the State was, and still is, part of the ordinary machinery of life in this island; and it is generally acquiesced in by children, who as a rule suffer from a great fear of varying from their kind.

But in this case there were influences behind the boy which suggested the thought of injustice; and there is no more flaming thought in the mind of a young child. There was the uncle in the workshop, type of the heroic and the divine; he was against the system, and did not hesitate to say so in the presence of the boys. Then there was the village blacksmith, whose "smithy," hard by the school, was a sort of village cave of Adullam; he said so between the clang of the hammer on the reverberant anvil, and what he said was law. No wonder that there stirred in the boy's mind the working wonder whether he should really submit.

There was, for instance, the yearly visit of the rector, the squire, and the gentry, in full feudal state, to hear the replies to the Church Catechism —a sort of annual homage to the powers that were, not unusual in village schools.

Then there was the visit of the Bishop, who was willing to confirm as many children, Baptist or otherwise, as the rector would present for him to lay hands on.

Now David admired his schoolmaster and worked hard and steadily in the only school accessible to him. But when the Church tried to turn his necessity to such uses he remembered that he was a Nonconformist child born of Nonconformist parents. Then he became a rebel.

The tales of these school revolts have already become part of the heroic legends of Wales. They have been told in many forms. I will try to tell the simple facts as gathered from contemporary witnesses and comrades.

The most famous revolt occurred over the Catechism. We can recapture the scene. There were the three village authorities-the Squire, the Rector, and the Schoolmaster, together with the Diocesan Inspector and a bevy of fair ladies-standing in front of the little class of Welsh children in the grey little building, expecting nothing but meekness and docility. Nothing fierce about these visitors, you may be sure-rather an attitude of smiling expectancy as they waited to hear the children repeat in chorus the comforting assertion that they were ready to order themselves "lowly and reverently" to all their "betters."

But look at the children. Their eyes look strangely bright and their lips are drawn together. There have been many whisperings on the way to school, and much flitting to and fro of the small Scotch cap with the ribbons that David wore. Some look flushed; others look grave and pale. Fear battles against resolve. Something big is struggling in those little minds.

The rector puts his questions; the squire affably awaits the reply; the schoolmaster looks stern. Little David looks unusually innocent.

There is a dead silence.

The rector raises his eyebrows and repeats the question:

"What is thy duty towards thy neighbour?"

Still, a dead silence.

And so the question is passed from child to child. The little heads are shaken. The little faces grow paler and paler. But still silence.

The rector turns to the schoolmaster questioningly. The schoolmaster is white with vexation. The squire smiles indulgently. Little David looks more innocent than ever.

But farther along the line, behind his little desk, sits a boy with a little troubled, anxious face, looking as if he were the centre of guilt in that little company. He watches with growing trouble the ashen face of the schoolmaster; for he loves his master with all his soul, and he cannot bear to see him suffer. For this is little William George —a boy of milder, quieter temperament, given to love his enemies; and when his much-distressed head master appeals to the children to recite the Apostles' Creed it is William George who suddenly breaks the silence with a strident "I believe," and all but two or three "infant" Die-hards join in the recital that followed. The schoolmaster turns to the class with a flush of pleasure; the rector smiles —"good boys" —the squire nods approvingly; and the scene ends as suddenly as it began.

So much for the Catechism revolt. The second revolt arose over the Church's claim to "confirm."[12]

It was little William Williams, one of David's intimates, who had been selected as a capture for the Bishop. His father, a Calvinistic Methodist, but with a kindly heart for the great, had surrendered the lad to the rector. William had been duly prepared and instructed. Confirmation day had arrived. William Williams, shining with soap, smart in his best clothes, was already on the road-walking to school to join the church boys. There the little catechumens, all duly marshalled, were waiting to be marched off to the church.

But on the way to school it was fated that William Williams should meet David Lloyd George. Seeing his friend so smart, David naturally asked what he was going to do. Williams told him. David's eyes flashed; his voice rang out. He argued; he persuaded; he urged. Not that! Not that! His winged words went home. In a few moments William Williams, aged fourteen, felt thoroughly ashamed of himself. His best clothes and his clean collar became garments of shame. He was willing to follow David anywhere.

The two boys managed to get out into the school-yard; and there, in the twinkling of an eye, they were over the wall. They hid behind the hedge. In a few moments out came the schoolmaster, hurried and eager; he could see no one in sight. He blew his whistle once, twice, and yet again. There was no reply. Time pressed. The Bishop could not be kept waiting. There was nothing for it but to go back and fetch the others.

So David and William Williams stood and watched while the little procession of children, with their nicely washed faces, walked across the school-yard to the church.

Then, when all had passed by, out came the two rebels. Without a pause they jumped over the wall, leapt into the road, and made for Richard Lloyd's workshop. Instantly, when he had heard their story, the bootmaker dropped his last and patted the boys on the back. "Well done, my boys!" he cried; "well done!"

I will suggest to any Anglican reader that he should, for the moment, try to look at the situation from the point of view of his Nonconformist neighbour. Suppose that he, an Anglican parent, were obliged by law to send his boy to a Baptist School because no other school existed in his village. Suppose then that the Baptist minister took advantage of this situation to baptize the boy up to the neck in the village stream. What would the Anglican parent do? Why, probably something much more violent than either uncle Lloyd or nephew David.

Yet the spirit of rebellion is rare, and the act is slow. Doubtless there were other boys in that school whose hearts waxed hot within them, and other parents whose blood boiled. But they did nothing. Where David Lloyd George differed from the other boys, and his uncle from the other parents and guardians, was just here-that they acted while the others merely raged. That is the startling difference.

They possessed that particular quality which explodes in deeds. There it was already-this care thing called courage, which was, in process of time, to become the driving-wheel of the whole machine.

It is not to be thought that a boy thus endowed was to prove a pattern boy in all directions. David was sound enough at heart; but he was certainly not a saint. He was not born with a halo round his curly head. In that little village he was often the leader of enterprises of pith and moment. He was not without suspicions of piracy. "It's that David Lloyd George," was the sure comment of the village mother when she found her fences down. Wherever those two ribbons were seen flying in the wind, you might be sure that the other boys were not far behind. You would scent mischief in the tainted breeze. There was indeed much to be done. There were fish to be caught; rabbits to be snared; dogs to be trained. There was even-alas! —at one time a privy "cache" in the woods where pipes and tobacco were stored to be fearfully tested on uncertain stomachs.

No, certainly David was no model of the boyish proprieties; no candidate for a stucco niche. He was already a Robin Hood of the woods, an adventurer of that winding, brawling stream. He led others into the adventures with him; for he was already gregarious to the finger-tips. He would draw along with him his more cautious brother; and, somehow, it always seemed to be the brother who bore the weight of the trouble that followed.

Not that David ever shirked the penalties of his youthful sins. He was ever ready to "face the music." He would bravely stand before his uncle in his sterner moods; and many an explosive of argument and reproof had to be expended on his well-entrenched defences.

Not that his uncle ever took up that relentless attitude which drives so many children faster on the downward path. He remembered the text —"Whom He loveth He chasteneth," or, as it has been rewritten, "lick 'im and love 'im." But Richard Lloyd never let the stripes blot out the love. He always believed in this boy David. That was the real secret of the uncle's influence. Beneath the rough, dusty ore he already saw the gleaming gold.

There were indeed some rare features about this boy's character. His early companions testify to some features that still shine in memory. "He was the most kind-hearted boy I ever met," said one who was an inseparable. "If he ever got a penny he would buy his sweets, and then divide up the whole among the other boys." He was very fond of animals —a glorious virtue in the young. There was always a dog in his train-and a dog, being ever young, loves youth and mischief. Then David was ever full of pity for the weak. Pity and audacity met in his nature. They made him at school, as in after-life, a terror to the bully and a trial to the boaster.

His youthful companions cannot remember that he was notably ambitious. But he was from early days a lover of books; and that often held in leash his passion for adventure. He rarely, for instance, played truant from school. There is one historic dawn, still standing out in red letters in the memory of his friends. On that morning the school-bell sounded to deaf ears; all that day those spirits from prison scampered by the river-side testing a new dog.[13] The deed was never repeated. That day of glowing delight was probably burnt into his memory by one of those reprimands from an uncle whose words cut deeper than another's whips.

There is, indeed, an epic story of a holiday hunt of a hare down in the Aberkin farm between the village and the sea. The boys followed the dogs and the dogs went through the river, but an old ganger on the railway refused to allow the boys to cross the bridge. But David was not to be daunted. "Come on, boys!" he cried; and straight through the river he went almost up to his shoulders!

As the years went on he became more serious. He conceived the idea of going to see the world. He spent weeks with maps and made a plan of a journey. Boys will do such things, and the difficulty generally comes when the tickets have to be bought. That was where David Lloyd George's plan broke down. But if he could not wander in the body, he could at any rate travel in the spirit. He read more and more as the years went on. After twelve, remaining on at school after his friends, he became rather a lonely boy. At that time he would often go off with a book into the woods; and he acquired the habit of climbing a tree and there reading for hours in some kindly fork of the branches far away from his romping friends.

There, alone in the woods, his mind formed; and the shadowy whims of youth-perhaps influenced, like Wordsworth's, by the surrounding mountains and sea-steeled into firmer stuff. When he was a very small boy he would say, boy-like, to his uncle, "I am going to be a giant, like that tree." This infantile yearning after something larger than his natal fate seemed to grow upon him. A sense of power seemed to be working within him. Strange, when you consider the cramping conditions of his life. Here was a boy living in a little cottage in a remote Welsh village; talking a despised language; an obscure member of a race scoffed at by the powerful of this earth. He had already proclaimed himself faithful to a religion contemned by all who wished to rise in life. He was surrounded by a peasantry long trained to humility; living in houses that belonged to others; with few rights in their own land-excluded from their own woods and fields by laws of trespass, and menaced with dire penalties if they killed the wild animals of their own land. He found himself born with little freedom beyond the liberty of the village street. There were few adventures for him that were not crimes in the eye of the law. In such a life there seemed enough to quell any growing spirit and to crush any latent ambition. For in those days the social power of the Welsh squires was still scarcely challenged; their claims shadowed all the large spaces in the world around him.

Yet this boy began to look at all this with candid, unprejudiced eyes. He began to grasp the fact that what was required was daring, and still daring.

In this vision he was by no means alone. It was a perception dimly stirring in the minds of all those multitudes of youth who were then, during those years, the first to pass through the new schools of the nation and to win the franchise of the mind. Again, where he was alone was in the courage to pursue this vision-the courage to act as well as to see.

At the age of fourteen (1877) it became necessary to choose a life-calling for David Lloyd George. The village National School had finished its work for the boy. The extra two years' schooling had brought him as far as that training could take him.

Richard Lloyd was not indeed compelled by any law, human or divine, to carry the boy's education any further. He would certainly have achieved as much as most men consider due to a sister's child if he had now taken David from school and apprenticed him to his own honourable handicraft of bootmaking.

But Uncle Lloyd knew only too well the carking cares of a workman's life. He knew what it was to feel a mind-hunger which cannot be sated. Those who saw much of the preacher-bootmaker in those days tell how eager he was for books-how in this eagerness he struck up a very admirable friendship with the kindly village curate; how, after his long day's work, he would read half through the night, and how the village doctor, going on some errand of midnight or dawn, would still see the light of his candle shining through his bedroom window.

Such a life is often filled with an aching regret. The hardly tasked body yearns for a fuller freedom-the freedom to follow, undisturbed, the clear call of the mind.

It was such a life that he dreamed of for his boys when he decided to send them, at all costs, into one of those learned professions which Britons hold in so much honour. His eager aim was to free them, at any sacrifice, from the great burden of manual drudgery.

That being decided, it was not so easy to make a choice between the professions. Richard Lloyd was not one of those men who think it a sign of strength to force children into careers against their own will. Above all, he wished to have the following wind of their free consent and help.

The "ministry" was practically closed to them by that rule of their uncle's Church which forbade Christian service as a means of livelihood. The Established Church, indeed, was an open road for them; there "Welcome!" was written over the door for every clever Welsh village boy. If David had consented to follow the lead of some of his village friends, who can say that he might not have ended as an Archbishop? The thought never took serious shape at Highgate Cottage. I scarcely dare to think of what would have been said in the village "smithy" or the uncle's workshop if David had turned his steps towards that primrose path-as both he and his brother were more than once invited to do.

Richard Lloyd's own desire was that David should be a doctor. But the lad had an instinctive, physical shrinking from disease and death. Richard Lloyd, being a wise man, sorrowfully agreed that David's temperament was unfitted for the hospital ward and the sick-room.

His mother, Mrs. William George, pondering the future in her heart, and watching the boy with a fond mother's eyes, desired him to be a lawyer.

The mother won.

In those old days when Mrs. William George was in the depths of sorrow and distress, through the long agony of her husband's illness, she had received much help and kindness from an old friend of her husband's, one of those tender-hearted family lawyers who are the crown and salvation of their profession-Mr. Thomas Goffey of Liverpool. The boys had heard much of this man at an impressionable age; and the effect left on David was a great desire to go and do likewise. "To be a lawyer like Mr. Goffey!" That was the shining quest before him.

At this critical moment the memory of this helper acted as a magnet to them all; and it was this lode-stone that drew on first David, and then his brother William.

In such pleasant guise did that useful calling present itself; in such Christian fashion came to the youth this summons. The lawyer's gown appeared to him as the robe of the Samaritan.

So far, so good. But the career of the law requires a long apprenticeship; and apprenticeship means money. The examination fees alone for a solicitor amount to a good sum, and there was a substantial premium on apprenticeship to a good firm to be paid in addition. Then there would be over five years without earnings. Where would they obtain the resources to face the strain?

At this point Richard Lloyd turned to the pooled family savings of himself and his sister, Mrs. William George, and dipped deep. Little was left when sufficient for this purpose had been drawn, and even so the supply was precariously meagre. Could they find enough to start the two boys on their careers?

It was clear, on a survey, that they could not send the boys either to a higher school or to a University. How, then, were they to acquire that considerable store of general knowledge required of the legal apprentice?

David had done well under Evans's faithful tuition. He had advanced into the higher mathematics; he had read a certain amount of history; he had now mastered the elements of French and Latin.

But much more was required if he was to pass that first obstruction in the great obstacle race set before the novice in the law-the Preliminary Examination. He must, for instance, know more French. He must read Cæsar and Sallust. The village dominie could not carry David as far as that.

Here seemed a formidable gulf to bridge. Less formidable barriers have closed careers to others and driven them back into the workshop.

But human love can leap over great obstacles; and Richard Lloyd was no ordinary man. He knew neither French nor Latin. Very well, he would set out to learn them.

So together the uncle and the nephew started into the unexplored. Hand in hand, they tackled the Latin and the French grammars, and thumbed the dictionaries. For this great-hearted man knew that if both be ignorant of the way it is better to go together. Company gives courage. So in the dark winter evenings, with the light of a candle, they together spelt out the sentences of Cæsar and Sallust and laboriously read Æsop in French. I will warrant that those lessons in Latin and French were not wasted. I even doubt sometimes whether the class-rooms of Eton or Harrow, with their picked teachers, can show anything so inspiring as this little village study-the uncle and nephew struggling along that unknown path, lit only by zeal and affection. May it not be, perhaps, that the accident of this laborious schooling gave a special nourishment to the boy's instinct of self-confidence, proved more potent than the spoon-feeding of some well-endowed college?

At any rate, this common struggle for knowledge gave the uncle a new insight into his nephew's powers. From this time onward the boy became his very special "Di" —the darling of his heart-the apple of his eye. He began to perceive that there were few things impossible for this boy to achieve.

At last this astonishing experiment in coaching came to an end. But his uncle was determined to stand by the nephew to the end in the first great trial of his life.

In December, 1877, he accompanied him to Liverpool, where the examination was to take place. Every morning-as he often told in later life-Richard Lloyd accompanied the youth to the examination room in St. George's Hall; and every evening, after the day's work, he met him on the steps of the hall and went home with him.

The examination lasted a week. Suspense was followed by triumph. David passed.

The young hopeful who had set out from Llanystumdwy with the good wishes and fervent prayers of friends and neighbours, returned on December 8th with the first flush of achievement on his cheek.

Nowhere was there a happier Christmas in that year of 1877 than at "Highgate."

There was only one man as happy as the uncle and the mother-and that was the village schoolmaster. It was a proud day when he could solemnly record the fact of David's passing in the Log Book of the Llanystumdwy National School.

---

[12] Implying a belief in Infant Baptism, "Confirmation" is regarded as inconsistent with the creed of the Baptists.

[13] "Bismarck" —a dog snatched from the streets of Hamburg and brought home by a sailor from the village —a bold and unscrupulous poacher.

CHAPTER III

YOUTH

"Who, with a natural instinct to discern
   What knowledge can perform, is diligent to learn;"
Wordsworth's The Happy Warrior.

Portmadoc is a little provincial business town lying on the coast some five miles to the west of Criccieth in the very heart of Cardigan Bay. It stands at the mouth of the Glaslyn, one of those little mountain rivers which flow southward through wild valleys from the Snowdon range. The river broadens to a port at its mouth and the town spreads on both banks. A hundred years ago the land here was below high-water mark. It was redeemed by an enterprising man who has given his name to the town and the estate.[14] The old high-water mark can be seen far up the valley, and it is an actual fact that every building in Portmadoc itself stands on land snatched from the sea.

Here in Portmadoc, just east of the Town Hall, stood the office of Messrs. Breese, Jones, and Casson, the firm to which David Lloyd George was articled after he had passed his Preliminary Law Examination. There the square-built, airy chambers still stand. Here, in this building, young David Lloyd George, aged sixteen, took his seat at the window on one of those high stools where the clerks of to-day still sit; and doubtless the young David's eyes sometimes glanced anxiously at the same old clock that still measures out the limits of work and play. The preliminaries of this articling took some time; but within six months-at the opening of 1879 —David had been fully articled by his uncle as clerk to Mr. Casson, the junior partner.

Portmadoc itself stands in prim straight rows of slate-roofed houses built at right-angles to the long main street. The great thing about the town is that from every corner of its streets you can see the mighty mountains of Snowdon on the horizon. It was still under those Eagle Rocks that David's life-work was to be carried on for the next few years.

It was no longer possible for him to live in the little cottage at Llanystumdwy, which was over seven miles from Portmadoc and two miles from Criccieth railway-station.

So it was arranged that the lad should spend the week at Portmadoc and go back to his uncle's home at week-ends.

During the week he lodged with some good people whose children had gone out into the world[15] and who looked after him for several years as if he had been their own child. Like many another young Welshman he was also taken into the kindly fraternity of the chapel folk, who looked after him on behalf of his uncle. He soon began to find friends. On Wednesdays he would attend the little chapel; and he was especially fond of frequenting the little candle-making workshop behind the main street, where the workmen can still be seen ingeniously contriving the special illuminant candles for the slate quarries of North Wales. There, as in the smithy at Llanystumdwy, he found much congenial company for discussion and debate; for it was a significant fact that in youth David Lloyd George was always drawn to the places where men assemble and discuss their affairs.

Here was a youth at the age of sixteen taken out of his village and thrown into the larger turmoil of the world's affairs. The solicitors' firm to which he was articled was an important legal centre in Carnarvonshire. The solicitors were Clerks to the Petty Sessional Division, and Mr. Breese was also Clerk to the Lieutenant of the County, besides being the Liberal agent for Merionethshire. Finding that the youth was handy and smart, they soon began to use him as deputy in their various functions. So David found himself immersed into all the affairs of a great county, besides being in constant touch with the stirring life of a little port. The ships and sailors were ever coming and going, and all the murmur of larger interests flowed in from outside. There, in that little corner of Wales, they could constantly hear "the great wave which echoes round the world."

From the vantage-post of his firm the boy could gradually gain an insight into the whole machinery of county administration.

In law, as in journalism, provincial experience is a far better school for a young man than that of London; for in the provinces work is less specialised, and the young clerk in a busy lawyer's office has a chance of such varied work as his powers show him capable of. David Lloyd George, for instance, now found himself often called upon to undertake responsible tasks; to watch the interests of his firm in the Police Court or in the Quarter Session; to collect rates and taxes; to find his way through that complicated network of wire entanglements which British wisdom had thrown around the exercise of the suffrage. The canvassing work which he did for his firm in their capacity as Liberal agents stood him in very good stead later on which he had to do the same work for himself. It was during this period that he acquired, too, that intimate mastery of the details of rural rating with which he afterwards astonished the House of Commons. During the same years he achieved an insight into the surprising affairs of many county families. There is no surer way of finding out the secrets of the English land system than to look at them through the peep-holes of a good lawyer's office.

No doubt the young Lloyd George lost much by being plunged so early in life into the urgencies of practical work. But he also gained. For it would have been difficult to devise a training more suitable for a coming statesman.

For a time the young man was absorbed by his new work; and, indeed, it was enough to take up his energy. David Lloyd George was from the beginning a keen lawyer. He was not content with practical experience; he read hard at the law; but in his case law did not take form in his mind as a fixed dead thing, but as a vital function of growth, with possibilities of perpetual change and reform.

Thus his apprenticeship began to feed and stimulate his instinctive interest in public affairs. His daily experience led him back at every turn into larger public interests and speculations. He had his week evenings free; and so gradually among the young men of Portmadoc he was led into that life of debate which has always been his very life-blood.

In 1880 his uncle, his mother, his brother, and his sister gave up the little cottage at Llanystumdwy and moved to "Morvin House" in Criccieth. Richard Lloyd and Mrs. William George, their mother, had now saved enough to enable Uncle Lloyd to give up the bootmaking; and his interest was now so much centred round David that he decided to make a move that would enable the youth to live at home. The little house where David was to live for the next ten years was just beneath the walls of that shattered Norman castle which crowns a precipitous cliff on the very edge of the sea. Now battered and worn by the assaults of man and the ravages of the ocean, that castle was once a strong link in that scheme of blockhouse fortresses which the Normans built to keep down North Wales. The ruins typify to-day the valour of this land of bards, and prove the power of a little nation over a mighty conqueror. At its strongest, the rule of the Normans extended very few feet beyond those castle walls. Now this fortress is in ruins; and all around the very portals of that ancient blockhouse you will hear few words of any language except the very tongue which the Normans tried to ban and to bar.[16]

To this house David Lloyd George now came home every evening and he was able to give up his kindly lodgings in Portmadoc. This return to the strongest influence in his youth perhaps explains a certain deepening of purpose which now becomes visible in his diaries[17]; but there emerges also a new independence of spirit. Somewhat to the alarm of the uncle, the youth was beginning to exhibit a rambling interest that went far outside that still lagoon of puritanism which was the home of that high, simple spirit. There was already a touch of that defiant self-confidence which has so often since puzzled and troubled both the followers and the counsellors of Mr. Lloyd George. The young man was reading widely and daringly-not merely sermons, but plays, histories, and novels. He was going through crises of spiritual doubt unknown to the securely anchored soul of his foster-father. He was catching the malady of his age, and finding its remedy, as so many others of that time found it, in the vague anodyne of books like Carlyle's Sartor Resartus.

His growing spirit was finding outlets in every direction. He was attending political meetings and listening eagerly and critically to such gospel as his elders preached. He had begun writing regularly for the newspapers; and over the challenging name of "Brutus," the North Wales Express was producing a series of articles,[18] vigorous and combative —a little young and flamboyant, but always arresting and stimulating to the audience of young Wales.

Already in the 1880 Election those articles, written by a boy not yet 18 years of age, played no insignificant part in North Wales: and now the people of Carnarvonshire were beginning to ask of the young David, as in the old days another people asked of a greater prophet —"Who art thou? What sayest thou of thyself?"

To these questions the daring youth soon began to give an answer with both speech and action. In 1881, the third year of his apprenticeship, he was elected a member of one of those little centres of intellectual energy which were growing up all over Wales in the dawn of this new time. The Portmadoc Debating Society may have meant little to the world; but it meant a great deal to itself and to the town of Portmadoc. This little assembly met weekly in a room over a shop in the Portmadoc High Street. There came together an eager throng of young Welshmen determined to discuss for themselves all the problems of the day. Their debates covered every great question of the eighties. David Lloyd George, now eighteen years of age, did not intend to be a silent member. He soon began to speak often. He took part in debates on all the great problems that occupied his later life-Franchise and Free Trade, Trade Unionism and Irish Land, even the Channel Tunnel. On all these subjects he expressed bold and progressive opinions, and in this little school he began to train his power of speech.

Such a passion for debate is a common disease of youth, and often passes like a fitful fever. But with the young Lloyd George it was not to be so. It was soon clear that the power of speech was with him a very special gift, and he threw into it a great deal of care and industry. Men at Portmadoc will still describe how he could be seen walking along the high-road gesticulating as he practised his speeches; and there is no doubt that at this moment of his life he already had some dim perception that he possessed the magic gift of oratory.

There are those in Portmadoc to-day who can still remember some of these youthful orations, and especially remember the wonderful speech which he made in 1881 on the Egyptian crisis of that year. At that moment conflicting opinions swirled round the figure of Arabi Pasha-the Egyptian Nationalist leader. Was he a hero or a villain? History has not even yet quite decided.[19] But the young Lloyd George was in no doubt. He saw in Arabi a hero of romance rightly struggling for the freedom of a small nation. The impassioned speech in which he defended Arabi gained for him the first attentions of the Welsh press. It revealed to his hearers that deep enthusiasm for freedom among the little nations which afterwards became his leading public characteristic. Men who heard the speech still speak of it as a remarkable event in Portmadoc.

At that time young Lloyd George was slim of body and pale of face; the portraits that exist possess none of that twinkling gaiety which came to him in later years. Youth with him, as with many, seemed to be the gravest period of his life; and indeed it happened that very heavy tasks were laid upon these young Welshmen at the opening of their lives.

For these were perilous years in Wales. The power of the old order had been shaken, but not shattered. The constituencies indeed could no longer be divided up by the squires at a private meeting in Carnarvon; it was not quite so easy now to woo a seat through a Welsh interpreter. The General Election of 1868 had revealed the power of the new order; but the day of Welsh Nationalism was still to come. The older men stood aloof; there was much of the old cringing humility still left in the social life. The squires had punished the Welsh farmers of Carnarvonshire for their votes in 1868 by ruthless, widespread evictions, and a certain fear had been spread through the county. It was clear to the young Lloyd George that this fear could only be destroyed by a new dose of daring and defiance. Thus beneath the shadow of Snowdon the new spirit of young Wales was working up to a storm.

It is not to be wondered at if his debating achievements caused in the mind of this eager young man certain stirrings of ambition that began to belie the opinion of his old schoolmates. In November, 1881, he visited London for the first time: and, like most young men with kindly London friends, he was taken to see the House of Commons. At this time he was keeping a fairly full diary; and the entry of this date (November 12th) is rather remarkable in view of subsequent events:

"I will not say but that I eyed the assembly in a spirit similar to that in which William the Conqueror eyed England on his visit to Edward the Confessor, as the region of his future domain. Oh, vanity!"

Perhaps it is scarcely fair to intrude on such self-communings of early aspiring adolescence-easily forgivable for their naïve boyish pride. But in the same diaries, a year or two later, this young articled clerk jots down another reflection rather strangely prophetic of what was to come. A quotation appeared in the Carnarvon and Denbigh Herald which signified that David Lloyd George was already in the public eye:

"When first the college rolls receive his name,

The young enthusiast quits his ease for fame,

Resistless burns the fever of renown,

Caught from the strong contagion of the gown."[20]

Young Lloyd George makes a curiously level-headed comment on this reference to his thirst for renown:

"Perhaps (?) it will be gratified. I believe it depends entirely on what forces of pluck and industry I can muster."

Strangely sober reflection for the eighteenth year!

The desire for fame-that "last infirmity of noble minds" —was already there. But it had not turned the head of the young man. Already he seemed to have some measure of the task before him, and of the effort that would be required to achieve it.

---

[14] Mr. A. Maddocks. One of the men who was interested in this project was the poet Shelley.

[15] Mr. and Mrs. D. Lloyd Owen, Auctioneer, High Street, Portmadoc.

[16] After writing this I came across the following passage in a speech of Mr. Lloyd George's made in the House of Commons: "Two thousand years ago the great Empire of Rome came with its battalions and conquered that part of Carnarvonshire in which my constituency is situated. They built walls and fortifications as the tokens of their conquest, and they proscribed the use of the Cymric tongue. The other day I was glancing at the ruins of those walls. Underneath I noted the children at play, and I could hear them speaking, with undiminished force and vigour, the proscribed language of the conquered nation. Close by, there was a school where the language of the Roman conquerors was being taught, but taught as a dead language."

[17] These diaries are very fully published in Herbert Du Parcq's excellent Life of David Lloyd George, London; Caxton Publishing Company Limited, 1912.

[18] A large selection of these articles can be read in the pages of Mr. Du Parcq.

[19] Lord Cromer always called him an adventurer. Mr. Wilfrid Blunt has always regarded him as a great patriot.

[20] From Dr. Johnson's "Vanity of Human Wishes" (135-138), an early poem, based on Juvenal's Tenth Satire. The third and fourth lines should run —

"Thro' all his veins the fever of renown

Burns from the strong contagion of the gown."

The poem was popular with such different judges as Sir Walter Scott, Byron, Cardinal Newman, and Matthew Arnold.

"UNCLE LLOYD": MR. RICHARD LLOYD,
THE UNCLE OF DAVID LLOYD GEORGE.

THE SMITHY AT LLANYSTUMDWY:
THE OLD "VILLAGE PARLIAMENT."

CHAPTER IV

EARLY MANHOOD

"Fame is the spur that the clear spirit doth raise
  (That last infirmity of Noble Mind)
  To scorn delights, and live laborious days"
  Milton's Lycidas.

During these years of the early eighties (1880-4) that great Government of Mr. Gladstone's which opened so triumphantly in 1880 was rapidly drawing towards its downfall. Checked in Ireland and stagnant at home, the Whigs who dominated the Cabinet had been gradually drawn abroad into enterprises for which they lacked both heart and capacity. Mr. Gladstone was losing the middle class, and not winning the manual workers. Meanwhile that astonishing young man from Birmingham, Mr. Joseph Chamberlain, had swiftly perceived the decline of the old Liberalism, and was building up a new and daring programme of social and political reform. He was speaking with a new voice. He was uttering his mind in simple language, and calling things by very plain names.

The heart of the young Lloyd George went out to this newcomer with a frank enthusiasm. It is quite clear from his diaries and newspaper-writings during these years that he was at the beginning a vehement supporter of Mr. Chamberlain.

In an article on Mr. Chamberlain written by David Lloyd George for the North Wales Observer of October 17th, 1884, there is a remarkable passage which is worth while recalling to-day as a flashing revelation of the mind of the young writer:

"Mr. Chamberlain is unquestioningly the future leader of the people. Any one who reads his speeches will know the reason why.... He understands the sympathies of his countrymen. It is therefore that he speaks intelligibly and straightforwardly, like a man who is proud of the opinions which he holds. He is a Radical, and doesn't care who knows it as long as the people do."

So strongly was he attracted by Mr. Chamberlain's personality that the young Lloyd George was always inclined to take his side. He supported him, for instance, in that struggle with the Whigs over his Radical Programme which, by the strangest possible twist, led later on to that great misunderstanding over the tactics of Home Rule and ended in splitting the old Liberal party. Mr. Lloyd George had perhaps some temperamental sympathy with that spirit of impatience which made Mr. Chamberlain resent so deeply the snubs and checks he received at the hands of the Whigs.

Although a fervent Nationalist and Home Ruler, Mr. Lloyd George was always inclined to sympathise with Mr. Chamberlain's methods of approaching the Home Rule problem. Looking at it from the view-point of Wales, he liked Mr. Chamberlain's feeling for federalism. It is a curious fact that if Mr. Lloyd George had stood for Parliament in 1886, he would probably have been drawn by his sympathy for Mr. Chamberlain into the ranks of that small section of Radical Unionists who followed Mr. Chamberlain in his opposition to Gladstonian Home Rule, but afterwards, recoiling from open reaction, rejoined the Liberal party-men like Sir George Trevelyan and Mr. W. S. Caine, a small, afflicted, but deeply interesting group.

In 1884 David Lloyd George went up to London to pass his Final Law Examination in order to enable him to be admitted on to the roll of practising solicitors. His comment in his diary on the admission ceremony shows his growing freshness and independence of outlook. He was not at all cheered by that atmosphere of dusty dullness which envelops the ritual of our law:

"The ceremony disappointed me. The Master of the Rolls, so far from having anything to do with it, was actually listening to some Q.C. at the time, and some fellow of a clerk swore us to a lawyerly demeanour at the back of the court, and off we shambled to the Petty Bag Office to sign the Rolls."

On the occasion of this visit to London, he again attended the House of Commons, and for the first time listened to a debate. He was fortunate enough to be present at a lively skirmish between Lord Randolph Churchill and Mr. Gladstone. "It was a clever piece of comedy," he said some years afterwards, recalling the scene. "I thought Churchill an impudent puppy, as every Liberal was bound to do-but I thoroughly enjoyed his speech." Then, as now, he could never sufficiently express his admiration for courage in any field of life and on any side.

He could now (1884) leave the high desk in the square room at the office by the Town Hall. He had served during the past five years (1879-1884) a faithful apprenticeship. He had allowed few diversions to draw him from his work. In those days the Puritan tradition of a little Welsh township held the young people in a fairly tight grip, and there were few light distractions. Portmadoc held no theatre or opera within its boundaries. The "Moving Pictures" had not yet taken Puritanism on the flank. Football was beginning to seize the Celtic fancy; but David had little taste or time for violent sports. In 1882 he became a Volunteer, and went into camp at Conway. But it is not recorded that he secured any promotion, or at any time suffered from the pangs of military ambition. Otherwise his amusements took that sober form of the Portmadoc debating society speeches, or essays for the Eisteddfod, for which the two brothers wrote a discourse on the "Cash and Credit System." They spoke of credit with a scorn unhappily rare in young men!

He was no longer any master's man. He could, if he liked, set up for himself. The firm for which he had worked all these years had, indeed, a high opinion of his powers; and they did not wish to lose him wholly. Mr. Breese, the head-partner, "a kind master and a thorough man," as David described him in his diary, had died in 1881; but the other partners did their best to give him a start. They secured him an offer of a managing clerkship in an old county firm at Dolgelly. It would have been a most attractive opening for a man who wished to follow the safe course in life. But David Lloyd George was one who preferred risks. He wished to be the ruler of his own fate.

He had now practically no one behind him. The long period of examination and apprenticeship had exhausted the slender stores of his mother and his uncle. He had even to wait for his first cases before he could purchase the robes required of a Welsh solicitor before he could plead in the County Court.

But he still preferred a small independence to a big dependence. Perhaps he was right. Probably he had ideas as to the way of conducting a legal business which would not have always gratified any old-fashioned firm of country solicitors.

The young solicitor started quite simply by putting a brass name-plate on the door of Morvin House, their little dwelling at Criccieth. He then began to practise in his uncle's back parlour.

It was a daring venture for an unknown village youth; but after a few months he began to get under way. His diaries of 1885 punctuate with thrilling eagerness the opening steps in his professional career-his first case in the Police Court, his first service of an order, his first plea in the County Court. On June 24th he records with glee that he won all his cases. "Never had a more successful field-day." On July 9th he is attending Penrhyn Sessions for the first time, opposing the transfer of a license. On September 8th he is in the Revision Courts. "Came off better than Liberals ever did." In fact, he marches in these first skirmishes from victory to victory.

So successful was he, in fact, that in this year (1885) he opened an office in the High Street at Portmadoc, not far from the building in which he had been articled. He began in a very small house, and remained there for some years before moving to the corner house where the legend "Messrs. Lloyd George and George" is still prominent in the window. This corner house was previously a public-house known as "The Fox Inn." There the brothers-for now William had joined David in practice-took the end of the lease, and finally secured the freehold. There, in that dispossessed hostelry, William George practises to-day (1920).

This year and the years that followed in David's life were crammed with intense activities. The diaries show that day after day he rose between five and six o'clock. He devoted the cream of his energies to the active pursuit of the law. But he could never be a man of one interest. He was also, during these same months, fiercely energetic both in religion and politics. He was constantly reading sermons and listening to sermons. He often spoke from the pulpit, after that liberal fashion encouraged in the Free Churches.

But gradually in these diaries the political interest begins to loom larger. When the autumn General Election of 1885 comes on, he takes an active part with pen and voice. On October 17th he goes to the Tory member's meeting, and is with difficulty restrained from taking part. On November 18th he makes an impassioned speech in defence of Mr. Chamberlain, and is tremendously cheered. On November 24th he goes to a Tory meeting and finds that he is the chief butt of their attack. He shows his precocious political shrewdness by the satisfaction he feels in thus drawing the enemy's fire.

Instead of injuring the practice of his profession by these public displays of courage, he soon found that he was really attracting to his house and office a new class of client, the discontented farmers of the county. First one and then another began coming to him, at first privily and then confidently. They came on tithes, and on rents, and on rates. He took up some of these cases and scored successes which resounded through the county. The result was that other men came who had never before been to lawyers, and he began to open up a new vein of business. Law, after all, can sometimes pay, even as a remedy for injustice.

He was, indeed, now becoming a very busy solicitor of the kind which in the provinces is not easily distinguished from a barrister. The fact that a solicitor can address a County Court and a Petty Sessional Court gives him, outside the great centres of English life, a practical command of both branches of the law and abolishes that rather absurd pedantry of divided function. This power of speech suited young Lloyd George very well. It gave him a new training in public address, and it provided him with a new weapon for asserting public rights. From the time of that great nation of lawyers-the Romans-the Law Court has always been second only to the Senate House as an instrument of popular power. Mr. Lloyd George showed to the Welsh people that, in the integrity of the British law, they had a new resource for the recovery of their ancient rights.

But never at any time did he allow the call of the law to divert him from politics. Day by day his diaries reflect his passionate interest in the struggle of 1885. When the first results come in he is profoundly disappointed. "There is no cry for the towns," he writes on November 26th. "Humdrum Liberalism won't win elections." Then, on December 4th:

"Great Liberal victories in counties. Very glad of it. Am convinced that this is all due to Chamberlain's speeches. Gladstone had no programme that would draw at all."

Throughout we can see his ardour for the forward course and the vigour in attack. "Humdrum Liberalism won't win elections" —that was to be the gist of his political teaching in later years: it almost summed up his political strategy.

Certainly young Lloyd George was not himself inclined to be "humdrum." Just at this moment, when the old and the new Liberalism in Wales, as in England, were wrestling for the mastery, he definitely took the forward side. It was significant of this that he first came out as a notable public speaker in a sphere beyond his own district at a great public meeting held at Festiniog on February 12th, 1886, and addressed by the famous Irishman, Michael Davitt.

The Liberal Party was not at that moment fully committed to Home Rule, and among the elder men there had been grave head-shakings over this invitation to Michael Davitt. Rebellion was more seriously regarded in those days; and Michael Davitt had both rebelled and paid the penalty. The law had laid its finger on him and marked him with its broad arrow; and respectable people whispered the word "felon."

Young Lloyd George was invited to the Davitt meeting. There were grave doubts in the family circle as to whether he ought to go. But he was urged on by one who had already a great and growing influence over him, a certain Maggie Owen living at a farmhouse about a mile from Criccieth and more and more mentioned in the diaries of this time. This young lady already had her definite views, and she had no patience with this attempt to make a pariah of Michael Davitt. "Of course you must go," she said simply; "why not?" And that seemed to settle the matter.

The difficulty was to persuade any one to move a vote of thanks to Michael Davitt at this meeting; all the prudent people stood aside. But there sat in a chair a brave and stalwart man-Mr. Michael Jones of Bala-and at the last moment he persuaded young Lloyd George to move the vote of thanks. The young David rose, and he instantly made a speech which was largely reported and which electrified North Wales. In this speech there are already some of those daring, flashing phrases with which he afterwards familarised the world. There was already that fearless touch which has since made the speaker a perpetual storm-centre.

Michael Davitt, always a shrewd judge of men, was deeply impressed with the speech. He advised Mr. Lloyd George to think of Parliament, and the other Michael-Jones of Bala-urged the same advice. From that time forward the young man's thoughts began to turn towards Westminster.

And yet his first approach to Parliament was not easy. Some of the young enthusiasts who now gathered round him wanted him to stand for Merionethshire in the General Election that soon followed in 1886. But here there was another son of young Wales already in the field with stronger local claims. This was none other than the man always known afterwards as "Tom" Ellis, son of a Merionethshire farmer. Ellis was four years older than Lloyd George; and young David readily and instantly stood aside in favour of the elder man. They met soon after; and a great friendship struck up between them which lasted until the premature death of Tom Ellis in 1899. It was a wonderful friendship between two men of common aspirations but utterly different character. Tom Ellis was by no means the "Welsh Parnell" —no description could have been further from the truth. He was a man of high enthusiasms and noble integrity. He was a real Welsh Nationalist. But, by going to Oxford, he had come within the governing English circle; he was touched with that Saxonism which tempers the native zeal of the Celt. He was no longer "racy of the soil." It was no mere chance that he was afterwards drawn before his due season into the circle of British power, and was fated to stand aloof from his friend when Lloyd George was asserting the rugged and relentless claims of Welsh Nationalism.

Thus David Lloyd George was for the moment delayed in his progress to Parliament. Perhaps this was a fortunate accident, because it gave him a breathing time in which to master the needs of his own people and to train himself more thoroughly for the public stage.

CHAPTER V

MARRIAGE

> "A Daniel come to judgment! Yea, a Daniel!
> O wise young judge, how I do honour thee!"
> Shakespeare's Merchant of Venice, Act I, Sc. iv.

Cut off from Parliament for the moment (1886) David Lloyd George spent no time in vain regrets. He resumed that life of combined public and private activity which was rapidly becoming his second nature. His diaries during the following years show that he was now absorbed in his growing "practice." But that did not prevent him from continuing his eager and active interest in public affairs. Then, as ever after, the two interests developed together.

From this time forward he steadily directed his energies to work on behalf of his own beloved little nation. Perhaps never did he quite lose sight of that high ambition to command "listening senates" which had come to him when he first sat in the Gallery at Westminster and looked down on the combats of the great parliamentary gladiators. But for the moment there was urgent work to do nearer to hand; and David Lloyd George knew the wisdom of Carlyle's great law of conduct —"Do the Duty that lies nearest thee."[21]

So he plunged into the great work for Wales which was already on foot at his own doors.

In 1886 he joined eagerly in the great Anti-Tithe campaign which was being carried on throughout North Wales by those remarkable men, Mr. Thomas Gee and Mr. John Parry. David Lloyd George became the Secretary of that League in South Carnarvonshire, and he addressed meetings throughout the district. He accompanied Mr. Gee and Mr. Parry on many of their most daring raids. He drove long distances in a small governess cart and addressed meetings in little villages away in remote districts.

It was characteristic of David that he actually provoked and promoted hostility. He would hold his meetings by preference in the neighbourhood of the Parish Church or of the National School. He would regard it as his greatest triumph if he could draw the parson or the curate to come out and meet him in open warfare. One of the visions of him at this period handed down is that of a day in June 1887, when he was seen coatless and in his shirt-sleeves arguing against the curate in the open green at the village fair of Sarn Melltcyrn. He did not shrink from passive sympathy with the mild rioting which began to take place at the tithe sales resulting from the distraints that followed. His whole heart went out in sympathy to Welsh farmers compelled by law to contribute from their pocket to what they regarded as an alien Church.

The "Tithe War" gave David Lloyd George that best of training for a young public speaker-the training of public controversy in the open air. It made him quick and resourceful. Here was the best possible whetstone for his natural gift of courage. These speeches made him already a rising public champion.

This was a new portent for the Welsh farmer —a lawyer who was not in league with the rich. It flashed as a shining light on the eyes of a people who had always been used to regard the law as the paid servant of power and property. It brought more of those farmers flocking to his office: and once more it brought him forward as the legal friend of the poor and the oppressed —"the poor man's lawyer" of Carnarvonshire.

The people gradually learned that here was a man skilled in the law who was ready on their behalf to face the tyrants of the Bench and to challenge their power.

In nothing had this power of the Bench been more ruthlessly exercised than in the matter of fishing. By a curious distortion of public rights, the rivers of this country have been mainly turned into private property. While fishing on the open sea is as free as the air, unlicensed fishing in fresh water in England outside navigable waters is often accounted a crime.[22]

This law of private property in fresh water fishing has fallen with peculiar harshness upon a people like the Welsh, who inherit a great passion for this particular sport. The pressure of the law has been made worse by the fact that the prohibition is perpetually being extended to waters where a customary right of fishing has existed.

Here has been a cause of perpetual conflict between the law and the public —a conflict in which the bias of the law has been mainly against the public.

Such a case occurred in North Wales in May 1889, when four quarrymen were prosecuted for fishing in a small mountain quarry lake.[23] The aim of the prosecution was to bring the lake within the definition of the word "river" in the Act of Parliament. It soon became quite clear from the proceedings that the bias of the Court was against the quarrymen. Mr. Lloyd George rapidly determined to bring this out in the most vivid manner possible. So when the chairman —a great local potentate and sportsman-gruffly interrupted his legal argument by saying that the legal point must be tried in a higher Court, Mr. Lloyd George swiftly replied:

"Yes, sir, and in a perfectly just and unbiassed Court too."

The result of this remark was precisely what Mr. Lloyd George expected. The chairman rather unwisely asked Mr. Lloyd George to what magistrate he was referring. To this the young advocate immediately replied:

"I refer to you in particular, sir."

Whereupon the chairman immediately rose with great pomp and dignity and left the court.

The other magistrates now felt that it laid with them to take some action. A second magistrate, allied to sport, protested. A third, noddingly acquainted, declined to proceed with the case: whereupon Mr. Lloyd George calmly remarked, "I am glad to hear it." A fourth rose and left the court. One of the few left asked Mr. Lloyd George for an apology, whereupon he replied:

"I shall not withdraw anything, because every word I have spoken is true."

The result was that all the magistrates left the court, and Mr. Lloyd George's purpose was fully achieved.

Here was an incident by no means the result of mere thoughtless impertinence on the part of a young lawyer. Mr. Lloyd George has always regarded this as one of the proudest incidents of his life. He is still of opinion that it came at a critical moment to shake the petty tyranny of the local Bench, and he still quotes it as a good example of one of his favourite methods of public action.

A short time afterwards David Lloyd George was the chief actor in another famous case which showed the people of Wales that the spirit of British justice, if boldly challenged, was capable of maintaining their cause. This was a case arising from that incredible ecclesiastical inhumanity which consisted in attempting to visit ignominy upon a man of another faith even after he had passed through the gates of death. Nothing did more to shatter the power of the Established Church of Wales than the refusal of the parsons to bury the dead of other sects within the walls of the old parish burial-grounds. Those parish "God's acres" had been in the possession of the people before the Reformation, and it was only by a chance turn of English history that they passed away from them.

The growth of the great Free Churches resulting from the immense religious revival of the late eighteenth and early nineteenth centuries made this an acute matter. The hostility of the Established Church to this revival led to a new use of the power of exclusion from the burial-grounds. Terrible memories have centred round that struggle. The late President of the English Divorce Court, Sir Samuel Evans, once told me that he had to carry by stealth the coffin of his first wife into his parish cemetery before he could obtain burial for her in Christian ground. The Established Church in Wales has had to pay heavily for the luxury of such adherence to a narrow and inhuman practice.

In 1880 the Welsh members returned to Parliament since the Liberal Revival of 1868 had succeeded in passing that famous Burial Act which now enables a British Nonconformist to be buried in a parish burial-ground according to the rites of his own religion as long as due notice is given to the parish priest. In most of the parishes in Wales this Act was accepted by decent parsons as a satisfactory settlement of a prolonged dispute.

But in the little village of Llanfrothen, at the very foot of Snowdon, there was a rector whose fanatical religious instinct led him to make one last daring effort to cheat his parishioners out of their rights of decent Christian burial. In 1888, an old quarryman died at Llanfrothen. He left it as his last wish that he should be buried by the side of his daughter. Now, this daughter had been buried in a piece of land which had been added to the churchyard as far back as 1864 by a certain Mrs. Owen of Dolgelly. The new piece of land had been enclosed by a wall built out of their own money by the parishioners. This "acre" had been recognised up to that time as part of the burial-ground. But the Rev. Richard Jones cared nothing for walls and little for precedents. This "churlish priest" raked up the old records and found that Mrs. Owen had made no legal conveyance of the land. In 1881, the year after the new Burial Act had passed into law, he persuaded that good lady to make a new conveyance, with a trust which confined it to those parishioners who used the rites of the Church of England.

The new grave had actually been dug for the poor old quarryman to rest by the side of his daughter. A notice under the new Act was served upon the rector. Then began the struggle. The rector filled in the grave and pointed out another spot for the burial of the old quarryman — a spot far from his daughter, "bleak and sinister," in the words of Mr. Lloyd George —a place reserved for shipwrecked sailors and suicides.

It was at that moment in the struggle that the relatives of the quarryman went to consult young David Lloyd George.

Without any hesitation Mr. Lloyd George advised them to act on their rights. Following his daring counsel, they entered the graveyard and reopened the filled-in grave. Then they made a pathetic appeal to the rector. He still forbade them to act. Then they made a demand on the rector. He still refused. Meanwhile young David had spent a night in foraging and rummaging through the church records, and he had discovered that in 1864 the rector had allowed the public to enclose the piece of ground without any conditions. He advised the relatives to go on. Let them, if necessary, break into the churchyard.

They went on. They broke into the churchyard. They borrowed a bier from the church. They gave the old man a Christian burial by his daughter. The Calvinist minister spoke the service, and the relatives went home happier-contented with the feeling that they had buried the old man where he had wished to lie.

Infuriated by their defiance, the stubborn rector sued the relatives for damages in Portmadoc County Court. Mr. Lloyd George took up the defence and asked for a jury. The jury decided that his facts were correct. The County Court Judge decided against him on the point of law. Fortunately for Mr. Lloyd George, the Judge made an incorrect record of the jury's verdict and refused to correct it. David Lloyd George appealed to the Divisional Court. He was heard by Lord Chief Justice Coleridge and Justice Manisty. In the middle of the case Lord Chief Justice Coleridge discovered the incorrect record by the County Court Judge. Result-fury of the Lord Chief Justice, anger of the Court, and, finally, a verdict in favour of the quarryman.

So that poor old quarryman of Llanfrothen was after all laid to rest in peace in that little burial-ground beneath the mighty precipices of Snowdon; and the fame of Mr. Lloyd George spread wider and wider throughout North Wales. It was felt that here at last the people had a man who had the courage to support them in their struggles against the powers in high places.

He now began to act as a popular pleader in cases of social injustice before the Petty Courts of the Principality.

It was during this period of dawning thoughts and powers that David Lloyd George wooed and won the woman who became his wife. The young man was at that time a keen-eyed, attractive youth; and the silver tongue which he was already using in Court and on the platform was also very social in private life. He was from the beginning a sociable, conservative man. Dowered with welded gifts of wit and wisdom, he had already the makings of a good talker. Above all, he had that gift of sympathy with the views of others which is more popular with women than with men. So it was that the cottage-born boy of Llanystumdwy, the promising son of Morvin House, was a prime favourite with the girls of Criccieth-and with one girl in particular who lived just outside Criccieth.

For about a mile inland from the sea, on a hundred-acre farm called Mynydd Ednyfed, there lived a farming family of old lineage and high standing possessing the proud, historic Welsh name of Owen. They claimed descent from Owen Glyndwr, and they faced life with that simple Homeric pride which lends dignity to worthy living. The yeomen farmers of Wales, like the "statesmen" of the Cumberland Dales, inherit the pride of landed men; and the Owens were no exception to this rule.

The Owens of Ednyfed had a daughter-Maggie by name-whom they loved passing well. She was the apple of her father's eye; and no man who sought her hand was likely to have an easy time. That, of course, was likely to make Maggie not less, but more desirable to David Lloyd George.

Maggie went to chapel at Criccieth, and the young people met in that simple but thrilling way-when the heart is at its best and highest-as they went to and from their little chapels. They did not worship together; for the Owens were Methodists. But love has leapt higher barriers than that between Baptists and Methodists.

Then there came those entries in the diaries-innocent, human entries-how David took Maggie home from meetings-how, later on, he began to go to the farm and talk. Little is said; but we see the old, old story developing along its ancient trodden paths. The son of the land is going back to the land for his wooing.

Then came those stones in the path without which the truth of love never was and never shall be proved. It was after 1885 that the young man began to go frequently to the farmhouse-solely, of course, to obtain sound political advice and counsel from a very wise young lady. Fathers have strange illusions, and at first Mr. Owen thought that David came to talk to him. Many fathers have often thought the same.

But the day came to Mr. Owen, as it comes to all parents, when the veil was torn asunder. It became only too obvious that this young man did not toil out so often to Ednyfed solely in order to enjoy the society of Mr. Owen-or even of Mrs. Owen.

Then Mr. Owen became less friendly. It is not Polonius only who thought himself wiser than youth; and in this case Mr. Owen brought Mrs. Owen over to his side.

Ah! If this young David could look forward to the secure tenancy of a good solid farmhouse and a rich, broad-acred farm, how different it would be! But there he was, a struggling limb of the law, scarcely emerged from articles, given to outrageous public forays, still under his uncle's roof! Farmers rarely love lawyers.

Happily the Owen parents had friends and relations, who took a sounder and longer view. Maggie had one of those friendly aunts who are the best counsellors of our youth. That good lady now urged Maggie to stick to the young man. "Mark you," she would say, "that young man has a great future. Don't give him up." Maggie was perhaps like any other young girl, at first a little divided and disturbed-distracted between the calls of love and filial duty. But in the end she did the sound, straight thing-she stuck to her man and won.

Once the victory was established, and bold heart had won fair lady, then the parental entrenchments surrendered. The white flag became the flag of loyalty; and Mr. and Mrs. Owen, once won over, became the devoted friends and worshippers of their son-in-law up to the close of their lives. I saw something of them in their home at a later time; and among all those humble folk who have helped David Lloyd George to achieve, those two wise elders, Mr. and Mrs. Owen, held no mean or unworthy place.

The years flew swiftly, and by 1888 it became clear that Maggie's aunt was the true prophetess, and that the young Criccieth solicitor was a coming man. The rumour of him was spreading through the county like the roar of a "spate" from the hills of Snowdon. What was more important, he was earning an income. Not even the thrifty, careful farmer of Ednyfed could doubt any longer.

So with the opening of that year it was decided that the marriage should take place.

On January 24th, 1888, just after the twenty-fifth birthday of the young bridegroom,[24] David Lloyd George and Maggie Owen were married. The wedding took place in a romantic spot, in the little chapel of Pencaenewydd, an inland Carnarvonshire village, a few miles from Chwilog. Uncle Lloyd took David over by train on that fateful morning to Chwilog; there they breakfasted, and walked over to Pencaenewydd. Uncle Lloyd and the Rev. John Owen performed the simple ceremony; and there were present only relations and a few friends. But it was recorded in the Carnarvon Herald that flags were to be seen everywhere in Criccieth, and in the evening, after the young couple had left for London, the people defied the drizzling rain with a bonfire and fireworks. Already the people knew their friend.

Twenty-nine years later (1917) a daughter of these simple spousals was married with the same simplicity in a little Baptist chapel in London. Only the welling, pressing crowd outside the chapel showed that the man who stood by the pulpit giving away his daughter was Prime Minister of England. One wedding was as simple as the other.

When they returned to Criccieth from their brief honeymoon, Mr. and Mrs. Lloyd George settled down at first at Mynydd Ednyfed, in the farmhouse of the Owens, and there they spent a few happy years under her parents' roof. There the elder children were born.

It was soon clear that the marriage was not going to bring any abatement of courageous action on the part of the young husband. Mrs. Lloyd George was not the sort of wife who encourages her husband to uxorious ease. She was, and always has been, on the side of daring. She faces danger with a simplicity which is disarming.

One night, for instance, there was to be held at Criccieth a meeting of the kind known as "Church Defence"; a species of gathering not free from offence to the people of Wales. David was suffering from a mild attack of tonsillitis. There seemed every reason why he should not go to the meeting.

But the people of Carnarvonshire had had to stand a good deal of this sort of thing; and David's blood was up. He wanted to go. Would his young wife mind? She? "Why not go?" she said.

So he went off, closely muffled up by a wife who was tender as well as brave.

He stepped into the meeting with one definite object. It was his deliberate intention to stop a practice that was growing into a scandal. It had become a habit in these gatherings to fend off the eager questionings of militant Nonconformity by disingenuous postponement. It is a method well known to the tricksters of public life. "Questions? Oh! yes, as many as you like! Only it is more convenient to answer them at the close of the meeting!" Then at the close —"So sorry! But our friend here has to catch a train-his invaluable time —" We all know this sort of thing.

But at the opening of this particular meeting-an important meeting, to be addressed by a very special Church advocate-there arose the young David Lloyd George, muffled but insistent. Yes, he wanted to ask some questions. No, he would rather ask them now. In fact, he intended to ask them now. So he stood, pale to the lips, but unyielding.

The audience, taking courage, began to clap and cheer. "To the platform!" shouted some one. So David quite deliberately stepped up to the platform, mounted it, and began to address the meeting.

In vain did the righteous rage. The chairman ordered David down. He held his ground. Nay, he began to address the people, simply, incisively, thrillingly. The chairman was forgotten. David had become the speaker of the hour.

Then a curious thing happened. Warming to the task, David began to take off his mufflers. He unwound them and cast them aside. His hoarse voice became clear and ringing. The sick throat was forgotten.

He captured the meeting. The platform was silenced. It was he who made the speech of the evening; and at the end the enthusiastic Free Churchmen in the audience took up the young man and carried him from the hall on their shoulders.

No, certainly, marriage had not pinioned the wings of this young stormy petrel.

---

[21] Sartor Resartus, Book II., chapter ix.

[22] In countries like Japan all fishing is free; and public fishing, of course, can be "preserved" as easily as private.

[23] The lower Nantlle lake.

[24] He was born on January 17th, 1863.

CHAPTER VI

ENTERS PARLIAMENT

"The day of the cottage-bred man has at last dawned." —Lloyd George.

Now (1888) happily married and well started on his legal career, Mr. Lloyd George was able to return to his larger ambition of sitting in Parliament. From this time forward he definitely aspired to sit at Westminister as the representative of his own native constituency, the Carnarvon Boroughs. The achievement was not to be easy. There were many lions in the path.

During the last few years, indeed, he had immensely increased his reputation. He had travelled through many parts of Wales and visited many courts, fighting the cause of the "underdog." The tenants of Wales, harried and evicted after 1868 and 1880, had begun to hold up their heads again. They felt that they had a new champion on their side.

But the old habit of sending to Westminster only the powerful and wealthy was not yet dead. Feudalism always dies slowly. It was a very sudden change indeed to pass from the squire and the manufacturer to the cottage-bred lad of Llanystumdwy.

David Lloyd George, indeed, neglected no opportunities. Besides being a lawyer and a public speaker, he was now an active journalist. Working with that fine spirit, Mr. D. R. Daniel-then one of the noblest sons of the Young Welsh movement-David Lloyd George founded at Pwllheli in 1888 a paper called The Trumpet of Freedom —a name which certainly did not lack sound and vigour.

Then, a few months after his marriage, with the consent and support of his fearless wife, he allowed his name first to be put forward as possible Liberal candidate for the Carnarvon Boroughs.

Then followed one of those personal struggles which test and try a man.

It is right that all claim to rise above our fellows should be narrowly scrutinised. There is even in jealousy some element of that instinct for equality which gives dignity to the meanest man. Here is a factor that takes multitudinous forms, varying from fair judgment to sheer malice. The strongest man will wince under the scorpions of spite; but he will accept the verdict of a fair jury of his peers. It was to such a jury that young David Lloyd George now fearlessly appealed.

Certainly it was scarcely to be expected that his claims to the seat should pass unchallenged. He was still (1888) only twenty-five years old. He was appealing to his own countryside; and a prophet is recorded to have authority anywhere but there. There was the inevitable question of envious neighbors —"Is not this the bootmaker's boy?" There was the man who had known "David" with the curls down his back-who had kept a record of his youthful pranks. Then there was "the County" —that fine essence of squiredom which had always regarded "the seat" as one of its own possessions. Above all, there were the little borough circles-the elders in the chapels, the grey-beards in the seats of the saints. There were some such seniors who shook their heads gravely at such madness. The boy must bide his time. Who was he to rule over them? For when David, the shepherd's youngest son, came up to face the Philistine champion, it was not only the Philistine enemy, but also his own elder brothers who scoffed and doubted.

Against all these doubts and envies only one thing could prevail. It was the new wave of Nationalism which was sweeping over the younger generation throughout Wales, and especially North Wales. Wales was tired of those respectable professional members who were so easily captured by the political machines at Westminster. They wanted some one endowed with the courage to revolt; and already they had a perception that David Lloyd George was such a man. He had shown this in his defence of the fishermen of Nantlle, and in his championship of that poor old quarryman of Llanfrothen. In both cases he had defied authority; and in both cases he had won. He had been the first to break the tradition of fear which brooded over the Welsh people.

He had already roused a new spirit of hope in the younger generation: and they were determined that he should carry their banner forward.

At first his candidature progressed very slowly. It was true that the constituency had fared badly of recent years. In 1886, when Tom Ellis was sweeping all before him in Merionethshire, the Carnarvon Boroughs had put forward an old-fashioned Liberal who had lost the seat to an able Tory.

At this time it was still in the possession of that Tory member-Mr. Swetenham, Q.C. Humdrum Liberalism, as David Lloyd George had already prophesied, had not proved a winning card in the Boroughs. But such an experience does not always remove prejudice. There were those who argued that a Q.C. could only be defeated by another Q.C. —or say, a professor; or perhaps, even better, a millionaire, if he could be obtained. We all know these dreams that haunt the minds of local committee-men in difficult and doubtful constituencies.

The first step towards achievement was taken in the spring of 1888 when he was adopted as candidate by the Liberals in the Borough of Carnarvon.[25] But for some months the other four Boroughs held aloof, and it was not until later in the year that he was selected as candidate by the Liberals of Nevin, Pwllheli, and Criccieth. For several months longer there was a hesitation among the respectabilities of that eminent cathedral city of Bangor, where even Liberalism has a tinge of blue. But on December 20th Bangor surrendered, and he was chosen as Liberal candidate for the whole constituency.

It is clear from the letters and diaries of the time that these months marked a period of great stress in his life. When he was selected at Bangor he wrote to his family one of those passionate youthful assertions of "will to win" characteristic of power in the bud:

"Despite all the machinations of my enemies, I will succeed. I am now sailing before the wind, and they against it."

It is clear from these sentences that there was keen personal opposition to his candidature. It was a moment in Welsh Liberalism of fierce tidal struggle between the old and the new forces. The old forces died hard. That type of Liberalism, still not rare in England, which aims at cashing its seat in Parliament for money favours or local privileges, was by no means yet dead in Wales. The strong wind of that great national spirit which has since swept through the Principality had not yet risen to hurricane force. There were many elements of fear and self-interest which viewed with horror the challenge to powers in high places which David Lloyd George set before Wales as the only sure road to liberty. These men found his doctrine too hard for them. Mr. Doubting and Mr. Feeble-mind hoped still to serve two masters and to get the best of two worlds. It yet required a great struggle before David Lloyd George could convince them that his was a sign in which they could conquer. These great victories are not achieved easily; it is only through great storm and stress that nations attain to freedom of soul.

But a great event in this progress was destined to take place the following year —1889. It was a singular curiosity of this period of reaction in British home affairs that there had crept into the Unionist Government a man of large and progressive views. Mr. C. T. Ritchie[26] had emerged from the British middle class to take his seat among the mighty of this land. He had not lost sight of his own people in the process. Mr. Ritchie was a bluff man, rugged of speech and ungainly of appearance. He seemed like a fly in amber in the midst of a Tory Government. But he happened to be very popular with Queen Victoria, and he was a power in the City of London. It has always been in England a part of the compromise of the great aristocrats who dominate the Tory Party that they should promote to high office a few shining lights of the middle class. In an earlier time they had to promote Sir Robert Peel-at a great price to their cause. Now they had to admit Mr. Ritchie; and the penalty was almost as great. For in 1888, by creating the County Councils, he struck a blow at the roots of county feudal government.

Young Lloyd George saw in a flash the tremendous opportunity thus given to Wales. He knew by long experience that the power of the squires was largely based upon their control of county government in Quarter Sessions. He saw that they would endeavour to prolong their power by capturing the new County Councils. He determined to do his utmost to defeat them.

He refused to stand for election himself, although he was offered four seats. His own ambition was larger. It was to capture the county. He moved about from place to place speaking everywhere and trying to rouse the whole of Carnarvonshire to the great chance now placed in their hands. He succeeded. He carried the county. Everywhere the candidates of progress were returned. "It is a revolution!" he cried. "The day of the squire has now gone!"[27] So profound was the conviction of the Welsh Liberals that he had won their battle for them that he was immediately chosen as county Alderman along with Mr. (now Sir) Arthur Acland, who, at that time, had a house in Carnarvonshire.

"The boy Alderman," as he was called, instantly threw himself hotly into the new work of the Carnarvonshire County Council. He became a conservator for those native rivers of his which he loved so dearly, soon winning for them that freedom for which he had always striven in other ways. He took an active part in every branch of administration. But his main purpose was directed to using the Welsh County Councils as a political stepping-stone towards the great goal of Home Rule for Wales. He was a prime mover in appointing a Committee to collect evidence for the Royal Commission on the Sunday Closing Act in Wales. He pushed forward the idea of an Association of County Councils for the whole of the Principality. During those months of 1889 David Lloyd George created a Home Rule weapon in Wales of which he was destined to make a mighty use in one of the greatest struggles of his later years. Perhaps he "builded better than he knew." But it is a very striking evidence of his early political instinct that he should have perceived so soon the full possibilities of the Welsh County Councils.

The tide of events now began to sweep him rapidly towards a larger political career. As recognised candidate for the Carnarvon Boroughs he already began to play an important part on the larger political stage. In October 1889 he had supported a Welsh Disestablishment resolution at a meeting of the Welsh National Council. In December he persuaded the National Liberal Federation at Manchester to accept the policy of the Local Veto on the drink traffic. On February 4th, 1890, he made at the South Wales Liberal Federation a brilliant and arresting speech on Welsh Home Rule —a speech which instantly marked him out as a coming figure in Welsh politics. He argued with force and power that, as compared with Ireland, the argument for Welsh Home Rule was stronger because they lacked the specific difficulty of Ireland-the Ulster problem. The speech made a deep mark. Already in his own country he stood for unity and daring, while even in England rumours began to reach the ears of Radical politicians that a new and fiery force was arising hard by the rocks of Snowdon.

It was at this critical moment that Mr. Swetenham, the Conservative member for the Carnarvon Boroughs, died; and suddenly the young David Lloyd George was faced with a supreme challenge. Probably, if he had been able to shape events himself, he would have preferred to wait a few years before standing for Parliament. But to some men the call of fate comes early and swiftly, and cannot be denied.

Certainly David Lloyd George showed no sign of hesitating to meet the call. On March 24th, 1890, he issued his Address —a brief, terse, dignified statement of his political faith. It was not the Address of an ordinary Liberal candidate. True, he gave his homage to Mr. Gladstone and the cause of Irish Home Rule; but then he passed on rapidly to a strong assertion of the claims of Wales-first and foremost, for religious liberty and equality; then for sweeping reforms in land and labour laws; last, but not least, for a liberal extension to Wales of the principle of self-government. In other words, Mr. Lloyd George stood for Parliament always before all things as a Welsh Nationalist. In subsequent years, when he was to be so often accused of disloyalty to the Liberal Party, that fact might perhaps have been more often remembered.

The sudden death of the Tory member threw the Unionist organisers into some confusion. At first they pushed forward a Liberal Unionist; but Wales has no liking for the lukewarm in politics. Finally, they selected the local squire, Mr. Ellis Hugh Nanney,[28] a strong Tory, but a man of considerable local popularity with those who admired him.

Here, then, was a thrilling contest-between the village boy and the local squire; between the rebel of the village school and its secular ruler; between the Robin Hood of the village woods and their lord and owner.

It was a sharp, keen struggle, fought to all appearances on Irish Home Rule; but the weapons of the fight were edged and pointed by the new spirit of freedom that was blowing hard from the Welsh hills. On Mr. Nanney's side was the old order, with all its powers and attractions, its graces and its condescensions; on the side of David Lloyd George was the keen, breezy hope of the future, with all its rough and rugged possibilities. In the end the veteran Liberals of Wales rallied to the support of the young David. Both Mr. John Parry and Mr. Thomas Gee-after a searching interrogation-came to his help.

We may be sure that in the fierce atmosphere of that contest there was little effort to spare the humble origins of the Liberal candidate. It was characteristic of David Lloyd George that he met these attacks, not with apology, but with bold defiance.

On March 28th, speaking at Carnarvon, he uttered this ringing reply:

"The Tories have not yet realised that the day of the cottage-bred man has at last dawned."[29]

It is clear that that idea had taken hold of his mind with mastering power.

We can recover a picture of that little by-election as the struggle ebbed and flowed in the streets of those little Welsh townships, far away there between the mountains and the sea. To the great world it was a mere episode in Mr. Gladstone's last great struggle.[30] It was only dimly that the shrewd London special correspondents began to perceive that something else was at stake also-something else for Wales, something else for England also.

We see the slow-moving drama working to a crisis through that far-away Easter-tide —the public still mainly absorbed in their holiday pleasures-the meetings at first feebly attended, and then, as the day of election draws near, more and more crowded-the squire-candidate at first amiably confident and aloof, pleading ill-health, then suddenly appearing constantly in public, feverishly canvassing, plainly alarmed by the reports of his agents. All through we can see the little "hamlet-lad" with the yellow rosette-boldly sporting his colours-flitting from town to town, urging on his supporters, speaking to the Welsh people in that sweet mellifluous, persuasive tongue of theirs, so magical to those who know it.

"A dull election," said the correspondents at first. The result seemed to them doubtful. These Londoners expected the Welsh to be very excitable; and they were surprised to find them so calm. They forgot that deep waters run still.

Then they began to notice the Liberal candidate. One who heard him speak in Welsh wrote to London: "I never heard any one speak Welsh so charmingly as Mr. Lloyd George. It was the first time I had heard him; and though I could not understand a word of it, it is exceedingly pleasant to listen to him."[31] Truly, a remarkable victory for the power of sound!

Then, as the election goes forward, we can see pale fear gradually creeping through the ranks of Tuscany. The Welsh Tory agent was hurriedly sent down from headquarters and wired back that the situation was serious. Exertions were redoubled. On those last days this election certainly was not dull. Deep cried unto deep; and the Welsh crowds began to murmur like the restless sea which beats on their shores.

Then comes the polling day-Friday, April 4th. Up to the last the issue is doubtful. It is a neck-and-neck struggle. The poll is very heavy. Carnarvon votes to a man-and Bangor almost to a man.[32] The shrewd observers are puzzled. They feel like those who watch the meeting of the tides. The signs are not clear. One coming from Nevin finds David Lloyd George in Carnarvon the solitary wearer of his own favours. He cannot understand it.

Then, the closing scene-the counting of the votes on the polling day in the room beneath the town hall at Carnarvon. It is midday of a beautiful spring day, and the street outside is packed with seething, expectant humanity. How slow they are inside there! How wearily the minutes drag on! But far away, over Criccieth, Snowdon shines, still snow-crowned, beautiful and serene.

Inside the town hall the issue wavers to and fro. From hour to hour fate oscillates in the balance.

The votes have now been counted. The Nanney heap is one side of the table, and the Lloyd George heap on the other. The heaps seem almost equal. But to the trained eyes of close observers the papers on the Nanney heap rise above his rival's by just a shadow of a shade. There can be no doubt about it-David Lloyd George is beaten. Better tell him at once.

David Lloyd George smiles bravely. His friends gather round him with sober solace. "Better luck next time" —when suddenly there is a stir in the throng which surrounds the ballot papers.

One of David Lloyd George's vigilant agents has been better occupied than in uttering words. He stands eagerly scrutinising the piles of papers: and now his keen eye has noticed something doubtful about one of the packets of papers on Mr. Nanney's heap. He picks it up and glances rapidly through the voting-papers. Below one or two Nanney votes there is a little unnoticed series of votes for Lloyd George. It is enough to make the difference, and to return David Lloyd George as member by a majority of 20.

Stung by frustrated hope, the Nanney agents insist on a recount; and one vote is transferred from Lloyd George to Nanney, reducing the majority to 18.

David Lloyd George is M.P. for the Carnarvon Boroughs!

The word goes swiftly forth. As soon as he appears, he is received by that hitherto silent crowd with tumultuous acclaim. The still waters break into foam. He is drawn in a carriage through the town by a tremendous crowd. At Castle Square he addresses them in Welsh: "My dear fellow-countrymen," he says, "the county of Carnarvon to-day is free. The banner of Wales is borne aloft, and the boroughs have wiped away the stains!"

Eighteen votes[33] —not a very large gap between defeat and victory. But it is enough. 'Twill serve. The moving finger has written.

---

[25] Now (1920) as then a constituency consisting of five Welsh Boroughs-Carnarvon, Bangor, Criccieth, Pwllheli, and Nevin. Out of consideration for the Prime Minister the constitution was left unaltered by the Act of 1918.

[26] Afterwards Lord Ritchie.

[27] In a speech at Liverpool on February 18th, 1889. The first mention of Mr. Lloyd George in a leading article was in the Carnarvon Herald over this speech.

[28] Now Sir Ellis Hugh Nanney.

[29] These words are taken from the verbatim report of his speech in the Carnarvon Herald.

[30] Mr. Gladstone wrote the following by-election letter:

"Dear Sir,

"Your sanguine anticipations do not surprise me. My surprise would be this time, if a Welsh constituency were to return a gentleman who, whether Tory or Liberal, would vote against the claims which Wales is now justly making, that her interests and feelings should at length be recognised in concerns properly her own. Even if he reserved or promised you his individual vote, by supporting the party opposed to you and keeping it in power, he would make that favourable vote perfectly nugatory.

"I remain,

"Your faithful servant.

"W. E. Gladstone."

[31] The Daily News, April 2nd, 1890: "He has a flexible, sympathetic voice, a silvery, mellifluous articulation, and his action is that of an accomplished orator."

[32] The Carnarvon Herald records that the Tories polled every possible man. One voter was brought all the way from Wolverhampton. Three Carnarvon plasterers were brought by car to Carnarvon from the beach at Pwllheli, where they were working.

[33] The full figures were:

David Lloyd George	1,963
Ellis Nanney	1,945
	— —
Majority	18
	— —

MRS. WILLIAM GEORGE,
THE MOTHER OF DAVID LLOYD GEORGE.

DAVID LLOYD GEORGE AT THE AGE OF SIXTEEN

CHAPTER VII

FIRST SKIRMISHES

> "And now,
> Out of that land where Snowdon night by night
> Receives the confidences of lonely stars,
> And where Carnarvon's ruthless battlements
> Magnificently oppress the daunted tide,
> There comes, no fabled Merlin, son of mist,
> And brother to the twilight, but a man."
> William Watson on Mr. Lloyd George.

Entering the House of Commons in April 1890, David Lloyd George walked straight into one of those great party struggles which in those days supplied the British public with an efficient substitute for the Prize Ring. The subject was a clause in the Budget of 1890 compensating the Drink Trade for abolished licences. The whole Liberal Party attacked this clause hotly under the leadership of Mr. Gladstone. The whole Unionist Party supported it.

On the face of it, the young Lloyd George, hot with temperance enthusiasm, could not have found a more congenial theme. But his letters and diaries reveal that he felt an immediate chill on contact with the House of Commons. He found the drink question being used as a great party weapon on both sides. Shrewd political calculations had annexed one party to drink and another party to temperance. But the young Lloyd George, drunk with the temperance faith, detected no real enthusiasm on either side.

"The debate," he wrote to his uncle on May 16th, "was rather an unreal one, no fervour or earnestness characterising it. The House does not seem at all to realise or to be impressed with the gigantic evils of drunkenness."

It was characteristic of young Lloyd George that he hoped for a great change in the atmosphere when the country was really aroused; and he proceeded to do his best to arouse it.

Often in the years that followed the young Lloyd George felt the same chill in the atmosphere of Westminster. He often used to say in those days that he found it necessary to renew his strength by constantly visiting the constituencies. He was always rather a platform man than a House of Commons man: he was never a great lobbyist. Often in those early years he used to find that he gained more inspiration from great popular meetings than from a week in the House of Commons.

He was a little timid of the House of Commons-perhaps wisely so. He saw in a moment that the House liked to be wooed carefully. "I shan't speak in the House this side of the Whitsuntide holidays," he wrote to his uncle. "Better not appear too eager. Get a good opportunity and make the best of it-that's the point." There, at any rate, he showed that he had the first qualification for parliamentary success-respect for his audience.

I can remember the ferment of expectation that gathered round Mr. Lloyd George among those of us who, in those days, watched the House of Commons from the gallery. We had heard vaguely of him as a great "spell-binder" in North Wales. We had been told that no man equalled him in his power of rousing Welsh crowds in the Welsh tongue. We had heard that he had the gift of the "hwyl"; and, not knowing quite what that meant, we expected to see something resembling a Druid appear on the floor of the House of Commons. Imagine our surprise, therefore, when we saw a slim, well-groomed young lawyer in a frock coat and with side-whiskers. The few questions he asked in the first week revealed that he had a soft, rather sweet voice, and was more inclined to speak in a whisper than a shout. All these things seriously upset our calculations, and considerably disappointed the hopes of all fervid sketch-writers.

It was on June 13th, 1890, that he first broke his parliamentary silence by a speech on the compensation clauses. He supported Mr. Acland's amendment for diverting Mr. Goschen's grant from liquor compensation to technical education.

It was by no means the speech of a fanatical Druid. It was a soft-spoken, skilful piece of debating expressed in excellent idiomatic English. It was full of swift debating thrusts and sharp-edged jests. It was in this speech that he described Lord Randolph Churchill and Joseph Chamberlain as "political contortionists who can perform the great feat of planting their feet in one direction and setting their faces in another." Here was just the kind of humour that the House of Commons loves. It came well within the line of that traditional parliamentary wit which has to be appreciated even by its victims.

In fine, Mr. Lloyd George's maiden speech seemed a good start for a promising parliamentary career. It was approved by Mr. Gladstone, praised by Sir William Harcourt, and cheered by the House itself.

For the moment the young Welsh victor was a conspicuous figure. He stood in the limelight. He received from many quarters those purple favours which have turned the heads of so many young members fresh from a by-election. For this return, coming after several defeats of other candidates, was a notable event in the close and desperate partisan warfare of those years.

It was an event, indeed, deemed worthy of special attention from the veteran leader of the Liberal hosts, Mr. Gladstone smiled on Wales. On May 29th Mr. Lloyd George was invited to Hawarden with a party of Welsh constituents, who sang hymns and folk-songs on that historic lawn. The young recruit was introduced to the Grand Old Man, who honoured him with a special oration. "The Carnarvon Boroughs," he said in his stately way, "are a formidable place for the Liberal Party to fight. Penrhyn Castle is an important centre. But truth, justice, and freedom are greater than Penrhyn Castle!" Mr. Gladstone was no doubt thinking of little more than his beloved cause of Ireland; but the words echoed through Wales with a meaning that perhaps Mr. Gladstone himself little dreamed of.

Thus David Lloyd George was initiated into the sanctities of the Liberal party. But he was not always to prove an easy and obedient acolyte.

For the House of Commons had not yet had any taste of Mr. Lloyd George's rebellious humours. The real test of this quality was yet to come.

It came on August 13th of this year (1890) when he let himself go with a touch of his own native daring on some of the items of the Estimates. He selected them from among those decorative payments which are far too easily granted by an assembly always inclined to be kind to the great and prosperous. One of the items was a payment of £439 on the installation of Prince Henry of Prussia as a Knight of the Garter. "What service," asked Mr. Lloyd George boldly, "has Prince Henry of Prussia ever rendered to this country? He has not yet rendered any service to his own country, to say nothing of service to Great Britain."

Then he passed to an item of £2,769 —"equipage money" to the Lord-Lieutenant of Ireland. "The Lord-Lieutenant," said Mr. Lloyd George, "is simply a man in buttons who wears silk stockings and has a coat-of-arms on his carriage." At this he was called severely to order by the Chairman, but that did not prevent him from a ruthless comparison of this expenditure with the recent report of a Sweating Committee and the terrible revelations of poverty contained in that document.

Here the House of Commons had a touch of the real Lloyd George whom they were to get to know so well in the future. It was for this that he had come to Westminster; not for conventional party speeches, but for plain homely utterance on the pomps and conventions and extravagances of the great world. Here we get a first hint of his mission: a difficult and even cruel mission-to tell the comfortable and wealthy that they were living on the poor-to tell the decorative that they must be decorative no longer, but must either be useful or come down from their high places. He knew that such talk was not going to be popular in the House of Commons, but he was looking to another quarter for approval. Writing in his diary the day before delivering the speech on Prince Henry of Prussia's Garter he made the following significant entry:

"My audience is the country."

It was to the country, indeed, that he was already making his chief appeal. His biggest efforts of this year were made outside the House of Commons. The first was made on May 7th at the Metropolitan Tabernacle, where the Liberal Party appeared in full force to support Welsh Disestablishment. He prepared his speech with the utmost care. He sent notes of it down to his uncle at Criccieth and received the comments and criticisms of the "Esgob" —the "Bishop" —as he loved to call Richard Lloyd.

Mr. Lloyd George was perhaps a little humanly disappointed when he discovered that, graded by party officialism, he had been given the lowest place in the list of speakers at the Tabernacle. But this was soon forgotten when he once got into his stride. Although the audience had been dismally thinned by a succession of dreary orations, they sat out his speech to the end. He had intended to go on for only five or ten minutes: but the cheering and laughter of his audience carried him on for twenty-five. This was the very thing-here was a man to whom Welsh Dis-establishment was an actual life issue, and not a mere new item in a party programme. When at last he sat down, the audience seemed surprised. Like a wise man, he left them unsatisfied, and the result was that the public soon demanded more.

After this success he was deluged with requests for speeches in every part of England. But wisely he accepted few. He decided to stick closely to his House of Commons work, and there is no sounder course for any young Member of Parliament. The result was that at the end of this first session of 1890 he had already secured a good parliamentary footing.

It may be taken that the transition to Parliament from North Wales was by no means an easy domestic revolution for a struggling young provincial solicitor who had only just begun to earn an income.

Politics did not come to him, indeed, with such a crushing burden as it brings to many young men. The total expenses of this, his first election, were little more than £200. He definitely refused the offer of his political friends to raise a fund to cover his election expenses. But he accepted gratefully the unpaid help of several friendly lawyers at Bangor and Carnarvon as his election agents. In his later elections the Liberal Association of the Boroughs covered his expenses. The labourer is worthy of his hire; and Mr. Lloyd George had wisely accepted the offer. To that arrangement the Association adhered until the time when he entered a Min-istry (1906) —thus creating one of the finest ties that can exist between a constituency and its member. Here, at any rate, was a member who was a public servant and not a public almoner.

But in spite of that great public aid the entrance of David Lloyd George into Parliament proved a great and growing strain on the young couple. Their eldest child Dick[34] was already fifteen months old when Mr. Lloyd George came into Parliament. The growing practice at Port-madoc had to be left during the Session to his brother, Mr. William George, whose splendid self-sacrifice and high public spirit have always fortified and entrenched the private fortunes of his elder brother. While profits diminished, new expenses grew. A domicile had to be secured in London. Mr. and Mrs. Lloyd George settled down first (1890) in a flat in Gray's Inn, then (1891) in the Temple, and, later on, for six years (1893-9) Palace Mansions, Kensington. There they set up a simple house, always open to their many friends. For from the beginning Mr. Lloyd George was always the most hospitable of men.

For the first year or two of his parliamentary life he continued to practice in North Wales during the recess and to live during the autumn months at Criccieth with Mr. and Mrs. Owen, his parents-in-law.[35]

On these returns to his native soil he continued to use his legal position for those daring assertions of popular right which had become his passion. At this time, indeed, occurred one of the boldest of these incidents, when he faced Mr. Casson, the very lawyer to whom he had been articled. That able provincial attorney had concentrated in his hands all those secular offices which combine to make a genuine social tyranny. He was at once Clerk to the Justices and agent to the Tremadoc estate, which practically covered the whole district. As agent to the estate, he had allowed some of the houses in Portmadoc to fall into grave disrepair. At last the thing became a scandal. The Urban District Council had to take action; and they instructed Mr. William George.

Complaint was in vain; it was soon necessary to prosecute. But the summons against Mr. Casson the agent could only be issued by Mr. Casson the Clerk of the justices: and Mr. Casson the Clerk of the Justices refused to issue it. He seemed safely protected by his own loyalty to himself.

Not an unusual incident in our happy countryside, in England as well as in Wales; but Mr. David Lloyd George there and then determined that it should not occur again in Portmadoc.

Mr. William George reported the situation to his brother, who said, "Leave this to me." Next day he went into court. He began by challenging the bench. For one cause or another he was able to disqualify all the magistrates except a schoolmaster and a bank manager, men of open minds. To them Mr. Lloyd George then began to denounce Mr. Casson with merciless vigour for a whole hour. He lashed him ruthlessly for his misuse of his powers. He demanded that he should sit where every other culprit had to sit-in the dock.

Mr. Casson did not remain quiet under these lashes. He protested and interrupted for a time, but was at last quelled by Mr. Lloyd George's attack. Then he subsided into silence until the magistrates sternly ordered the issue of the necessary summonses. The result was that the dangerously crumbling walls complained of by the Urban Council were put in a state of safety for the public.

When Mr. Lloyd George opened this scene the court was almost empty; but in a few minutes the public outside had seemed to get wind of what was happening. Long before the attack ended the court was crowded with people who made no attempt to conceal their approval. To this day Portmadoc will tell you that Mr. Lloyd George never did a more necessary piece of work, or did it more thoroughly, than on this notable day.

It is not remarkable that, feeling these powers growing within him, he should have thought seriously at this time of being called to the English Bar. His friend Samuel Evans urged this on him. He put his name down. But at that point some rare strain of diffidence held him back-some instinctive shrinking. At any rate, he never carried the matter further; but went on attempting to combine with his parliamentary duties the conduct of his solicitor's practice at Portmadoc.

But he could not go on permanently with this double strain. More and more the public demanded speeches from him in the autumns; and he had less and less time for work at Portmadoc. In May 1897 he sent for his friend Arthur Rhys Roberts, a solicitor who was practising at Newport in South Wales. He asked him to join him in starting an office in London. They took rooms in 13, Walbrook, E.C.,[36] where they opened with no prospects except the vague promises of friends; and for the first three years David Lloyd George gave a great deal of time to this venture. He went to the office every morning and to the House in the afternoons. He worked hard for the firm. He wrote all important letters; he conducted all important interviews-often at the House of Commons. He was still a partner at Criccieth, and thus for a time he maintained a double position in the law-the partner in two firms. But Criccieth counted less and less, and gradually passed entirely into the hands of his brother.

He earned a fair income; but it was a hard life, and he had to supplement it with journalistic work for Welsh papers and for the Manchester Guardian. He was quite a vigorous writer in those days. The burden was heavy. But he had beside him the great courage and thrift of his wife, and behind him the high and splendid spirit of his "Uncle Lloyd."

His life in those early days was full and serene, crowded with work and play. The children began to fill his quiver-Dick, Mair, Olwen, Gwilym-those young voices that speak with our enemies in the gate. He loved children; and he loved life. He was already surrounded with friends, and especially with that bright band of young Welshmen who were gathering to Westminster-Tom Ellis, Herbert Lewis, Frank Edwards, Sam Evans, Llewellyn Williams. So girt, he ever took life "with a frolic welcome."

His was a spirit welded of laughter and tears, moulded for great adventures. He learnt even in those early days the great art of varying grave with gay. But then, as now, the gay never took the place first. It was always there as a servant rather than master —a foil to grave endeavour; a background to serious purposes.

He had, of course, those little weaknesses that require the forgiveness of affection. He could always, when he wished, write letters with the best-especially when letters were really required for business or affairs. But he would not write the small letters, or answer the small letters. He was not very precise over social engagements. He was always more faithful to his humble friends than to the great and fashionable; and he sometimes forgot Gilbert's great discovery-that even Belgrave Square has a heart behind its stucco.

Behind all the colour and zest of his young, eager life there was always that same quality of courage that knit his character like an iron girder. He had a serene confidence in his own star. He did not know the word "impossible." The greater the obstacle the greater his security of success. It was this note that dominated his thought and speech.

But, after all, it was at those gatherings of his friends, when the pipes were lit and the laughter rang free, that the true Lloyd George was to be seen and heard-the Lloyd George who has since won the hearts of nations. Those were wonderful meetings of young souls at that little flat in Kensington. How that symphony of laughter and speech rings across the years, the echo of those grave debates of youth in which, though we knew it not, opinions were moulding and a will forming which, in the coming time, were to fashion and shake the world!

---

[34] Now Major Richard Lloyd George.

[35] At first on the farm, and later in Criccieth. Mr. Owen built there two semi-detached houses, Llys Owen and Brynawel, and there the Owens and the Lloyd Georges lived for some years next door to one another.

[36] In 1900 they shifted to 63, Queen Victoria Street, E.C., which is now the office of the firm of Rhyn Roberts & Co., as it has been called since Mr. Lloyd George severed his connection with it after taking Government office.

CHAPTER VIII

PITCHED BATTLES

"Though it appear a little out of fashion,
    There is much care and valour in this Welshman."
    Shakespeare's Henry V, Act I, Sc. iv.
    David Lloyd George had gone to Parliament as a Welsh Nationalist; and, as the months passed, it became clear that the task of moulding and defending the new national cause in Wales would absorb his main energies.

It was not a popular task at Westminster, where it cut right across the party divisions. It was not even yet wholly an easy task in Wales, where the old spirit of feudalism had many strongholds and was still "an unconscionable time in dying."

Throughout the following years (1892-7) David Lloyd George had to fight a double battle-at Westminster and in Wales. At Westminster he took the lead of a small group of Welsh members-often only four-who greatly dared to put the cause of Wales before the cause of party-never an easy task in a House where the party system is the very oxygen of the political atmosphere. On all great public questions that arose in those years-tithes, free schooling, local option, clergy discipline-he steadily and daringly pursued the national course and built up a national policy.

The influence that kept him straight on this course came ever from his own native soil. For he was in daily touch with that faithful little family group-those four loyal souls-his uncle, his brother, his sister, and his mother-who kept for him, while he battled in London, the fires burning on the home hearth, helped his wife by looking after the children in moments of stress, and steadily aided him with counsel and inspiration. David wrote to that little family party a daily record of his doings; and day by day Uncle Lloyd wrote to his "Di" long letters, partly in Welsh, partly in English, advising him on every question that arose, always taking the bold side, always bringing his nephew back to the goals of his pilgrimage-faith and fatherland. "Land of our Fathers" was the key-phrase in Uncle Lloyd's politics; and, amid the stress and distraction of Westminster, his boy was never allowed, for a single day, to miss hearing that clear call from the Eagle mountains.

Here was the source of his strength in the struggles that now lay before him, calling for the utmost exercise of will and decision. For, if the Welsh cause was to be kept to the front, it was necessary to fight continually against the submerging influence of the party machines.

The most remarkable among these contests of the early nineties was undoubtedly that memorable fight undertaken by Mr. Lloyd George and a small band of Welsh fellow-members against Mr. Gladstone in the zenith of his power and frame over the Clergy Discipline Bill.

The Bill seemed a very innocent and reasonable measure. It aimed at strengthening the control of the Anglican Bishops-always weak enough-over their clergy. To Englishmen reasonable enough; but not so to Welshmen, to whom the very word "Bishop" was almost as hateful a sound as to the Presbyterian Scotch. Not until the Bishops released their hold on Wales would they consent to give them a stronger hold over their own clergy.

Now the Bill happened to be a very special favourite of Mr. Gladstone, who still loved his Church with a mighty love, and Mr. Gladstone was at that moment a very formidable opponent. It is difficult now to realise the power of his authority at that moment. The Liberals who had remained faithful to him regarded him with a loyalty that amounted to a passion. To dispute his word would seem to them the nearest secular approach to heresy or sacrilege. It was that spirit that Mr. Lloyd George dared to defy.

It was a sight for the gods to see those young Welshmen, night after night, facing the Grand Old Man. There he sat, almost alone on the Front Opposition Bench, battling against those eager young members. He took them very seriously. He argued with them, pleaded with them, rebuked them. Mr. Lloyd George thoroughly enjoyed the experience. "Ah! But he is a great debater!" he would say. But one thing he never forgot-the Grand Old Man's eye. He has often said that to face that eye in anger was one of the most trying experiences in his parliamentary life. Years after, when some of us were discussing the points of likeness between the Grand Old Man and that gallant grandson who so splendidly gave his life for his country, Mr. Lloyd George suddenly burst out: "Ah! But he has not got the Old Man's terrible eye!"

Mr. Gladstone pursued the matter to the end. He took a seat on the Grand Committee that was to consider the Bill. He and Mr. Lloyd George fought the matter out. It was only towards the end that Mr. Gladstone realised one day that his own speeches were prolonging the fight; and then the Old Man would sit glaring at the impudent youngsters in speechless anger.

But Mr. Gladstone bore no grudges against a good fighter who stood up for his own honest faith; and some years afterwards, when he met Mr. Lloyd George at Sir Edward Watkin's house on the slopes of Snowdon, he made a special point of singling him out for special friendly speech.

Such revolts did not make Mr. Lloyd George more popular with the orthodox English Liberals. But things were to become worse before they became better. In the years 1892-5 came that great and prolonged contention between the Welsh members and the English machine over the position of Welsh Disestablishment among the Liberal fighting measures. In that contention Mr. Lloyd George took a leading part.

Welsh Disestablishment in Wales, ever since 1868, had taken the same position and grown to the same power as the Home Rule Movement in Ireland. The Welsh was a Nationalist movement in a religious dress. But English Liberalism had been chilly towards this movement, and treated it with scant favour. Mr. Gladstone opposed it in 1870, and it was only in 1891 that he first supported it, and allowed it a place in the famous Newcastle Programme. But so greatly was the Liberal Party absorbed in the Home Rule struggle that in 1892-3 the Welsh cause slipped back and the Liberals showed a definite tendency to shelve it.

It was at that moment that that small group of young Welshmen again stepped forward and definitely demanded that Welsh Disestablishment should be carried through the House of Commons and sent up to the House of Lords.

Mr. Lloyd George was the leader of this revolt; and for those two years he conducted it with a ruthless persistence which galled and embittered the Liberals, wearied by the great fatigues of the Home Rule struggle. For it was precisely in 1893, just after the great disappointment of the rejection of the Home Rule Bill by the House of Lords, that he roused the whole of Wales to demand the production of the Welsh Disestablishment Bill.

There followed one of those intense sectional struggles which in our party system are largely veiled from public view, but are none the less bitter for that.

Those of us English Liberals who were actual spectators of the battle certainly regarded Mr. Lloyd George as far from reasonable. We were looking at the matter from the angle of English Liberalism. His was the angle of Welsh Nationalism. Those angles sometimes crossed.

Mr. Gladstone resigned on March 1st, 1894; and Mr. Lloyd George instantly demanded of the new Government that the Welsh Disestablishment Bill should be carried through the Commons in 1894, unless they were prepared immediately to take up the struggle with the Lords, in which case he was prepared to forego the claim of Wales based on the Newcastle Resolution to legislative attention immediately after the Home Rule Bill.

The harassed Liberals-sensitive from weakening vitality-struggled on their bed of torture. Sir William Harcourt, the new leader in the Commons, at first refused. Mr. Lloyd George pursued his offensive with a fierce attack at Holywell. Then came Mr. Asquith with a vague speech at Plymouth; and at last on April 26th, 1894, the Disestablishment Bill was introduced. Again came delay. But the revolt went steadily forward; and the unhappy Government, with its dwindling majority, squirmed like some victim under the mediæval torture of the peine forte et dure.

At the opening of the Session of 1895 the Rosebery Government were perforce obliged to push the Disestablishment Bill forward. It was carried by a majority of 44 on April 1st, 1895.

But yielding brought no peace. The Government was forced to pass the Bill through Committee; and during that stage Mr. Lloyd George and his friends fiercely pressed certain nationalist amendments which the Government reluctantly accepted. These convulsions proved too much for a sick Ministry. On August 11th, 1895, while the Welshmen were away in Wales devising new measures of torture, the Rosebery Administration fell over the "cordite vote."

Mr. Lloyd George was fiercely attacked by orthodox Liberals for his conduct in this affair. He was roundly accused of hastening the downfall of the Government. He answered by saying that the Government was already doomed from internal dissensions.

But in Wales his attitude was greeted with acclaim; and in the General Election that followed, he was able to defeat Mr. Ellis Nanney once more with a majority practically identical with that of 1892.[37]

The reason was clear. The Welsh now cared more for their own causes than for the causes of the Liberal Party. The spirit of nationalism had spread from Ireland to Wales. They cared nothing for the Rosebery Government. They did not believe that the Commons could any longer legislate-not until the Lords were fought and crushed. What they were looking to was that the future claims of Wales should be pegged out as clearly as the claims of Ireland.

It was for that spirit that Mr. Lloyd George stood now in Wales.

Not that, even in Wales, the victory of Welsh nationalism was achieved without a struggle. During these years (1893-7) parallel with his activities at Westminster, David Lloyd George was engaged in a great campaign within Wales itself. It was a campaign for unity and concentration.

He found in 1892 the political energies of Wales divided between a number of purely party organisations, precisely after the fashion of England. Parliament Street had carved up the Welsh counties in the same spirit and method as Canterbury had carved up the Welsh dioceses. There were the North Wales Federation and the South Wales Federation, and a number of other similar bodies, with all the various staffs and camp-followers who find their meat and malt in local distinctions and differences. The worst of it was that these local divisions often blazed up into national divergences on points of policy.

On the other hand, there were simultaneously growing up among the younger generation of Wales a vast number of common national organisations and societies, literary, social, and political. There was the same ferment that we have of late years seen in Ireland-the ferment of a new national growth, shown in language, literature, and even in costume. There was the Cymru Fydd ("Wales of the Future"), the Cymmrodorion, and, above all, the revived Eisteddfod, that remarkable annual Welsh festival of poetry and song which seems to combine the spirit of classical Greece and of Celtic Britain.

Mr. Lloyd George aspired to bring into Welsh politics some of the strength and hope of this new national rebirth.

His definite aim, in the long series of great orations which he delivered on this subject between 1889 and 1896, was to bring patriotism to the help of Welsh politics in place of party —

"The spirit of patriotism has been like the genie of Arabian fable. It has burst asunder the prison doors and given freedom to them that were oppressed. It has transformed the wilderness into a garden and the hovel into a home."[38]

It was his aim that the same spirit should transform Wales.

A simple aim, it would seem. But no sooner did he set finger on the various political Arks that had been set up for worship in the different competing capitals of Wales than he found himself faced with the fiercest hostility. Among his bitterest opponents was one of his own followers in the House, Mr. D. A. Thomas (afterwards Lord Rhondda). Mr. Thomas set himself up as the champion of the South Wales Federation; and he succeeded in maintaining the cause of local independence.

So tense and prolonged was the struggle that Mr. Lloyd George was content in the end to achieve his purposes in another way, by way of a Welsh National Council. "A rose by any other name will smell as sweet"—that is an important thing to remember in politics. Mr. Lloyd George has never forgotten it.

Here, in Wales, was evidently a case of nationalism only slowly struggling into consciousness, with many forces still to contend against. But if we take a long survey, and cast our eyes over the last half-century (1867-1920) how great is the contrast! Then (1867) there was a Wales almost entirely subject to its feudal chiefs, scarcely daring to assert its own language or nationality. Now (1920) there is a Wales returning an almost unbroken national party, and a majority of Welsh-speaking members.

In this great change David Lloyd George played a leading part.

The division between Welsh Nationalism and British Liberalism did not last long. British Liberalism, essentially in sympathy with Nationalism, soon forgave Mr. Lloyd George. Welsh Nationalism, always essentially Liberal, soon made its peace again with Liberalism.

It was during the struggles of 1896-9 that the reconciliation came. Then in the great parliamentary strife over the Agricultural Rates Bill and the Voluntary Schools Bill, Mr. Lloyd George first showed his mettle as a leader of parliamentary guerillas. Nay, more. At the moment when British Liberalism was bereft of leadership he gave it a lead. That was the great point.

Mr. Lloyd George's great fight against the Agricultural Rates Bill in 1896 marked, indeed, his first great advance towards an assured parliamentary position. It was the first of the measures put forward by our Agrarians for the special relief of agriculture from the misfortunes which had befallen them in the seventies and the eighties. A small affair as compared with later proposals; but Mr. Lloyd George conceived against it an implacable hatred. It was not the relief that he hated; but he argued that under our land system the money would all go finally into the pockets of the landlords. He believed this sincerely; and he fought a great fight against the whole proposal.

The struggle went on through the early months of the Session of 1896. The Unionists at first took it lightly; then they grew angry. Here, it seemed, was a man who must really be reckoned with. This little Welsh attorney, this chapel-trained Nonconformist, actually seemed to know a thing or two about the sacred land system of these islands. He could not be ignored. His pertinacity and resourcefulness seemed to be inexhaustible. The fight went on from day to day, and there seemed no end.

On May 21st the Government moved and the Chairman accepted the "block" closure on the vital clause of the Bill-Clause four.

When the Chairman called the House to go into the division lobbies it was seen that a little group of members were sitting still on their seats, refusing to move. They were Mr. Lloyd George and Mr. Herbert Lewis, backed by a little group of sympathetic Irishmen-Mr. John Dillon, Dr. Tanner, and Mr. Donald Sullivan-and by one Radical-Sir John Brunner.

"I must request honourable members to proceed to the division lobbies," said the Chairman.

"I decline to go out under the circumstances," said Mr. Lloyd George, speaking with his hat on, as in duty bound.

It was a new event. The Chairman was puzzled what to do. So he called the House back, summoned the Speaker-then Mr. Gully-from his repose, and reported to him what had happened.

"Do I understand," said the Speaker sternly to Mr. Lloyd George, "that you refuse to clear the House?"

Mr. Lloyd George was quite unshaken by all this awful panoply of parliamentary terrorism.

"That is so, sir," said he; "as a protest, I declined to go out."

Then came the turn of that valiant and faithful soul-the Fidus Achates of our Æneas-Mr. Herbert Lewis. Did he too-so quiet and dutiful-refuse to go out?

"I regard this Bill, sir, as legalised robbery," he said with a sudden outburst of honest vehemence.

After that there was nothing more to be said. The sacrilegious word had been spoken, and it was time for the high-priests of the temple to act. So the Leader of the House moved the suspension of these wicked men-the House voted the suspension by 209 to 58 —and the Speaker called on them to withdraw. Mr. Lloyd George cheerfully rose to obey.

"For how long, sir?" he asked the Speaker, with the spirit of a schoolboy making sure of his holiday.

"For a week," said the Speaker; and they all withdrew.[39]

But the week was to be well used. The rebel went off immediately into Wales and was received with acclamation. The grey veterans of the Welsh Party in the House had shaken their heads. But the Welsh people knew better. They realised the value of a dramatic protest.

There were others who knew better even in the House of Commons. Sir William Harcourt, always a great parliamentary leader, recognised in a moment that there was stuff in this new fighter. "My little Welsh attorney," he said to me once, "is worth the pack of them."

"My audience is the country" —that was still the clue to all "Mr. Lloyd George's parliamentary actions. He and Mr. Herbert Lewis "stumped" through Wales, rousing the people. That week's holiday bade fair to cost the Government dear.

The English people were not far behind the Welsh in their applause. He was now fighting a battle in which not Wales only but the whole country was concerned. Invitations to speak showered in from all over England.

It is, indeed, from this period (1896-7) that we must date a very important and vital development in Mr. Lloyd George's career. The guerilla warfare which he opened in this year was carried on by him over the Voluntary Schools Bill of 1897 and the Tithes Bill of 1899. But from a "guerilla" he was gradually developing into a leader of Parliament. Instead of his following the Front Bench, it was the Front Bench that began to follow him!

For it was a moment of deplorable strife and weakness in the Liberal leadership. Lord Rosebery had resigned over Armenia in 1896, and both Sir William Harcourt and Mr. Morley resigned over Fashoda in 1898. The throne was constantly being vacated; and Sir Henry Campbell-Bannerman, who succeeded to the purple, seemed at that time only a "stop-gap," with Mr. Asquith as the real and only successor.

The country was weary of these personal issues; and they turned with refreshment to the little warrior below the gangway who, at any rate, seemed to care for the cause more than for himself. During those years it was he who checked the Tory ascendancy; and it was largely owing to his vigour and vehemence that in 1897-8 the tide began to turn in the country and the by-elections began to go against the Government —a landslide that was only stopped by the outbreak of the South African War in 1899.

In 1896-7, then, came the critical new departure in the career of Mr. Lloyd George. Up to 1895 he had seemed to be a Welsh Nationalist, pure and simple-that and nothing more. It looked then, indeed, as if he might become the Parnell of Wales —a Parnell of a different kind both in speech and character, but like him in his sole devotion to a national cause —a Parnell in the sense of a leader of a national revolt.

Mr. Lloyd George gave to Wales the opening call. But Wales was not ready for such a complete break with the old order. She was too deeply committed by sympathy and conviction, both political and religious, to the British Liberal allegiance. The feud was healed.

The Welsh Party in the House flinched from electing the rebel as their Chairman. So they left England to share his services. They allowed him the freedom of a wider and more splendid career. They refused to adopt his policy of an independent Welsh Party; so they threw him into a larger contest.[40]

He still continued, after 1895, to push the Welsh National cause-he has never ceased to push it. In the new House his enthusiasm was directed to "Home Rule all Round"; but he found few supporters.

He began more and more to merge the cause of Wales in the larger cause of Britain. He began to believe that the Nonconformists of Britain were in much the same case as the Nonconformists

of Wales. Thus from being a Welsh Nationalist only he became a Nationalist on a larger scale —
a Nationalist of Britain.

Wales practically gave him to England.

---

[37] 194 votes as against 196 in 1892, when he defeated Sir John Puleston, the popular Tory champion.

[38] October 1894.

[39] These details are based on contemporary impressions and verified from Hansard.

[40] At a Welsh Party meeting on May 19th, 1899, an "independence" resolution moved by Mr. Lloyd George was definitely shelved.

CHAPTER IX

SOUTH AFRICA

"God defend the right!"

When the South African War broke out in early October, 1899, Mr. Lloyd George was touring in Western Canada. The mutterings of the coming storm had already reached him in the distant regions of the Rocky Mountains, and that swift political instinct of his had warned him of grave events. He turned in his tracks, abandoned his holiday, and made for home.[41] While crossing the Atlantic he had abundant time to meditate on the great issue between the South African Republics and the British Empire.

By the time he arrived in England he had already a very strong impression that a great wrong was being perpetrated. But before uttering any decisive word in public he made a very careful study of the many State Papers which set forth the case on either side in that momentous strife, especially the minutes of the negotiations between President Kruger and Lord Milner at Bloemfontein. For it has always been the habit of Mr. Lloyd George to study his documents in politics with fully as much care as a good judge preparing for the courts.

We all know the conclusion he reached in regard to the Boer War.[42] He took the view, on the facts of the case, that the war was by no means inevitable. He held strongly throughout the following years that the war was the result of bad statesmanship. He did not deny the wrongs of the Uitlanders; but he believed that the results of the war could have been achieved by the patient pursuit of peaceful diplomacy. This view has certainly been strengthened since those days by that very remarkable book, The Autobiography of Sir William Butler.[43]

Throughout the most bitter period of the controversy that followed Mr. Lloyd George always admitted that there were two sides to the case. He absolutely refused to join in the utter damnation of those Liberals, such as Mr. Asquith and Sir Edward Grey, who supported the war. "We take a different view of the facts," was his way of putting it; and perhaps this view explains why he refused to make the quarrel over the Boer War a dividing issue within the Liberal Party. There were extremists on both sides who wanted to part company; and there were pro-Boers who even rejoiced when that strange creation, the Liberal League, came into being. Mr. Lloyd George was not one of these. Sir Edward Grey on the side of the war Liberals, and Mr. Lloyd George on the side of the peace Liberals, did their utmost to prevent a permanent split; and they succeeded. When the war was over the two branches of the party were able to come together, and found that they still agreed on the main issues of domestic politics.

We can now see a little more clearly why it was that Mr. Lloyd George refused to found a separate party on the basis of his opposition to the Boer War. It was not merely his practical perception that the South African War was an issue that would pass: it was also that he was in no sense a "peace at any price" man. Although he found himself in the company of the pacifists, he never wholly belonged to that faith. He has always been conscious that the ultimate support of power and freedom must be force-force guided by right, but still force.[44]

His passionate sympathy with wars of freedom is in itself evidence on this side. His greatest heroes abroad are men like Garibaldi, and at home those great Welsh patriots and princes who maintained the forlorn fight of his own little nation against Saxon and Norman-men like Glendwyr and Llewellyn; fighters like De Wet often reminded him of those indomitable Welsh guerillas. He used to point to the great Norman castles along the coasts of North Wales and the Welsh borders as the "block-houses" which the conquerors had to build to control his own people.

Not, indeed, that he ever maintained the view that a little nation was a law unto itself. His support of the Boer cause was not due merely to his belief in little nations.

Order has to be maintained in the world, and little nations cannot be allowed to run amuck. That was why his opposition to the war was mild at first and grew stronger as time went on.

He felt that the Boers had made a grave mistake in issuing their Ultimatum. As long as the war was on our part a war of resistance to the Boer invasion his criticisms were restrained by that fact. But in his view that phase ended with the capture of Bloemfontein and the British claim to annex.

From that time forward (1900) Mr. Lloyd George opposed the war tooth and nail. It was after that date that he determined to enter upon a campaign against the war throughout the length and breadth of Great Britain. Many of his parliamentary friends refused to join; but Mr. Lloyd George went straight on and faced the music in every part of the kingdom.

Since John Bright's great fight against the Crimean War nothing of the kind had been seen in England. It is no light thing to meet the war-passion full front.

But none of these fears held back Mr. Lloyd George at this great moment. He went everywhere and faced hostile crowds in the very heart of the war country. He faced a violent mob at Glasgow; he defied Mr. Chamberlain's own followers at Birmingham; he narrowly escaped death in one of his own Boroughs-Bangor.

Whatever men might think of his views, no one could deny his courage. It was no easy campaign to conduct. The charge of treason was always in the air. "Do you wish the Boers to win?" shouted a heckler after one of his most eloquent defences of the Dutch Republicans. He was silent for a moment, then he said, slowly and impressively: "God defend the right!"

He has often been severely criticised both then and since for consenting to put on a constable's coat and uniform in order to escape from the Town Hall at Birmingham. An armed mob had possession of the hall itself. They had pinned him and his friends into a back room: they threatened and partly intended to achieve both his death and theirs. It is contended that he was to wait meekly for his doom.

Such criticism is surely the very extravagance of blame. If an unarmed public man faced with a mob so organised cannot resort to a "ruse of war" to save both his friends and himself, then surely the bully will rule the world. As a matter of fact, the Chief Constable of Birmingham found it difficult enough to persuade Mr. Lloyd George to put on the uniform; and it was only when he had convinced him that his friends too were in danger that he reluctantly assented. But if he had actually himself asked for the uniform he would surely have been fully justified.

To achieve an honourable peace-that was the object of his great campaign in 1901 and 1902; and undoubtedly he played a great part in an achievement which saved British South Africa. It is true he had beside him that brave and honest man, Sir Henry Campbell-Bannerman, who helped as far as it was possible for the official chief of a party deeply divided by the issue. It is also fair to say that Lord Rosebery played a great and honourable part in the final settlement. But all the risk was taken by Mr. Lloyd George-at the time when every phrase and word meant danger.

It is a curious fact that, when the Boers finally agreed to peace, Mr. Lloyd George seemed for the moment to lose his interest in them. He afterwards met and made great friends with General Botha and General Smuts; and he has since taken General Smuts into his War Cabinet. But I think he had at the time a sentimental sympathy with General De Wet in his "no surrender" policy. His reason was with General Botha; but his heart was with the men in the Back Veldt.

His interest did not revive until that occasion when Sir Henry Campbell-Bannerman persuaded the Cabinet of 1906 to make the "clean cut" by giving self-government to the annexed States. Of the speech which "C. B." then made to the Cabinet, Mr. Lloyd George always afterwards spoke with a sincere and passionate admiration. He felt that it was the undoing of a great wrong.

All through the time of the Boer War (1899-1902), Mr. Lloyd George would spend his Sundays in that simple little house by the side of Wandsworth Common —2, Routh Road. There he could escape from the tumult and turmoil. On those Sunday afternoons he would often walk over Wandsworth and Chapham Commons, and he would play and sing with his children as if no great shadow overhung the country. He was especially fond of singing hymns on those Sunday afternoons. He would always join with tremendous gusto; and although his voice was untrained, he was certainly a very hearty singer. But his greatest joy was when the children brought a book of Welsh hymns and Welsh folk-songs. He would sing these with a thrilling delight which made him really for the moment a singer of power.

Then he would come back to discuss the situation; for he was never tired of discussion. He would talk over every detail of the war; he would follow it out with the greatest precision on large-scale maps. He developed a most uncanny military skill; and he would prophesy with the most remarkable astuteness the next move of the Generals on either side. He knew every battle and skirmish; and, though he had never been to South Africa, he seemed even to know the lie of the ground. He appeared to know to what spot a column was going to move before it got there. He had the same instinctive military perception with which Botha himself was gifted. I remember De Wet once saying in conversation, "The only military training I ever had was the same as that of Mr. Lloyd George-parliamentary tactics." May it not be that there is some intimate relation between the tactics of Parliament and the battle-field? Cromwell was a Member of Parliament before he was a soldier; is it not possible that, if opportunity had afforded, Mr. Lloyd George might have become a successful leader of armies?[45]

One afternoon especially comes back to my mind-hot summer afternoon when we sat in the garden of the Wandsworth house and listened to Miss Emily Hobhouse as she read to us her diary of her life in the concentration camps. She had come hot-foot from South Africa with these bare daily records of her experiences; and her idea was to work them up into a book. Mr. Lloyd George gave an instant opinion: "No, publish it as it stands!" was his pronouncement; and so the diary was published with its fearful record of daily horror. Simultaneously with its publication Mr. Lloyd George arranged to move the adjournment of the House of Commons, and the double event blew up the whole policy of the concentration camps.

Thus did he ultimately redeem the British name from the charge of barbarism.

In the midst of the struggle Mr. Lloyd George determined that he must have a London daily newspaper on his side. Committees had been formed and subscription lists started, but little progress had been made. At last he concluded that this was not a case for founding a new journal. What was wanted was to buy up an established Liberal paper. A whisper of trouble in the Daily News office gave the compass-bearings for this venture. Imperialism was not suiting the Daily News readers; the proprietors were willing to sell. But a hundred thousand pounds were wanted for the purchase. Mr. Lloyd George determined to raise the money. For once in his life he wrote two very careful letters-one to Mr. George Cadbury and the other to Mr. Thomasson. He placed before them the issues in very clear and searching language. Those two generous and large-hearted men replied by offering £25,000 each; and the battle was practically won.

He read me those letters at the time-we were dining at Gatti's —and he read them over the coffee and cigars. All I can say is that the letters were fully worth the money they brought to his cause.

It was not very pleasant for the "prize crew" to take the places of old colleagues like Sir Edward Cook and Mr. Saxon Mills, both of whom from their own point of view had honestly and patriotically maintained their faith. Nor was the struggle easy for the new proprietors. I remember consoling Mr. George Cadbury by pointing out that he saved at least as many lives as he lost pounds sterling; and with that reflection that excellent man was more than satisfied.

But the personal crises through which journalists and proprietors had to pass during that time were dust in the balance compared with what Mr. Lloyd George and his family had to endure. His professional work in the City came almost entirely to a stand. His office was boycotted; and one day a lump of coal was thrown through the window. Towards the end of the war things got so bad that he had to contemplate breaking up his home. "They shan't starve me," he said to his wife one day, "even if I have to send you all to Criccieth and live in a garret myself." Peace happily came before this event; but at every turn in the struggle he had to look ruin in the face. His boy Richard[46] had such a bad time at school in London that they found it necessary to transfer him to Portmadoc County School when the facts were drawn from the reticent boy.

Throughout these troubles he was as considerate of those around him as he was regardless of his own interests. Mr. Arthur Rhys Roberts, his partner in the city firm, has always given to Mr. Lloyd George his devotion and loyalty; but he is the first to claim that Mr. Lloyd George has earned it. At the most critical moment of the struggle, when threatening notices were coming with every post, old clients vanishing like melting snow, and companies discarding their services, Mr. Lloyd George came to Mr. Roberts. "What are your views?" he said to him. "I don't mind smashing up my own business, but I have my qualms about injuring you. Tell me what I shall do to protect you." Mr. Roberts, feeling that Mr. Lloyd George was risking everything, refused to claim any immunity; but these simple touches of consideration explain the devotion which Mr. Lloyd George has so often inspired in those who have worked for him.

Down in his own constituency he seemed to have sacrificed everything. They burnt him in effigy in three of his Boroughs-at Criccieth, Nevin, and Pwllheli. When he went to Bangor all his friends warned him of the grave risks he was running. But he insisted on speaking there in the Penrhyn Hall. The mob broke every window. He refused protection, and walked openly through the crowd out of the hall. In the High Street he was struck on the head with a bludgeon and only saved by his hat. He staggered, half stunned, into a café in the High Street, and there he was besieged for hours by a raging mob. On the advice of the police, he climbed out at the back of the house and got away in a cab that was brought round to him. The crowd waited until two o'clock in the morning in the hope of being able to "finish" him.

All through the fearful episode Mrs. Lloyd George shared her husband's danger, and was stoned in her motor-car as she was waiting for him.

At last he paid a visit to Nevin, his own special Borough, where as a rule the people worshipped him. But there at first his only friend was a lame old shoe-maker. The people did not attack him, but they held absolutely aloof. When he held a meeting, they refused at first to come into the hall. Nothing daunted, he spoke quietly, and at length, on every subject under the sun except the Boer War. As they heard him through the door talking about their favourite subjects people slowly crept in, man by man, and gradually filled the hall. Then, when he found himself with a good audience in front of him, he really approached the subject. Gently and tentatively he addressed them in their own Welsh language, and it is very, very difficult for a Welsh audience not to listen to him in that melodious tongue. But though they listened they showed no enthusiasm; he felt that he was not moving them at all. Then suddenly he changed his tack. Facing them in his grimmest way he said to them sternly:

"See here now-five years ago you handed me a strip of blue paper to give to the Speaker as your accredited representative. If I never again represent these boroughs in the House of Commons I shall at least have the satisfaction of handing back to you that blue paper with no single stain of human blood upon it."

The effect was electrical. The whole audience rose to their feet with a shout. He had won them back to his allegiance.

It is a curious historical fact that in another great struggle another great Celtic orator, fighting a lone fight against an unjust war-passion in these islands, uttered very much the same proud boast. When Mr. Edmund Burke sent to the Sheriffs of the City of Bristol in 1777 that famous letter on the affairs of America he wrote:

"If you and I find our talents not of the great and ruling kind, our conduct, at least, is conformable to our faculties. No man's life pays the forfeit of our rashness. No desolate widow weeps tears of blood over our ignorance."

"A conscientious man would be cautious how he dealt in blood." Comparing the two passages, Mr. Lloyd George's words are a curious unconscious echo of Edmund Burke's —showing how, under similar stress, great minds will ever leap to the same expression.

Throughout all these storms Mr. Lloyd George always showed that steady, clear-headed shrewdness which is perhaps his supreme characteristic.

Never was this more conspicuously shown than in his contest with Mr. Chamberlain over the connection with Kynochs. Here was difficult, dangerous ground, where he had to tread delicately. On one occasion, in that attack, he was constrained to make use of some figures published in a newspaper. Shortly before the debate, he sent to his partner an urgent request that he should verify his figures at Somerset House. A clerk was sent along, and after careful checking it was discovered that there was an error of no mean dimensions-an excessive 0 in one of the statements of share-holdings. At the last possible moment the error was telephoned to him at the House of Commons.

As Mr. Lloyd George waded his way through the figures in the press report, Mr. Joseph Chamberlain, sitting on the Treasury Bench, leaned forward, waiting to pounce. He, too, knew of the error, and he was intending to use it for his assailant's destruction. He well knew the cost of one such slip in the House of Commons.

But when Mr. Lloyd George came to the figure, he paused, and passed it by. Mr. Chamberlain leaned back in his seat pale to the lips, disappointed and baffled. He had met his match.

The climax in this crisis in Mr. Lloyd George's career came when Mr. Chamberlain, in September 1900, suddenly dissolved Parliament. In the famous Khaki Election that followed certainly Mr. Chamberlain seemed as if he might look with security to one great triumph, and that was the final political extinction of Mr. Lloyd George. It was surely improbable that a constituency which had just burnt him in effigy would return him to Parliament. But if Mr. Chamberlain staked much on that throw it only shows that he did not know Wales.

I happened to be with Mr. Lloyd George through that election. It was a very astonishing affair. When he first came down to Carnarvon he seemed to have few friends in the Boroughs. The people were sullen, if not hostile. Then he began talking to them in their own language; and it was curious to watch, in meeting after meeting, all their old tribal loyalty gradually coming back to him. He moved from town to town, slowly and cautiously recapturing their affections. He left no stone unturned. In private he calculated his chances with all the close shrewdness of a business man. Daily he reckoned up the voting probabilities in his pocketbook. In public he worked indefatigably. He had against him a retired military officer, Colonel Platt, chosen doubtless for the khaki suggestiveness of his title. All the feudal powers of Wales put forth a supreme effort to destroy their life-long terror.

We all know how it ended. Mr. Lloyd George was returned to Parliament on Saturday, October 6th, 1900, with the largest majority he had yet achieved —296. Some of the inflammable material which had been bought for burning him in effigy at Carnarvon was actually used in the manufacture of the torches which lit up his triumphal procession. The same crowd which had been ready to destroy him a few months before led him home on the night of the poll with a pomp and enthusiasm fit for a king returning from his wars. A few months ago they had stoned him; a few weeks ago they were still against him: but now with silver tongue he had won back their hearts, and his people were with him again.

Outside his own house, Mr. Lloyd George stood up in his carriage and bade them sing that great anthem of Wales, "The Land of our Fathers." The darkness above us gave to the scene a ghostly majesty; the earnest, melancholy harmonies breathed an undying hope; the sea of resolute faces gave a sense of vast, indefinable strength. The great hymn ended, and then in perfect quiet the great multitude dispersed.

That last scene gave a clue to his hold over his people. At the critical moment he had recalled their minds from adventures abroad to the thought of their own dear land at home. On the very edge of abandoning him they had recoiled. They had remembered him as their own Welsh leader; and their loyalty had gone back to him.

It marked a great step in his career. For it proved to the whole world that he had behind him a people that would support him in his direst need. With such a support behind him a man can serenely face the future.

---

[41] A letter from British Columbia on September 18th, 1899, records his horror, and his resolution to return (Du Parcq. ii. 216).

[42] His first public utterance was on October 27th, just before the House rose.

[43] Sir William Butler: An Autobiography. By Lieut.-General Sir W. F. Butler, G.C.B. (London. Constable & Co., Ltd. 1911.)

[44] He made a remarkable speech before the war at Manchester, in January 1899, defending the use of force in cases of defence.

[45] See the article by Mr. Herbert Sidebotham in The Atlantic Monthly for November 1919, in which he discusses the question.

[46] Now (1920) Major Richard Lloyd George. Both Mr. Lloyd George's sons fought in the war, and both became majors.

CHAPTER X

FOR WALES AND FOR ENGLAND

"No poor man can afford to be ignorant; leave that to the rich." —Mr. Lloyd George at Hartley (1913).

Mr. Lloyd George was not to remain idle long. In 1902 the Conservative wing of the Unionist combination once again asserted itself. The war was over. The Unionists found themselves with that great affair wound up and the whole world before them. It was a tempting position. They were still in supreme command of a Parliament which had five years to run. The House of Lords was their obedient servant. They could practically pass what Bills they liked. It was almost too much strain on human nature to expect that they should not pass some of the Bills that they really wanted.

True, there had been certain promises made during the General Election of 1900 which were rather difficult to explain. Various Unionist leaders had indiscreetly laid it down that that Election was for the war and the war alone. But the Government seemed content to rely on the humane view once put forward by an M.P. victorious through the strength of many promises-that promises made in the heat of an Election do not really count. So in 1902 they took the bit in their mouths and boldly brought in a Bill throwing the Voluntary Schools on to the rates. It was the very policy which had been openly declared impossible from the front Conservative bench in 1896, and it was known to be extremely distasteful to Mr. Chamberlain.

Mr. Lloyd George took a leading part in the parliamentary opposition to this measure. He once more let "all out" as a guerilla fighter. There he was always supreme. His knowledge of the law made him extraordinarily resourceful in the invention and discovery of amendments; while he displayed a skill equally astonishing as an agile draftsman. Night after night he turned up fresh and smiling; always calm and moderate, serenely persuasive, and, to his enemies, distressingly cool. It seemed an outrage to speak of such a humane fighter as an obstructionist; and yet there is no doubt that few of the most savage of that tribe succeeded so well in delaying the progress of Bills.

Now, as in 1896, he became once more the heart and soul of the Opposition. The Government found themselves compelled to accept a great many of his amendments, and in this way very much weakened their Bill. Mr. Balfour found him a shrewd and agile opponent worthy of his steel.

This time, of course, he was not fighting alone. He was supported with the full power of the Front Opposition Bench, now ably led by Sir Henry Campbell-Bannerman with Mr. Asquith as chief lieutenant. But Mr. Lloyd George always contributed something peculiarly his own. To the heavy thunder of the Front Bench guns he added the fret and jar of machine-gun fire, galling the flanks of the Government forces, driving them from their chosen positions, often annihilating their best offensives.

There is no doubt that his opposition to the Education Bill played an effective part in weakening Mr. Balfour's Government, and considerably improved the new Act when it came to be applied to the schools of the country.

But his real triumph came after the Bill had passed through Parliament. On the main objection of principle to that measure he agreed with the Nonconformists of England; but he did not see eye to eye with them in the policy to be employed to resist the application of the Bill. He was never a "Passive Resister." The English problem, indeed, was different. The English Nonconformists had no certain control of the English County Councils. But in Wales Mr. Lloyd George had long ago ensured his hold over those bodies, and he had deftly amended the Bill so that they should have a decisive control over the administration of the Act.

He now laid before the County Councils of Wales a very ingenious scheme of resistance, destined to be far more effective than the heroic but vain martyrdoms of the English Non-conformists.

In January 1903 he issued to the people of Wales an Address embodying his policy.[47] It was in appearance a law-abiding policy, with the careful intention of avoiding any element of offence to legality. It was ingeniously based on provisions introduced into the Bill in the course of the long parliamentary fight.

It was laid down in the new Act, for instance, that all schools must be passed as efficiently equipped before they received rate-aid from the Councils. That was a provision already existing in regard to the Parliamentary Grant; but always more honoured in the breach than in the observance.

Mr. Lloyd George proposed that this provision of the law should be carried out. He suggested that all schools should be inspected and surveyed by the County Councils before rate-aid was contemplated; and that only those which were passed should be capable of receiving it. Mr. Lloyd George knew enough of the condition of these schools to be sure that few would pass any honest scrutiny. But none could deny the reasonableness of this request. "The sectarian schools," he said in his Address, "should be properly cleansed and clothed before they are allowed to associate on equal terms with more decently clad institutions." It seemed a fair and proper condition.

That was the first stage. The second was that rate aid was then to be given only to those schools that would accept genuine public control by the Councils and would suspend religious tests for teachers. Otherwise, nothing was to be handed to the schools except the Parliamentary Grants.

Meanwhile, it was characteristic of Mr. Lloyd George that it was part of his policy always to hold out the olive branch as an alternative to the sword. He suggested to the Councils that rate-aid should be given to any schools where the managers would accept the plan of "facilities" for sectarian teaching on colonial lines-the sects, that is to say, to teach after school hours. This was a plan which had always attracted him. It seemed to him to combine equity with the least possible interference with education. It was the part of his proposals which roused least enthusiasm in Wales on either side.

But, though fighting fiercely, he never at any moment gave up the hope of peace. All through the hottest moments of this strife, through 1903-4-5, he kept the door open for a settlement. He struck up a remarkable friendship with that large-hearted man, Dr. Edwards, the Bishop of St. Asaph,[48] and largely through the efforts of these two there were frequent meetings and conferences-at Llandrindod and in London-but all to no effect. It always happened that just when peace seemed in sight the quarrel broke out afresh. The real fact was, of course, that the two sides never desired the same object or meant the same things.

"My advice is-let us capture the enemy's artillery and turn his guns against him." That was the heart of Mr. Lloyd George's policy of resistance to the new Act. His idea was to defeat the spirit of the Act by obeying the letter.

It was no easy task to swing Wales into line on this policy. Some authorities wanted to go further and defy the Act altogether. Some —a very few-wanted to carry it out. Many individuals craved for the prison martyrdom of the English Nonconformists. There is fascination as well as courage in suffering for a cause.

But Mr. Lloyd George preached his doctrine north and south, east and west. In the spring of 1904 the triennial election for the County Councils was due. His advice was-to make this policy the test of those elections. If the electors decided in his favour, well and good-if not, then they must bow to democratic control and carry out the Act. At no point did he encourage the idea of personal individual resistance.

The elections came; and the results surpassed his most sanguine expectations. In every one of the twenty-eight counties the supporters of his "no rate" policy were returned with a strong majority. In many cases the supporters of the Act had been almost annihilated. In Carnarvonshire itself they were reduced to a minority of six. In Merionethshire there were fifty-two supporters of Mr. Lloyd George's policy as against three opponents. Even in Brecon, where the Church was at its strongest, thirty-nine members out of sixty were in favour of his policy.

Such were the events which completely paralysed the exaction of the new Voluntary Rate throughout Wales.

The Government decided to coerce Wales. In April 1904 they brought forward a measure called the Defaulting Authorities Bill, but instantly nicknamed the Welsh Coercion Bill. This Bill provided that, where a Welsh County Council refused rate-aid to a Voluntary School, the Treasury should have the right to pay the money direct to the Church Schools. They were to deduct it from the Parliamentary Grant, thus compelling the County Councils to make up out of the rates the loss to their own "provided" schools.

It was an ingenious proposal; but it reckoned without the spirit of Wales under the leadership of Mr. Lloyd George.

The Bill did not pass through the House until the close of the Session of 1904. The "Kangaroo" Closure was called for by Mr. Balfour and granted by Mr. Lowther from the Chair. There was a scene of passion. Once more (as in 1896) Mr. Lloyd George refused to leave the House. Mr. Lowther brought to bear that invincible good-humour of his, and Mr. Asquith suggested another and a better way. In the result, the whole Liberal Party, headed by Mr. Asquith, accompanied Mr. Lloyd George and his Welshmen in a solemn exodus from the House. Such incidents were not likely to make Wales more conciliatory.

In October Mr. Lloyd George definitely raised the flag of defiance against this Coercion Act.

He persuaded a gathering of 600 representatives of Education Authorities, assembled at Cardiff, to agree on a refusal to surrender.

In the memorable speech he made on this occasion he carried the war into the enemy's country. He accused these law-makers of lawlessness on their side. He pointed out to them that for years the Board of Education had broken the law on behalf of Voluntary Schools. They had not enforced the efficiency imposed by law. "They broke the law in order not to levy a rate." Very well. Wales would not levy a rate until the law was obeyed. That was their position. He boldly maintained that the law was on the side of Wales; and thus most wisely did he avoid that perilous identification of his policy with the idea and habit of lawlessness which has needlessly injured so many good causes.

He defied coercion. If the Defaulting Act were enforced and the rate-aid deducted from the Parliamentary Grant, he boldly advised that the Welsh Councils should close their schools. It would be a better thing that the children should be brought up to reverence freedom of conscience than that they should learn even the three R's. Besides, they could provide buildings where they could teach them that freedom of conscience was a greater thing even than knowledge.

Once more, courage won the day. It was not going to be an easy thing to dispute Mr. Lloyd George's reading of the law in those High Courts which know nothing of politics. Only a very few Welsh Authorities got out of hand, and, going ahead of Mr. Lloyd George's astute advice, rendered themselves liable to prosecution.[49]

But even then the Government did not venture to act. They had not enough public opinion behind them. From 1904 to 1906 there was no moment in the history of that divided, tempest-tossed Government when they could safely have entered upon a strife so perilous and so doubtful. So Mr. Lloyd George was left in Wales still unassailed and triumphant until the General Election of 1906 swept away the Government and practically killed the Coercion Act.

Meanwhile, during those years David Lloyd George had been all the time steadily adding to his reputation as a speaker and debater both in the House of Commons and in the country. There, after all, we always come back to his supreme political weapon-the power of public speech.

Born in those village debates within the bootmaker's shop and the smithy at Llanystumdwy, that power had been sharpened and developed on the village greens and in the town halls of Wales, trained to finer uses on the public platforms of England, and quickened by the quick thrust and parry in parliamentary debate. It had passed through the fire of stern combat during the South African struggle, and now it had emerged in swift, keen sword of combat, at once supple and strong.

That weapon he had used in all the great parliamentary fights of those years, when Mr. Balfour was carrying on, like the great Arthur of old, the last great combat for that pleasant, serene, feudal England which was already so sorely wounded by the hunters.

Feudalism seemed to win for the time. The Bills became Acts of Parliament-the Schools Bill, even the Licensing Bill. Mr. Balfour, himself a supreme master of the parliamentary arts, seemed to survive. But all the time David Lloyd George was inflicting mortal wounds, until at last, like the old defeated royalist in the Civil Wars, Mr. Arthur Balfour gracefully yielded his sword. He was actually the first, in that generous way of his, who recommended to Sir Henry Campbell-Bannerman that, in whatever Cabinet he might be called upon to form, Mr. Lloyd George must in any case be a Minister.

It was in 1903 that a great diversion occurred in the development of this drama. Striking across the orbit of both the great political parties, with some of the strength and ruthlessness of his old Radical days, Mr. Joseph Chamberlain put forward his famous Tariff Reform proposals.

One of the first results of that event was to divert all political energy for the moment from Bills to debate. Both in Parliament and on the platform from 1903 to 1906 the energies of public men were mainly absorbed in that great titanic controversy-so absorbing to the British mind-between Free Trade and Protection.

Mr. Lloyd George shared this diversion with all the others. He was called from progressive tasks to the essentially conservative business of defending the existing economic order. He did it well. He proved himself a faithful Free Trader. But this was not principally and specifically his especial task. In this field Mr. Asquith took the lead, and Mr. Lloyd George was always his faithful "junior."

But Mr. Lloyd George's defence of Free Trade soon began to develop a character of its own. His tactics gradually began to take on a note of attack. His defensive became an aggressive.

He had recognised, from the opening of the struggle, that the strength of Mr. Chamberlain's case lay in his frank recognition of the grim, shameful facts that lay beneath the smooth surface of English life. He realised that Mr. Chamberlain was the first great statesman to recognise fearlessly the existence of that England which so few statesmen had yet recognised-the England of the poor. Mr. Chamberlain, in fact, had brought "Darkest England" into the political landscape.

As the campaign went on Mr. Chamberlain grew bolder and bolder along these lines. He contended that tariffs, and tariffs alone, would provide the money for Old Age Pensions. He hinted at even vaster boons which were coming to England if she would only turn her back on that sour and pinchbeck old lady-Free Trade.

Mr. Lloyd George perceived at once the danger of this attack. He, at any rate, knew the "deep sighing of the poor." He realised the black abyss which lay below the surface of England's wealth. He feared the appeal to the hungry mouths of our neglected masses.

From that day forward he set out to prove that Free Trade also could remedy poverty-aye! and remedy it all the more easily because it brought wealth in its train. The great need was that that wealth should bear its due burden. That was to be his cure for the trouble.

At that time his phrasing was large and general. He had not yet worked out his later plans. Earlier he had served on the Rothschild Pensions Committee, and he had thrown all his energies into that inquiry. He was ever studying the problems of the land. But he kept a mind open to details. In that year (1904-5) he was storing impulse and collecting knowledge, preparing for the great moment that lay ahead of him.

That moment was now to come.

In December 1905 Mr. Balfour resigned, and Sir Henry Campbell-Bannerman immediately undertook to form a Ministry.

It was already clear that Mr. Lloyd George must be a member of the new Cabinet. Sir Henry offered him the Presidency of the Board of Trade, and he accepted it. To the public the appointment came as a surprise. It seemed the last post for that brilliant parliamentary free-lance, that gay leader of forlorn hopes.

They were to find that, behind that flashing exterior, there was a cooler personality, well fitted for the control of the calmer and shrewder side of our national life.

---

[47] "Address to the people of Wales," January 17th, 1903.

[48] Cousin of Sir Frank Edwards, M.P., one of the most faithful of the Welsh Nationalists, but himself an Anglican.

[49] Carnarvonshire and Merionethshire.

CHAPTER XI (1905-1908)

A MINISTER

"If they take part in public life, the effect is never indifferent. They either appear like ministers of divine vengeance, and their course through the world is marked by desolation and oppression, by poverty and servitude, or they are the guardian angels of the country they inhabit, busy to avert even the most distant evil, and to maintain and procure peace, plenty, and the greatest of human blessings, liberty." —Bolingbroke in The Patriot King on his "Chosen Men."

The Department which fell to the control of Mr. Lloyd George on the formation of the 1905 Liberal Administration presented no easy or simple task. The Board of Trade stood at a moment which comes to every great office of State —a moment when it may either increase or decrease, gather power or lose it. Its official name gave little clue to the distracting combination of powers varying from complete control at one end to vague influence at the other. British Departments are like wild-flowers —they grow and spread without plan or scheme, just as the chance caprice of Parliament or some fugitive Ministry may decide. It is often just a throw of the dice as to what new powers or functions may be laid upon them.

The Board of Trade had withered under the shadow of the great fiscal deadlock of the previous three years (1903-6). Poised between two theories of commerce, it had lingered in the "doldrums," like a ship waiting for a wind.

Thus there awaited in the pigeon-holes of the office a great number of untouched and unfinished projects, loose ends of legislation, belated steps towards giving method and authority to the powers of that great Department.

For the Board of Trade reflected in every branch of its administrative powers the spirit of the age in which it had grown up-the timid, tentative, apologetic touch of the nineteenth-century administrator. The scope of its powers, indeed, bulked vast and tremendous-extending from bankrupt firms at one end to shipping, railways, and labour at the other; but over all these branches of national life its sway was mild and illusive. The very Consuls who control our trade abroad were appointed and controlled by another Department.[50]

The Labour Department, founded in a spasm of progress, was still mainly advisory. British railways had to be supplicated rather than controlled. The great shipping interests had discovered new sea-ways through obsolete laws.

Mr. Lloyd George soon realised the opportunity that lay to his hand. The time had come to give to the Board of Trade a new grasp and stretch of authority. New laws must be passed. But also, and even more important, there must be a new spirit in the administration of the laws that existed.

He did not act in a hurry. He spent his first weeks in a thorough study of the work of the Board. He appeared little in Parliament. He took the sensible course of first learning from the able officials of the Board the general outlines of its functions and problems.

Then, after some months, he began to legislate; but, before bringing in his Bills, he developed what was then a new system of preparation and anticipation.

It had been too often the custom of Ministers in such Departments as the Board of Trade to frame Bills without consulting the interests concerned. Here was the truly "bureaucratic" spirit of the olden days-to assume that the Civil Service must of necessity know better than the public about their own business-to enforce on great private interests measures as to which they had never been asked their opinions, to wait for the inevitable complaints and grievances until it was too late to remedy them without public confessions of ignorance and folly. Such methods have been responsible for many bad laws and for many parliamentary disasters.

Mr. Lloyd George changed all that. Take the first question in which he decided to legislate-the control of merchant shipping. Here he found things in a very bad mess. The British merchant sailor was still far behind most British land-workers both in comfort and in wages.

While fabulous fortunes were being made by shipowners, sailors were still badly fed, badly housed, irregularly paid, often cheated of their pay altogether. The result was that the more prosperous classes of British wage-earners were refusing to go to sea or leaving the sea as soon as possible. Our gigantic merchant fleet, the pride of the British Empire, was already half manned by foreign seamen, whose ignorance of the English language often put English ships and lives in grievous peril.

Many efforts had been made to remedy these things-one by Mr. Chamberlain, still remembered at the Board of Trade as the best administrator up to that time. Mr. Lloyd George proposed to carry Mr. Chamberlain's efforts to completion.

What had defeated all efforts up to the present moment was the powerful resistance of the shipowners in the House of Commons, where the rights of the many too often escheat to the bold and flagrant championship of the few.

Mr. Lloyd George determined to call the shipowners together and to consult them before he introduced his Bill into the House. But, if he was to consult the shipowners, he must also consult the sailors. So he ended by consulting both interests outside the House; and this sensible method proved so successful in the case of shipping that it soon became his favourite method in preparing all his Bills, and has now been adopted by many Ministers as the obvious and necessary preliminary to legislation.

In the Merchant Shipping Act of 1906, indeed, he carried this process a step further. Not only did he, by agreement, establish for the British sailor a new charter of rights,[51] but he also effected a new load-waterline agreement with foreign Governments. Thereby he established a new precedent for international legislation.

The working of the famous "Load-line" —so dramatically secured by that fervent and determined man, Mr. Samuel Plimsoll, a generation before-had undoubtedly saved thousands of innocent lives. It had given the seamen a new guarantee of security. There was always the fact that a ship could not be weighted down below a certain depth. But meanwhile a new evil had arisen. Foreign ships, without the British "Load-line," were using British ports to snatch British trade. Deeply laden "foreigners" could afford to carry goods at lower freights; and Great Britain was penalised for her humanity.

Mr. Lloyd George determined to stop this. He compromised the "Load-line" —raising it slightly for British ships, but enforcing this modified line on all ships that came to British ports. There were protests from foreign Powers. Mr. Lloyd George proceeded to negotiate. He bargained with the right of entry to British ports, and finally he came to an agreement with most of the great seafaring nations which enforced the new "Load-line" on all ships trading to Great Britain.

Such was the first of the new measures which came from the Board of Trade under his presidency and passed through the House of Commons in October of 1906. Now for the first time piloting his own measures from the Treasury Bench, Mr. Lloyd George showed new parliamentary powers that astonished the critics. The wiseacres had shaken their heads. "Too much of a rebel to govern!" they had said. "So accustomed to obstruction, that he will obstruct himself!" said others, scoffing. But they were wrong. He developed new powers of adroit persuasiveness that surprised lookers-on. He was patient and conciliatory. He could be firm when necessary; but at other times he seemed all open-mindedness. He had won his way very often just when every one else thought that he had lost it. He knew when to sacrifice details in order to win principles.

Now that the Board of Trade found that they had secured a good law-maker, the progressive officials who distinguish that Department pressed on him other tasks. There was, for instance, the question of the law of patents, crying for consolidation and amendment. There, too, legislation was long overdue.

Consolidation was easy. But, in looking into the state of the law, Mr. Lloyd George soon discovered that there was one glaring British grievance which no Minister had yet dared to touch.

Mr. Lloyd George refused to be paralysed by the terrorism of the Protection controversy. He has never admitted the view that Free Trade means discrimination against your own country.

And yet that was how the existing patent law worked.

For he found that a custom had grown up by which foreign firms would employ a British citizen to take out a British patent with the deliberate intention to work it abroad. In that case it could not be worked in Great Britain. For there was actually nothing in British law to prevent this British privilege from becoming a direct cause of loss to British trade.

This seemed to him intolerable. Accordingly, he introduced into the Patents Bill which he brought into the House in 1907 the following clause:[52]

"At any time, not less than four years after the date of a patent, and not less than one year after the passing of this Act, any person may apply to the Comptroller for the revocation of the patent on the ground that the patented article or process is manufactured or carried on exclusively or mainly outside the United Kingdom."

Looking back on this clause now, with all the excellent results that have flowed from it,[53] it is clear that it represented the merest justice to the British trader. The Tariff Reformers congratulated Mr. Lloyd George on conversion; the Free Traders reproached him for desertion. Neither had any leg to stand on. The mere fact of granting patents is, in a sense, a form of protection for the patentee. But to ask that a nation should grant so great a privilege in order that it should be used against its own citizens is surely the very ecstasy of "freedom."

Then, just before leaving the Board of Trade, he finally settled up the Port of London by buying out the Dock Companies. There again he arranged the terms of purchase by bargaining before he brought in his Bill.

One company stood out. He went straight on without that company. It was awkward; but it would have been fatal to show weakness. He was just about to move the Second Reading of the Bill, leaving that company out, when the announcement of its agreement to his terms was brought to him in his room at the House of Commons before he went in to the Committee. Thus a problem was settled which had defied several Governments and paralysed London as a port.

"Not an ideal way of legislating," it will be said. Certainly not. Nor was then our Parliament an ideal legislative machine.

In a speech made at Liverpool on May 24th, 1906, Mr. Lloyd George described how the menace of the Lords then threw its shadow over all Liberal policy. He told how, in framing every Bill, the Cabinet, even before the Bill was drafted, had to take the attitude of the Upper Chamber into consideration.

This was, in fact, still his own governing consideration in these Board of Trade measures. He was soon to show that he was quite ready to fight the Lords when it seemed to him a necessary stroke of high policy. But he did not believe in half-defiances. So he modelled these Board of Trade Bills to pass by agreement.

But, after all, it was not in law-making so much as in administration that he was destined to make his highest reputation at the Board of Trade. It was not only that he sent into every tentacle of the great organism a new vigour and intensity of purpose; it was also that he showed in a very high degree a genius for conciliation in great labour disputes.

It was in the late autumn of 1907 that there came to him the great test of the threatened Railway Strike. He had just achieved in October a very surprising triumph of peace-making at the Welsh Convention summoned at Cardiff to denounce him for some supposed weakening on Welsh Disestablishment. They were just preparing to sacrifice him with his own borrowed weapons when he appeared in the midst of them, claimed to speak, and won them over to spare him.

But all Englishmen always took it for granted that Mr. Lloyd George could manage Welshmen. English railwaymen and English railway directors seemed a very different affair. For both parties seemed very resolute; and the powers of the Board of Trade seemed remarkably weak.

But the crisis was too grave to consider legal powers. The country was faced with a paralysis of transport. Such an event might prove a national danger.

Mr. Lloyd George swiftly acted for the nation. With no power to enforce his summons, he boldly called directors and men to the Board of Trade to discuss the situation. There he held them for days, prolonging the discussion by every resource of persuasion until the moods of both parties were cooled to a more reasonable temperature. Then he made his proposal-the famous Conciliation Boards-and he won both parties to agreement.

Those who, like myself, saw much of him from day to day during that struggle could not but be amazed at his resourcefulness and persistence. He appeared never to contemplate the possibility of a breakdown. He seemed one of that rare band of whom the Roman poet said — "They can because they think they can." It was impossible to dream of failure in his presence. Infected by his magic faith, weak men grew strong and sceptics radiated with faith. He appeared one of those of whom, in a famous poem, a great English singer has said[54] —

"Languor is not in your heart,
Weakness is not in your word,
Weariness not on your brow.
Ye alight in our van! at your voice,
Panic, despair, flee away."

Here was a tangle of time-worn hatreds: the men were suspicious and resentful, the directors dogged and prejudiced. How bring together human beings so divided? How bridge such a gulf?

Well, first he brought into the conferences those men who stood between the quarrelling parties-the railway managers. Here he found a remarkable body of Englishmen-alert, resourceful, self-made, unprejudiced.

How often he used to praise those railway managers! Ten years after, in a still greater emergency, his mind went back to those men; and in the gravest crisis of the Great War he called them in to aid the hard-pressed British lines in France.

What is it that has made Mr. Lloyd George so great a conciliator?

It is not merely his power of using speech for purposes of persuasion. "Speakers attack too much," he often used to say. "They ought to aim at persuasion." That has always been his own central aim in the use of speech.

There is also in him an even greater power-the power of making two conflicting parties see one another's point of view. That is partly because they learn to see it through his eyes. It is like some arrangement of looking-glasses in which men see one another's faces at a new and more attractive angle. There, again, he works on a theory. "Men quarrel too much," I have heard him say. "They become slaves to words and phrases. They miss the reality."

It was such beliefs and perceptions that have so often made him persevere in peace-making when all others have given up hope.

In this case of the Railway Strike of 1907 it earned him the universal applause of the nation, voiced by King Edward, who always entertained a keen and subtle admiration for good peace-making. For a few brief months Mr. Lloyd George was the hero of the nation. He seemed almost a case for the warning —"Beware when all men speak well of thee!"

But in the career of this man of storm it is always fated that no peaceful interval lasts long. On November 6th he settled the railway strike; on November 30th he lost his eldest daughter Mair, the apple of his eye. While still bowed with that bitter grief, in December he was called to stop a threatened strike in the cotton trade. He is wont to say that it was the only thing that saved him. But there was clearly to be no peace for him.

Then, four months later, in April 1908, Sir Henry Campbell-Bannerman, broken by work and domestic sorrow, resigned the Premiership, and Mr. Asquith stepped into his place. Mr. John (now Lord) Morley was offered the Chancellorship of the Exchequer, but he refused it, and that high post was now allotted to Mr. Lloyd George.

---

[50] The Foreign Office, which still (1920) appoints them.

[51] A fixed standard of food and ship accommodation, a certificated cook on board ship, a guarantee that distressed seamen should be looked after and abandoned seamen paid, a restriction on the scandalous practices of overloading and under-manning, and on the employment of foreign sailors.

[52] Clause 27, Patents Act of 1907.

[53] Many patents are now being worked in England which were previously worked abroad.

[54] Matthew Arnold in "Rugby Chapel."

CHAPTER XII

A GERMAN TOUR

"In small, truckling States, a timely compromise with power has often been the means, and the only means, of drawling out their puny existence: but a great State is too much envied, too much dreaded to find safety in humiliation. To be secure, it must be respected. Power, and eminence, and consideration, are things not to be begged. They must be commanded." —Edmund Burke, Letter I on A Regicide Peace.

In the late summer of 1908, at the end of the parliamentary session, Mr. Lloyd George traversed Germany from west to east and from south to north. It was a very thorough and systematic motor-tour. He was the travelling guest of Mr. (now Sir) Charles Henry,[55] a Member of Parliament of great public spirit and strong Liberal views, who invited me also to accompany the party. It was a journey of profound interest for us all. The object of the tour was to investigate the German system of National Insurance. Parliament had just passed the Old Age Pensions Act; and Mr. Lloyd George had already publicly promised to round off the British pension system by a general scheme of national insurance. Before drafting the actual Bills he wished to make a complete study of that very comprehensive system which had been operating in Germany since 1893. The German Government gave us access to all their Central State Insurance Offices, and gave us facilities for interviewing all their leading Insurance civil servants. We visited most of the largest towns of the German Empire, and had conversations with employers and workmen-Socialists and trade unionists-as well as with officials. Never was a statesman's holiday spent in a more thorough investigation of a great problem of the lives of the people.

We started the motor-tour in France. We trained to Amiens, where the motor met us, and travelled on the great northern French national roads through the very region where so much of the fighting has taken place during the last three years-through Compiègne, Soissons, along the valley of the Aisne to Rheims, where we visited the Cathedral-that great masterpiece of Gothic architecture which has since suffered such sacrilegious injury. Thence we travelled south by Châlons-sur-Marne, following the river valley by Vitry and Bar-le-Duc. We crossed the Meuse and passed through Nancy, that most lovely of valley frontier towns, which has since so bravely borne such fierce enemy attacks. Nancy looked very peaceful on that August day when we passed through her pretty streets and pressed on towards the Vosges Mountains, hoping to reach Strassburg that evening.

At that point we made a happy miscalculation in our time; and we were benighted in a little French village just on the edge of the frontier at the very summit of the Vosges. We found that we could get supper and beds at one of those clean little auberges which are scarcely ever lacking in the smallest French village. As we supped on the excellent meal of bouillon and cutlets improvised by the ready hostess, she stood and talked to us. She spoke to us of the memories of 1870-71, when the tide of war had so swiftly passed by that little village. She was a school-child at that time, and she had missed two years of her schooling. For the Germans had remained in occupation of that part of the country on the Vosges frontier for fully a year after the end of the war. The withdrawal of the army took place, Department by Department, as the indemnity was paid; and this Department was the last to be evacuated. Before the war she was living well within France; at the end she found herself on the edge of the new frontier.

We asked her how she managed to make an inn pay at such a spot. "Oh, quite easily," she said. "We are kept going by the people of French birth who come up on Sundays from Alsace!" "Why?" "Oh, just to feel the joy of living for a day on French soil!"

Next day we motored down to Strassburg, climbed the towers, and saw the marks of the German shells fired nearly forty years before, and spent a pleasant afternoon in the picturesque streets of that ancient town. As far as man could do it Alsace had been painted black, white and red with Teuton colours. Nowhere in the streets of Strassburg did we observe any sign or notice in any language but German. Everywhere were German soldiers, and in the evening we attended a concert of massed German bands at which the music was purely Teuton, and Teuton of the most patriotic kind. But the people seemed to us to listen with a certain strange dull indifference to all this brazen wooing; and beneath the surface we seemed to hear the whisper of a coming storm. Next day, motoring across the country, we had occasion to ask the way from an Alsatian peasant. The question was asked in German, but one of the party slipped in with French. The peasant's face instantly lighted up. "Ah! do the gentlemen speak in French?" he said. "Ah! I prefer to speak in that language myself." So little had all the arts of suppression succeeded in crushing the spirit of that race.

At Stuttgart we were witnesses of a strange event, which comes now back to memory with a significance which was then hidden. Count Zeppelin was then experimenting with his airships, and one of those new miracles had been advertised to start on a voyage from a spot near Stuttgart. The whole town had flooded out in a vast multitude to see the airship make a start; but at the critical moment there arose a hurricane of wind. The ship was torn from its moorings and fell in utter wreckage and confusion in the midst of the crowd. We arrived on the scene just after this had happened, and met the people returning from witnessing the disaster. What was notable about that multitude was the passion of grief which at that moment was sweeping over them. It was as if they had all suffered some acute personal loss. Men and women were gesticulating, some were almost weeping; all their faces were troubled and perplexed. As the people coming from the city met those returning we could hear exclamations of sorrow and almost of anguish. "Ah!" they cried, "is the airship down? What a horrible calamity!" We heard afterwards that the crowd surrounding the airship had just sung that famous national hymn, "Deutschland über alles." They had been worked up to ecstasy when the airship crashed.

So we motored through that land in that happy peace time, little foreboding all the great calamities that were to break from that storm-centre on to an unsuspecting world.

Bethmann-Hollweg was at that time "Home Secretary," a vigorous, amiable Minister of the official kind, sincerely keen on social reforms; a Junker of the better type. He treated Mr. Lloyd George with great courtesy. He returned from his holiday, and specially entertained him and his party in the famous restaurant at the Zoological Gardens at Berlin. He invited many eminent members of the German Civil Service to meet us. Every one was very gracious and polite-almost too polite for comfort. After dinner we went into a large reception-room, and there we remained standing all the evening talking and looking at one another. Towards the end of the evening we began to feel very fatigued. I ventured to ask one of the German officials whether it would be the correct thing to sit down. "Oh!" he said. "We have all been waiting for you to sit down! We, too, are very tired!"

In the middle of this rivalry in fatigue, they brought round great glasses of foaming beer in Prussian fashion. Mr. Lloyd George, who is almost a teetotaler, looked at the glasses with a scared expression. Then suddenly his face grew resolute. "We must show that Great Britain is not to be left behind!"

Bethmann-Hollweg did not talk politics until towards the end of dinner. The conversation drifted to King Edward's visit to the Russian Czar at Réval. That visit had caused a great ferment in Germany, and grave suspicions of British intentions. Bethmann-Hollweg voiced those suspicions in the frankest manner. "You are trying to encircle us!" he cried to Mr. Lloyd George. "You and France and Russia are attempting to strangle us!"

Mr. Lloyd George assured him of the friendliness of Great Britain towards all the great Powers; but for the moment he refused to be appeased. He thumped the table with his hand. "The Prussian Government has only to lift a finger," he cried, "and every living Prussian will die for the Fatherland!"

Mr. Lloyd George listened to all this with his characteristic calmness and good-humour. "But what about the other Germans?" he put in at this point.

A shadow passed over the face of the Prussian Minister.

"Oh! they?" he said with a gesture. "They, too, will come along!"

But this was only a flash. On the whole, Bethmann-Hollweg was very friendly; and the facts of his family life showed him Anglophile. He had sent his son to an English University; and admiration for English education was, curiously enough, just at that moment almost as much a fashion in Germany as admiration for German education in England. When we were lunching with a judge at Frankfort Mr. Lloyd George discovered that the daughter of the house had actually been at school along with his own daughter at the famous English girls' school near Brighton-Roedean.

Of course, it is always foolish to imagine that social courtesies seriously affect the grave pursuit of national interests in any country. But they produce a friendly atmosphere; and he would be a criminal who, with all the causes of difference and conflict in the world, did not always try to improve the human atmosphere.

The people of Hamburg were remarkably friendly to us. The merchants trading with England gave us an especially enthusiastic reception. They feasted us at a banquet at which sat the Hamburg Prussian Minister-for Berlin keeps a Ministry in the "Free Towns" as a last relic of their former independence.

It was on the occasion of that banquet that Mr. Lloyd George threw out the idea of regulating armaments by a Plimsoll "Load-line" fixed according to population. It is strange to-day to remember with what enthusiasm that suggestion was received by the Hamburg merchants.

The authorities of Hamburg provided a launch to take us into every corner of their famous port, so as to show us all the power and pride of their new creation-with all its marvellous up-to-date devices for handling ships and cargoes, its wonderful new docks and elevators, its ingenious and multifarious resources for expediting sea-traffic. It was good to see that port; if only to realise the wisdom of the King's advice to us at home —"Wake up, Britain!"

It is difficult to exaggerate the part played by the personality of the Kaiser in German imperial politics at that moment. If one probed any great German question to the bottom, one always came back to that fact. Take the question of the Navy-that vital Anglo-German problem of the early century. The Army chiefs were, I think, quite ready to contemplate a naval "deal," if only to keep England out of the land-wars of the Continent. The Social Democrats, of course, were more than willing; they were anti-naval as well as anti-militarist. But to the Kaiser the Navy was always prime favourite; it was his toy, his darling dream, his cherished ambition. His sincerest belief and hopes were expressed in the phrase, "Our future lies on the ocean." He stimulated the popular zeal for the Navy in every possible way. The Nord Deutsche Lloyd Liners had elaborate pictures comparing the respective navies, and showing the smallness of the German in comparison with ours; the great German Navy League was constantly pushed forward; and no Minister could long remain in power who did not sympathise with this cult. The curious thing was that the German populations along the sea-board were not half so enthusiastic for the Navy as the inland populations, who seemed enthusiastic in proportion to their ignorance of the sea.

Many Germans used to put down the Kaiser's passion for the Navy to his English blood. He was a very enthusiastic yachtsman; and, as most yachtsmen are Englishmen, that threw him into constant relations of intimacy with English sailor-men. The English yachtsmen on the North Sea found him almost excessive in his friendliness. I remember an instance given to me by a famous English yachtsman, fond of cruising in northern waters. A German torpedo-boat had accidentally one evening broken the bowsprit of his yacht. During the night, while the owner was asleep, a body of carpenters came on board of the English yacht and mended the bowsprit. In the morning, after breakfast, the Kaiser arrived himself. He had sent the carpenters. "Well!" he said, "how do you like your new bowsprit?" Then he looked at it whimsically. "When you go back to England," he said, "tell them it was 'made in Germany'!"

And yet at that very time this friendliness towards English yachtsmen-of which this was only one example-was not preventing the Kaiser from regarding the British naval power with a haunting jealousy that led him into the constant intrigues against England, of which we gain a glimpse in the secret correspondence discovered in the palace of the Russian Czar.

The Kaiser, indeed, was at that time always a great trouble to all the diplomats. He was like a perpetual cracker explosively zig-zagging about in all the Foreign Offices of Europe. Nobody ever knew what he would do or say-to whom he would talk, and with whom he would correspond. He had a touch of freakish irresponsibility. "I always knew that Willy would come to no good," sighed an English Princess of the old school; and she seemed to have an eye for character. After Agadir, he calmly protested that the British Government had no right to object, as he had told some one of his intentions when he was visiting the British Court! His telegram to President Wilson seems to show that he carried this view of the British Constitution right up to the eve of the Great War.

"He is a bad neighbour," said an official of the British Foreign Office at that time; and that really seemed to sum it up.

His constant changes of mood made German foreign policy very difficult to forecast, and I do not think that any one can claim to have foreseen the future.

The German officials told me that they had never had a visitor with a quicker mind than Mr. Lloyd George. After a long day spent in the Central Insurance Office at Berlin, the men who went round with us were very enthusiastic. "He grasps the system more rapidly than any student we have ever had." Mr. Lloyd George, indeed, made a very exhaustive study of the German system. But in his Act he improved upon it and added to it in many important respects.[56]

It was a strange visit, curious to look back upon at this distance of time. Our days were filled with the insistent calls of a great social inquiry. But we could not ignore another aspect. After all, there was a greater problem darkening the air than insurance against individual sickness and unemployment. What about insurance against another and greater human sickness-the sickness of war? The thought of that kept recurring, like a secondary theme in some piece of music.

The impressions gained during this tour (1908) partly account, no doubt, for the firmness of Mr. Lloyd George's language in that famous City speech with which, after consultation with Sir Edward Grey, he faced the German Agadir threat in 1911. He himself always contended at the time that that speech saved Europe from war. A firm, clear, real attitude-an attitude that would convince Germany that we meant what we said-that is what he always in those days advocated. He argued that here was the most positive realistic Power in the world-with no regard for sentimentalism or even humanity where the interests of Germany were concerned. Very well; let us treat them as they treated us. Let them know definitely where we stood. Let our language to them be plain and frank. They would respect us all the more for it.

He was very fiercely attacked for this speech by the pacifists at the time, both in public and private. He made a characteristic reply to their pin-pricks. "Perhaps it would have been better if I had not made the speech! There would have been war, and the Prussian bully would have got the thrashing he deserves!"

Then, as since, nothing irritated and angered him more than the attitude of Germany to France. "It is simply persecution!" he used to say. "The world cannot be carried on along these lines!"

So he had already a dim perception of the great issue which was so soon to divide the world.

Between 1908 and 1914 came that "Turtle Dove" period (1912-1914) during which Germany wooed us. Never had Germany been more friendly to Great Britain than she was in the spring of that fatal year, 1914; never had our relations been more smooth; never had her protestations of affection been more numerous. The change from 1911 was almost startling.

Perhaps it ought to have startled us more. It is so easy to be sages after the accomplished fact. But it is not often that the architects of suspicion build wisely; their day comes once in a while, and they rejoice exceedingly. It is, perhaps, the worst crime of Germany that she has strengthened that sinister creed of doubt, and lowered faith between man and man.

---

[55] Died January, 1920.
[56] He raised the level of the sick benefit; he added several new benefits; and he paid the doctors better.

CHAPTER XIII

CIVIL STRIFES

"It gives me a serious concern to see such a Spirit of Dissention in the Country; not only as it destroys Virtue and Common Sense, and renders us in a manner Barbarians towards one another, but as it perpetuates our Animosities, widens our Breaches, and transmits our present Passions and Prejudices to our Posterity. For my own Part, I am sometimes afraid that I discover the Seeds of a Civil War in these our Divisions; and therefore cannot but bewail as in their first Principles the Miseries and Calamities of our Children." —Addison in the Spectator, July 25th, 1711.

During his foreign tour in 1908 Mr. Lloyd George always carried with him a small pocket-book, in which he jotted down ideas and suggestions as they came to him in thought or talk. These were jottings for that great Budget of which he already perceived the necessity.

For when he took over the Treasury in April 1908, he found British finance at the parting of the ways. Old Age Pensions had just been promised; a Bill was already drafted on non-tributory lines. He quite approved. But no provision had been made in the Budget of 1908 to pay for this great social boon.[57]

Here was a great opportunity for the Tariff Reform cause, at that time still languishing from the staggering blow of 1906. It was up to Free Trade to show that it could meet the coming deficit.

We all know how Mr. Lloyd George faced that crisis at the Exchequer-by what audacious drafts on the great reserves of our national wealth-by what determined levies on the luxuries of all classes. The Budget of 1909 is still one of the landmarks of English history. Its rejection by the Lords and its final triumph in the first General Election of 1910 are thrice told tales.

How did Mr. Lloyd George bear himself through the stress of these tremendous evils?

He did not spare himself. He bore the burden of the midnight sitting as well as of the day labour. He revolutionised the habits of the Treasury.

He had now left his private house and come to live in Downing Street. His life was practically lived in public. It was at about this time that he instituted his famous habit of breakfast parties at which the affairs of the nation were discussed. Strenuous gatherings were these, opening with merry chaff, but soon passing to earnest debate and discussion over coffee and bacon-debates always human and thrilling, enlivened by the swift jest and epigram of the host, always one of the best of talkers. But he never allowed these talks to drift into triviality. He always directed them to moulding and shaping policy. He compelled his guests to face vital decisions.

Great gatherings! Where the best of the nation met, not with idle gossip or silly scandal, but with high converse and swift, eager discourse, ever touched with hope and light!

He could not have lived this strenuous life without some relaxation. He found it, like so many other busy moderns, in golf. It was shortly after the opening of the twentieth century that he took to this game, and found in it his physical salvation. Up to 1900 he had never been robust. Often he had long periods of ill-health. But the steady tramps round those wonderful courses that now surround London made a great change. Golf has given him a tough physique, equal to resisting great strains.

Those of us who, during 1909, worked in the "Budget League" to help forward this great cause saw something of the energy and resourcefulness which went to achieve the hardly won victory of the first 1910 General Election.

One of our methods was to cover England with posters. I remember one glorious poster of an ermined and coroneted duke. We were very proud of it. But it passed through great troubles. Mr. Winston Churchill protested against it because it was too much like his cousin, the Duke of Marlborough. So we changed the face and darkened the colouring. The result was that the new duke came out precisely like our splendid and energetic chief, Sir Henry Norman, M.P.!

All this poster business was very expensive. We spent till we were exhausted; we swamped the Budget Protest League in paste. But, however much money we spent, we got more money. We only had to send across to Downing Street. Mr. Lloyd George seemed to have the key to the treasures of Golconda. He had the amazing gift of being able to persuade millionaires to subscribe in order to be taxed.

The Liberal Cabinet, as a whole, refused to believe that the Lords would throw out the Budget; and it was steadily set about through the summer of 1909 that Mr. Balfour and Lord Lansdowne were in favour of passing it. But Mr. Lloyd George persisted in believing the contrary. "They will throw it out all right!" he would always say cheerfully enough; and the only shadow that would pass over his face would come when some one would half convince him to the contrary. I believe that up to September there was some real doubt. But then the Tariff Reform League came into the fight; the first flush of the Budget popularity seemed to pass; our street-corner orators were met by rivals-often hired Socialists; and the "Die-hards" grew more powerful. The Lords determined to face the great risk. They threw out the Budget in November; Mr. Asquith was forced to dissolve; and in January 1910 came the General Election.

The Lords nearly won. The Liberals emerged with a diminished majority of 124 as compared with the 1906 majority of 354, meaning a loss of 115 seats, and a turn-over of 230 votes.

For a moment this fall in the majority shook the constancy even of that strong Cabinet. There was talk of resignation. Even Mr. Lloyd George was bitten for a moment by the idea of substituting House of Lords Reform for the policy of the Parliament Bill.

In a few weeks they steadied. They found that if they were disappointed, the other side were more so. The Lords had staked all; the Tariff Reformers had assured a win. The Opposition was as much "down" as the Government.

It was fated that a tragic event should give sudden pause to this rending strife. Just when the first shadow of civil war was falling across the nation, on May 6th, 1910, King Edward died. The presence of death brought a calmer mood; men saw realities for a moment, and shrank from the edge of the abyss. They were like travellers from whose path the mist suddenly clears, and lo! they find themselves stumbling along the edge of a precipice.

Mr. Lloyd George made a suggestion to the new King which was taken up and resulted in the remarkable conference of party leaders which lasted from June to November 1910. It was a pause of halcyon calm in the midst of storm.

Mr. Lloyd George was a member of that conference; he was always among those who took a sanguine view of its prospects; and he has always infinitely regretted its failure. He took a long view. He foresaw the civil perils that lay ahead of the country. He was ready to come to a large and comprehensive settlement. He knew that a settlement could not mean a victory for either side. He was ready to accept that view; and there were those on the other side-especially one, Mr. Arthur Balfour-who were large enough to accept it also.

But neither of the great parties, organised for combat and victory, could be brought to the height of so great a treaty. The secrecy of the conference had been perhaps all too faithfully observed. There had been no "spade-work" in preparing the parties for a self-denying ordinance so sweeping. The "Snakes" they say, "committed suicide to save themselves from slaughter." But in this case both parties still hoped for life and victory.

So, in November 1910, the conflict was resumed; and in December there took place the second General Election-this time, by agreement between the Prime Minister and the King, a test Election on the Veto Bill. The decision of January was practically repeated; and Mr. Lloyd George, again leaving his electioneering chances in Carnarvonshire to his local friends, was returned by a second sweeping majority.[58]

The second Election proved too much even for the strength of Mr. Lloyd George. After speaking up in Scotland with a strong fever actually on him, he was struck with a touch of serious throat trouble. His voice was threatened. After many efforts to go on, he finally accepted the verdict of seclusion, and spent a prolonged rest in a spacious, restful mansion behind the

Sussex downs, lent to him by Mr. (afterwards Sir Arthur) Markham. He grew to a genuine love of this peaceful life; and when he returned to the turmoil, it was with a certain reluctance.

Driven back on reading as his sole diversion, he rambled widely through literature and read a great deal of history.

But his chief occupation during these months was the preparation of the famous Insurance Bill of 1911.

All who saw much of Mr. Lloyd George at that time knew that that measure was inspired by nothing less than a profound compassion for the sick and the suffering—a passion sobered by reflection, but still burning with an intense fire behind all his cool and calculated moves.

He was moved by a spirit best expressed in Blake's golden verse:
"I will not cease from mental strife,
    Nor shall my sword sleep in my hand,
Till we have built Jerusalem
    In England's green and pleasant land."
Before drafting the Bill he took a prolonged and careful survey of the condition of the people: in Mr. Charles Booth's books, in the Poor Law Commission Reports, and from every possible source of the written and spoken word. He was appalled; and he expected every one else to be appalled. Carried forward by his own emotion, he did not perhaps realise the power of familiarity, the force of usage, the strength of vested interest.

He was greatly surprised and disappointed by the attitude of the doctors. He had always held the medical profession in the highest admiration[59]; and perhaps he expected more from them than any organised profession could supply. He had been so absorbed by conferences with the Friendly Societies that he perhaps did not sufficiently realise the importance of constant consultations with the doctors in the preparation of his schemes.

He was also sincerely surprised at the attitude of the well-to-do classes. He had imagined that the enforcement of contributions would disarm their hostility. As it was, he lost on both sides; though he never regretted his decision in favour of contributions. With all his sympathy-perhaps because of it-he entertained a great horror of a pauperised working-class.

Here, too, he had to face a revolt of the timid within his own party. There arose in the autumn of 1911 the same cry for "postponement"—always the first step to abandonment. He resisted it steadily; pushed forward his Bill, this time with the help of the strongest closures; and in December the House of Lords, perhaps chastened by events, allowed the Insurance Act to pass into law.

So ended the first stage of that great scheme of social reform with which he designed to change the face of England. Insurance against sickness and kindred ills was combined with an Act for insurance against unemployment; and for the first time in our history labour was backed by security.

Then, in 1912, amid the distractions of the growing crisis in Ireland, Mr. Lloyd George proceeded to approach the greatest of all fastnesses of privilege-the English Land Laws. Here was a more formidable enterprise than any he had yet undertaken. He had to carry out his own inquiries-for it had been proved by experience that the tenants of English land were in too precarious a position to venture an open disclosure of their wrongs to an open Commission. He appointed an able Land Committee, of which Mr.(now Sir) Arthur Acland became the Chairman. That Committee carried out its work with great courage and ability, and published two books which are still classical summaries of the main features of our land system, stated with fairness and thoroughness.[60] In a series of great speeches, Mr. Lloyd George in 1912 and 1913 announced his intention of making legislative proposals and carrying out the conclusions of this Committee.

But, in the meantime, across this great endeavour, there had arisen a hue and cry which had given new hope to the friends of the existing order. The great controversy of the Marconi shares seems now very far away. The whole case fabricated against Mr. Lloyd George in those days seem very ridiculous now. The perspective has changed very much since one of the great

English political parties could deliberately set out to ruin a political opponent on account of one act of carelessness.[61]

But it does not do to throw stones. Party strife is an ugly business at best; and he would be a bold man who should say that, in similar circumstances the Liberal Party would have shown a spirit very much better. In this matter of rushing readily to false accusations we have all sinned pretty deeply in our public life. Suspicion is the peculiar vice of democracies; and he would be bold who should say that the real scandal of the Marconi affair-the scandal of accusation so poisoned and exaggerated as to amount to calumny adopted as a policy and a cause-will not occur again.

Mr. Lloyd George suffered very much through this affair. For the moment it achieved its object of holding up his whole activities in furthering his Land Campaign. But at last the fever of the assault died away, and men began to return to the light of common reason, and to see the thing in its real proportions. Then there succeeded in the public mind a fit of remorse which worked in Mr. Lloyd George's favour; and both in London and in Wales he was banqueted and acclaimed. For, if the victims survive the rigours of the "ordeal by torture," then the populace applauds.

From another campaign of the same sort at an earlier date (1908) Mr. Lloyd George had emerged victorious in the Courts with damages of £1,000, which enabled him to adorn his native village of Llanystumdwy with a very handsome Institute, where all his fellow villagers can now read the newspapers and enjoy the advantages of a well-chosen library. So out of evil sometimes good proceeds.

In 1914 Mr. Lloyd George resumed the preparations for his Land Bills. It was his intention to introduce them into the House of Commons during the Session of this year, thus placing them before the country with a view of the General Election already looming ahead.

But across all these designs there came, in June and July 1914, a flood of reverberating events-the Ulster crisis, the officers' revolt, the gun-running, first of Larne and then of Dublin. Like other Ministers, Mr. Lloyd George was absorbed in a situation which threatened instant civil war.

Then once more, across the threat of civil war, came the even greater menace of an even vaster peril-world-war.

In the tremendous crisis that followed Mr. Lloyd George took the middle course. He was not for war against Germany at all costs. On Saturday, August 2nd, he was inclined to vote for peace; and if, necessary, to resign for peace.

On that day-as he has told the world-the biggest financiers in the City, including the Governor of the Bank of England, came to him, as Chancellor of the Exchequer, and urged that peace should be preserved, and that we should stand aside from the strifes of Europe. On Monday it was known that Germany had invaded Belgium. At once all these men swung over to the side of war.

Mr. Lloyd George himself, separately and independently, followed the same course. Eager as he had been in the past for peace, he had no hesitation from the moment that Germany invaded Belgium.

We had pledged our word; and we must keep it.

On Monday he was for war.

He had definitely chosen his part.

---

[57] Old Age Pensions were then estimated to cost £9,000,000, but were found to cost £13,000,000 (now (1920) £28,000,000). There was also the new Dreadnoughts, and so forth. The deficit for 1909 thus amounted to £16,000,000 even in prospect.

[58] His majorities in the Carnarvon Boroughs have been rising on the whole steadily since the first election in 1890. In 1892 he defeated Sir John Puleston by 196, as against 18 in 1890. In 1895 he again defeated Mr. Nanney by 194. In 1900 he defeated Colonel Platt by 296. In 1906 he won by 1,224; January 1910 by 1,078; in December by 1,208.

[59] There is a remarkable and eloquent passage on the doctor's work in the Limehouse speech.

[60] The Land. The Report of the Land Inquiry Committee, Vol. I. Rural, and Vol. II, Urban. (Hodder & Stoughton, 1913.)

[61] It is a strange fact that nothing worse was ever distinctly charged against him by his worst foes, although much was insinuated.

CHAPTER XIV

A WAR MAN

"O Statesmen, guard us, guard the eye, the soul
  Of Europe, keep our noble England whole."
  Tennyson.

From the moment that war was declared (August 4th, 1914), Mr. Lloyd George put aside all his doubts and hesitations. The perplexities of the previous week passed away like so many clouds from a summer sky. He became from that instant a war man, intent on nothing but achieving victory.

"I can understand a man opposing a war," he used to say, "but I cannot understand his waging a war with half a heart." In regard to the attitude of various friends in political life, he would always express a certain whimsical tenderness for those who were entirely opposed to the war. "Ah," he would say, "I was in that position once myself, and I know how difficult it is!" Wholly wrong as he thought them, dangerous as he thought their activities to the country, he could not shake off a certain admiration for their courage. But the men for whom he had no tolerance were those who waged the war with a backward glance over their shoulder all the time at the lost vision of peace. That seemed to him a confusing and weakening attitude. Peace was to be achieved, of course; that must always be the very aim of war; but once war began peace could only be retrieved across the gulf of war itself. That being the situation, he saw nothing for it but to bend the whole energies of the State to the sole purpose of conducting the war with the utmost power.

He realised at once that Great Britain was up against the most terrible danger that had ever faced it in the whole course of its existence. He knew Germany; he had a thorough understanding of German efficiency. Especially did he grasp the full strength and power given to the German Government by the patriotism of the German people. In entering upon this mighty enterprise, he approached the matter with the utmost gravity and seriousness. I never saw him so grave-minded as he was during those first months of the war. We rallied him one morning at breakfast for refusing to laugh at some jest. "The times are very serious," he said, and once more he seemed lost in his own thoughts again. He used to describe the moment when the Western world paused from peace to war as the most solemn and awful in his whole life. "We sat waiting for Big Ben to strike the hour when the ultimatum expired. We all fell quite silent. As the great blows of the hammer sounded on the bell we seemed to be passing into another world."

From the very first he took Lord Kitchener's view of the seriousness and probable length of the war. He was not a war "pessimist." He would not accept that phrase. "I look at the facts," he would say, "I merely refuse to live in dreamland." When people used to come to him in that bouncingly cheerful mood which patriots tried to cultivate in those days, he used to look at them gravely and say, "Have you read all the bulletins?" And then he would go on: "Have you read the bulletins on both sides?" Or to another he would say, "Have you looked at the maps?" For he always saw the war as a whole: he grasped it in the East as well as in the West. It was not that he was particularly disturbed by untoward incidents; he rarely discussed any such incident. It was the proportions of the vast forces at issue which filled his mind and imagination.

There were several consoling theories popular during the first year of the war for which he had little taste. There was the idea, preached in many powerful quarters, that German man-power would soon be exhausted. Mr. Lloyd George was an open sceptic on that point. It was not merely that the Germanic Powers had far more men than most English people realised at that time; it was also his fixed imaginative feeling that the resisting power of a country does not ultimately depend on numbers. It was the spirit of Germany that he feared-ruthless to others, merciless to itself. In a public speech he expressed that once as the "potato-bread" spirit.

Then there was the theory that Germany would soon be starved into submission. There again his imagination came to his help. "How do you know?" he would say. "How can you tell at what point a nation will cry for mercy? That does not depend upon the amount of food; it depends upon the spirit of the nation. History shows that there is little limit to what some nations will endure before they surrender."

The practical upshot of all this was that he could see no alternative to a clear and clean military victory. The only reason, in fact, why he combated such theories as "attrition" and "hunger-surrender" was that he regarded them as excuses unconsciously put forward to avoid the strain and stress necessary for that achievement. He saw men at that period cultivating optimism as a means of concealing from themselves the stark realities. He saw others preferring short views to long preparations. He perceived that too many were seeking for any or every other means of a softer outlet; and yet, to his mind, the sole chance of obtaining a satisfactory close to the war lay along the iron road of victory. It was in that way that he came to regard the people he met as too sanguine; for that reason he set himself to preach a more sombre view.

So much did this view afterwards prevail that it is difficult to recall now those amazingly cheerful forecasts so popular during the first six months of the war. Public opinion soon recovered from the first shock of the retreat from Mons. There were even a considerable body of people who persuaded themselves to regard that valorous series of rear-guard actions as a crowning victory. When, on September 9th, 1914, the Germans stopped their advance and began to retire to the line of the Marne, there were some who talked as if the war were already ended.

This was not by any means entirely the fault of the public, for a strict censorship had concealed from us in Great Britain that gigantic defeat of the Russians at the end of August known now as the battle of Tannenberg. There the Russian General Samsonoff had been drawn on to the lakes of East Prussia by Hindenburg, and a second Cannæ had been achieved. A vast number of Russians had been killed and captured; 90,000 had been taken prisoners, and no less than 516 guns captured.[62]

All these things were known to Mr. Lloyd George; and he did not possess the faculty, somewhat common in high places, of persuading himself that an inconvenient fact must necessarily be untrue. Nor was he so bemused by the censorship as to believe that you could make an unpleasant fact untrue simply by keeping it secret. He knew by the beginning of September that the theory of the Russian "steam-roller" must be set aside. He had realised already that the main effort would now lie with England. That was what gave so much sobriety to his outlook.

As the last months of 1914 passed by, the situation as a whole certainly did not improve. The Russian invasion of Eastern Prussia was definitely stayed. There were indeed certain compensations. In September the Russians seized Eastern Galicia and the Bukovina. In those months the Serbians, with heroic valour, three times drove back the invading Austrians from their little country. But it became obvious that the Russians, however daring in combat, lacked the generalship required for reaping the fruits of their successes. At the beginning of October Germany came to the help of Austria, and there was a great rally of the Austro-German forces. The Russians were driven out of Western Galicia, and in October a large part of Western Poland was seized by the Germans. In November there was another spasmodic recovery of the Russians; but again in later November they were driven back to within forty miles of Warsaw, and the opening of 1915 saw Russia practically on the defensive.

The meaning of all these events to Mr. Lloyd George was, that if we were to achieve victory we must prepare for a very great and prolonged effort; and he determined to set himself to the task of tuning the country up to the pitch of the highest endeavour.

It must be remembered that at this time he was still Chancellor of the Exchequer, and therefore not directly concerned with war matters. All his arguments and interventions both in war policy and foreign policy were liable to be regarded, according to the prevailing traditions of our Cabinet rule, as trespasses from the straight and narrow path of direct responsibility.

Still, he felt it his duty, as a citizen and a Minister, to run all the risks of personal misunderstanding that might arise from honest and vigorous expressions of his own mind. For, rightly or wrongly, he took a very serious view of the situation at the end of 1914. He felt his responsibility all the heavier for the knowledge which he possessed. The British public were looking only at the splendid achievements of our armies in the West. What they did not see was the heavy thundercloud in the East-the great German armies gathering themselves for a mighty, tigerish spring on to some of the fairest provinces of our great Eastern Ally.

Here was the loss side to this account-the achievements in the East of those German divisions which had been withdrawn from the advance on Paris, and had left their diminished armies to fall back on the Marne.

Mr. Lloyd George refused to regard those defeats of the Russian armies as inevitable. He would never consent to be a fatalist. He represented the vigorous energy of the Western man-eager and insistent to strive against the shocks of fortune.

Frankly he was not content with the measures taken to grip the situation. He did not feel that any military plans were being considered adequate to face the perils that threatened us. He was unhappy and dissatisfied with the plans he knew of; he felt little confidence that others would be devised more fit to avert these perils.

It was at this time that he first suggested day-to-day sittings of the War Committee for the conduct of the war. It was the first appearance of that proposal for a small War Cabinet which afterwards developed so stormily from the stress and travail of the war. Not before three years of trying the old bottles was the new wine to find a vessel fit for its feverish ferment.

During the Christmas holidays Mr. Lloyd George carefully surveyed the situation. With the opening of 1915 this is how he saw it.

Russia was in danger of a blow at the heart. In the West the military situation had reached a deadlock[63]; and it was not yet physically possible that the armies at this time raised by us should drive back the German invader in any time that then seemed reasonable from the North of France and Belgium. On those lines the war seemed certain to last a very long time, though not even he at that time cast his eyes beyond the historic three years fixed by Lord Kitchener. He wished, at all possible costs, to avoid a long war.

Looking across Europe, he asked himself-Was there not some alternative way? Some road to a quicker ending of this world-agony?

He found it in the Near East, at that point where the Teuton power touched the Danube, and was still at that time held back by the heroic resistance of the Serbians.

The plan that framed itself in his mind was to combine the Balkan States-to revive the Federation-to send a great British army to their help, and attack with these combined forces-perhaps amounting to 1,000,000 men-the Eastern flank of the Central Powers.

This great scheme must not be confused with the subsequent expeditions to Gallipoli and Salonika. It was something far larger in conception, and far more splendid in grasp and sweep of action.

It was a proposal for employing the new British armies, before they were wearied by being set to the tasks that break men, for fortifying our Allies, and for snatching success before the watching neutrals of the Near East-Bulgaria, Greece, and Rumania-were divided and distracted by doubt and failure.

It was also an essential part of his larger hope that such an effort would relieve the pressure on Russia and finally perhaps draw off the bulk of the German armies from the West to the help of Austria.

In his view the plan entailed far less risk than shaped itself in the minds of the timid. A visit to the Western front had impressed him with the feeling that this was not then the easiest place for a successful assault on the Central Powers. Here you would meet them just at the point where they had the greatest mastery over their defensive. The West, it seemed to him, was the proper place for a persistent, concentrated, and even vigilant defensive. But at that time the spot for a more prosperous offensive had, in the view strongly impressed upon him by observation, to be sought elsewhere.

His policy was to make the Western line impregnable; but, with the forces that could be spared beyond that necessary effort, to prepare and execute a great strategical diversion along the line of the Danube, striking into territory inhabited by men sympathetic to the Western Allies, and supporting our own weaker Allies among the Balkan States. In this way he hoped to save Serbia, to prevent the German "break-through" to the East, and in the end to divert the great German hosts from their assaults on Great Britain and Russia.

Such was the "Near Eastern idea" in its large scope and purpose. Those who held it were necessarily opposed to the earlier frontal assaults in the West, chivalrously and splendidly undertaken before we had an unquestionable superiority in numbers and guns. Like Botha in South Africa at the later stage of the Boer War-like every great general when he is outnumbered and out-gunned —they were seeking a "way round." It was a very big "way round" —by Durazzo or Salonika-but the point is that it seemed at the time the only possible way round.

We must remember that the submarine menace had not yet developed, that Bulgaria had not yet declared war, that we were still as much masters of the Mediterranean as ever in our long history. Austria had not yet stiffened her army with German troops, and Russia was still uninvaded. All these were governing facts in this great scheme.

It was characteristic of his buoyant faith that he firmly believed that the appearance of a great British army in the Balkans would surely bring in both the Rumanians and the Greeks to our aid. In his view those nations were at the moment hypnotised by the fate of Belgium.

They genuinely feared the military power and terror of Germany. What they wanted was a convincing proof of our land strength. They knew us as a naval power; but that was not enough for this war. Here was this new thing-our growing military potency. Very well, let us display this side of our strength to the world. Let us land our new armies in the Near East.

Such was the large design, boldly schemed and boldly started, which he set before his political and military colleagues in the early months of 1915. He firmly believed that it would inspire our arms with a new force and vigour. It would give our young soldiers a new hope. It would confuse and embarrass the German defence. It would present them for the first time in this campaign with that dash of the sudden, secret, and unexpected which was so often their own special way. It would knock away the German props by threatening her Allies; and it would build up new props for us by heartening ours. Such were the broad and daring ideas which underlay his thoughts.

We know that this great scheme did not prevail at the time, although pale ghosts of it lingered on and haunted the stricken fields of war. The flesh and substance of the plan evaporated in the atmosphere of doubt. Between all the Allies and the Chancelleries of the Allies, in the chilling alleys and by-ways of debate and diplomacy, this great enterprise lost "the name of action." It was "sicklied o'er with the pale cast of thought." Tradition, convention, convenience- all combined to strangle it.

We cannot say now how it would have prospered. The fortunes of war are always, after all, on the knees of the gods. No mortal can command success; we can only deserve it.

Such opportunities do not occur twice. The Near Eastern vision faded. The country set itself grimly to solve by direct methods the problem of the West. How heroically, how tenaciously the British race would set its teeth into that endeavour perhaps no one could then quite foresee; but, casting our minds back over these bloodstained years, the question cannot but again recur- Might there not have been a shorter road?

---

[62] See the full account in Ludendorff's War Memories (vol. i. pp. 41-72).

[63] See the remarkable survey of the military situation in January 1915, contained on page 19 of the Dardanelles Commission's First Report (Cd. 8490). That survey confirms Mr. Lloyd George's views at that time.

CHAPTER XV

EAST OR WEST?

"For East is East, and West is West,
    And never the twain shall meet."
    Rudyard Kipling.

It is characteristic of Mr. Lloyd George that, when his mind once seizes hold of an idea, he is wholly possessed with it until either he can bring it to accomplishment or he is fully convinced of its impracticability. It was so with regard to this great scheme of outflanking the Central Powers by an attack from the Near East. The more he reflected upon it the more there seemed to lie in this plan one great chance of bringing a speedy decision to the war. But, for better or for worse, the reinforcements were now being directed to the Western Front; and the policy of the Western Allies was more and more concentrated on that sphere of offence and defence-France, from absorption in her immediate danger, and Great Britain for her instinctive military preference for campaigning nearer to her sacred seas.

Out-voted in that larger proposal, Mr. Lloyd George now fell back on a smaller design. The cautious diplomacy of the Allies had shrunk from the large, bold strokes necessary for combining the Balkan States as an eastern wing of our offensive against the Central Powers; their military chiefs had hesitated to supply the means. Never at that stage did the Governments of the Allies fully realise the full proportionate value of the Balkan States in the vast scheme of the great European struggle.

But it was soon clear that, if the Western Powers were inclined to leave the Balkan States to themselves, the Central Powers had no such intention. Quite early in the war Mr. Lloyd George and Mr. Winston Churchill scented the danger of German intrigue in the Balkans, and the vast lure of that easy "corridor" to the East offered by the trans-Balkan railway system. In September 1914 they induced the Foreign Office to send the Buxton brothers to Sofia; and the proposals which those delegates brought back in January 1915 played an important part in the negotiations of February.[64]

Some time before the end of January 1915, indeed, the British Government got to know that Germany was already preparing a large army for the invasion of Serbia. Mr. Lloyd George instantly realised the gravity and urgency of this peril. It was largely due to his initiative that a note was sent to Greece and Rumania, urging those states to come to the assistance of Serbia.

No note was sent to Bulgaria. It was already dimly realised that this State was being drawn into the far-flung net of the Central Powers. The "Prussia of the Balkans" presented too rich a field to be left unharvested by the needy gleaners of Germany. The anxious and hard-pressed diplomats of Berlin, seeking eagerly for friends in a world growing more and more hostile, were already tapping at the doors of Sofia, offering golden and honeyed gifts to a State which had fed too long on the east wind.

Rumours of these approaches grew so strong and convincing that Mr. Lloyd George was moved by them to take fresh action along his old lines. It was now no longer a question of a great offensive with a gigantic army on the Near Eastern flank of the enemy. Fate does not repeat her opportunities; and the chances of that great diversion were already slipping away. It was now rather a question whether we should be in time even to save our smaller friends in the Near East-whether we should be able to prevent this threatened gigantic "sortie" of the Central Powers from the siege of the Entente Allies. Already, in January, Mr. Lloyd George saw, in that flashing way of his, all the tragic possibilities that might flow from a German "break-through" in the Balkans. Already he foresaw the fearful and disastrous fate of a conquered Serbia.

With this tragedy ever clearly in his mind's eye, Mr. Lloyd George left no stone unturned to avert it. In the middle of January he succeeded in persuading his colleagues to offer a whole army corps to Greece on condition that she would agree to join us in the war. Lord Kitchener agreed to spare the troops, and approved the wording of the offer. But it was necessary to obtain the approval of the Allies.

France was not for the moment happy at the idea of sending troops to the Near East. There came from across the Channel a breath of acute anxiety, the anxiety of an invaded and ravaged country.

The result was that the official note was held back and somewhat modified. The military offer of help to Greece and Serbia began to become vaguer. The army corps began to become a little ghostly. We can see the great plan still further dwindling into shadows.

Then, on January 26th, a new development occurred. M. Venizelos sent to London the Greek reply to the first note of the Allies, asking for help on behalf of Serbia. The reply was that, on certain conditions, Greece agreed to join in the war on the side of the Allies. If those conditions were fulfilled, then Greece-so the answer ran-was willing to give its assistance to Serbia, and to place the whole of its resources at the service of a "just and liberal cause."

But the chief of the conditions was that Bulgaria should come in as well on the Allied side. If not, then Rumania must come in and Bulgaria remain neutral.[65]

So far, so good. It now remained to persuade France.

On February 5th there was to be held in Paris one of those Allied Conferences on policy and strategy which have been held periodically throughout the war.

These Conferences were, indeed, originally Mr. Lloyd George's own special and favourite plan for bringing the Allies into a better sympathy of mind and purpose; and he had always promoted them with zeal and enthusiasm, which grew with his friendship for M. Albert Thomas. On this occasion-February 5th, 1915 —he had been selected to go over himself to Paris as the British delegate.

He proposed that M. Venizelos should come from Greece and meet him in Paris. But the domestic crisis in Greece was now passing into a stage far too acute for M. Venizelos to leave Athens. That eminent man was making his last effort to work with King Constantine.

Mr. Lloyd George went to Paris and won his case. That gallant nation, anxious to help the weak, and threatened even in the midst of her own agony, consented to join in the expedition. The French Cabinet were willing to send a French division to work with the British division to which Lord Kitchener had already agreed.

Returning to London, he informed the British military authorities, who in their turn offered to "go one better," and to spare two British divisions.

Mr. Lloyd George was now all eager for instant action.

He urged that the new Joint Note, offering military aid, should be sent at once. He brushed aside for the moment the idea of arriving at a general Balkan agreement on the lines of the proposals brought back by the Buxtons from Sofia. The Bulgarian suggestion that Serbia should make a considerable surrender of territory seemed to him impossible for Serbia after their recent struggles and sufferings. He had already a very deep perception that Bulgaria was hardening against the Entente. He saw definite evidence of it in Germany's known willingness to lend her money. It did not seem to him conceivable that Germany should be advancing money to Bulgaria without some assurance as to Bulgaria's action in certain contingencies. The Germans were not such fools.

Besides, Rumania seemed to him now less friendly. All the more need, then, for prompt and energetic action to clinch the friendliness of our most probable ally, Greece.

He felt very acutely at this moment the evil and harm of a dilatory policy. It was on his mind all the time that, if they failed to act in time to save Serbia, their responsibility would be a terrible one. Even days seemed to him to count in the great issues that lay before them.

It was a great design, greatly urged. It is impossible to say now whether it would have fulfilled the hopes of its chief sponsor. He had won over to his side all the chief forces in the West. The expedition that was about to start would have probably forestalled and averted that ill-starred enterprise of the Dardanelles-Gallipoli attack which opened on February 25th.

But just on the eve of fruition other forces intervened. While Mr. Lloyd George had been working in the West of Europe, the Central Powers had been busy in the Near East. On January 26th had come the conditional Greek offer to intervene in the war. On February 6th came their definite refusal.

The crash came suddenly. Russia had just promised 10,000 men towards the new Balkan enterprise. Then, at that moment of apparent success, M. Venizelos suddenly informed the British Minister at Athens that Greece had decided not to join the Allies in the war.

The refusal was abruptly worded, and the grounds given were very definite. They were that Greece found herself unable to obtain the conditions laid down in the reply of January 26th. One of those conditions was that Bulgaria should either join Greece in declaring war, or should promise neutrality. She had refused to do either. Another condition had been that Rumania should join. But Rumania, still hesitating between the two belligerent groups, would give no decided answer. It was at that moment the fear of Greece that, if she sent an army northwards to the help of Serbia, then Bulgaria would move to the south, seize Kavalla, and would strike westwards into Macedonia to drive a wedge between Greece and Serbia. In such a case it seemed more than possible that Greece would be crushed.

It is fair also to say that Bulgaria's refusal of a promise of neutrality was for Greece an ominous and formidable fact. It is inevitable that Greece should have been looking rather at her resentful neighbour than at those larger aims of European interest which filled the policies of the Western Powers; it was natural and human that their first and possessing fear should be lest the work of the war of 1913 should be undone. For in that terrible war the price of victory had been appallingly high for so small a nation. No less than 30,000 Greek soldiers had been killed within a few days in that tremendous onslaught which had driven back the treacherous Bulgarian attack. Greece, with her small supply of men, could not lightly contemplate the repetition of such a sacrifice, or the loss of the gains which had been so fearfully purchased.

Mr. Lloyd George did not give up hope. He knew enough to foresee, for instance, that the new attack of Bulgaria was bound to come, and that the most prudent course was to forestall it. It was at this moment that the suggestion came from Greek sources,[66] that Mr. Lloyd George should himself go out to the Balkans as a Commissioner to bring together the Balkan States. Mr. Lloyd George himself consented; and Mr. Asquith approved. But it was soon found that Mr. Lloyd George was wanted too urgently at the centre to be spared for distant missions.

The Greek Government held to its refusal. The Greek General Staff had pronounced strongly against Greek military intervention as long as Bulgaria remained even neutral; and M. Venizelos had now grave cause to believe that Bulgaria was pledged to the Central Powers. He hesitated to bind himself with the Army and the Crown against him.

As for the Greek King Constantine, he was already drifting along that fatal course which led ultimately to his exile. It was reported to the British Government that he saw the German military Attaché every day, while he refused to see the British Attaché at all.

Thus cut off for the moment from effective intervention on the Danube, the British Government drifted towards that tremendous Dardanelles enterprise[67] which took the place of the Serbian proposal. The first bombardment of the Dardanelles forts (February 25th to 26th) seemed to go prosperously; and at the opening of March Russia began to do well. Once more there was a new twist in the designs of the Greek Crown Government; and on March 6th the Crown Council assembled at Athens offered the whole Greek fleet and one Greek division for co-operation in the attack on the Dardanelles.

But already the curt refusal of the previous overtures had driven the Allies to other designs; and the pro-Bulgarian influences in Russia were now very strong. Bulgaria was now astutely offering to lend her armies for an attack on Constantinople from the north-west while the fleets were hammering at the Straits. The old Russian Court Government, always fearful of Greek designs on Constantinople, leaned towards Bulgaria, and, now that a choice seemed possible, preferred Bulgarian help to Greek.

As far as we can peer through the mists of Balkan intrigue, the success of the earlier bombardments of the Dardanelles outer forts swung Bulgaria for the time away from her Teutonic bearings. She was for the moment inclined to join the Entente, if only from fear of the consequences.[68] Whether she had signed an agreement with Germany or not, does not seem to have troubled the statesmen at Sofia, and certainly not the King.[69] The sanctity of a treaty would probably not have affected the policy of a country already strongly bitten with the virus of Prussia's world-politics. Bulgaria was, in fact, during that time making offers to both sides; she was, in vulgar language, waiting to see "how the cat jumped." For the moment, therefore, she became "pro-Entente." But immediately that the failure of the Dardanelles attack became apparent she swung back into the Teutonic orbit. The diplomatic situation was, as Lord Grey fairly claimed,[70] "overshadowed by the military."

Deeply disappointed with Greece, Mr. Lloyd George now held aloof from her overtures, and was inclined, for the moment, to hope something even from the Bulgarian alternative. During the spring and summer of 1915 the Russian campaign diverted the German resources for a while from the meditated attack on Serbia. The position along the Danube became less threatening. It became the German design to throw back Russia from Galicia and Poland before she entered upon her great Near Eastern enterprise. The result was a temporary lull for Serbia.

The British Government hoped to avail herself of this lull to bring together the Balkan States. Bulgaria assumed a willingness to join the Allies on the condition of certain large concessions of territory from Greece and Serbia. M. Venizelos even went so far as to imperil his position in Greece by suggesting consent. Mr. Lloyd George was now more hopeful of bringing together the old Balkan Federation on these lines. His general idea was that the Allies should occupy the zone of Macedonia as disputed between Serbia and Bulgaria, on condition that if they could secure Bosnia and Herzegovina for Serbia in the final settlement they should then hand the disputed territory over to Bulgaria.

But the sacrifices of the Serbian people in the previous three years had been too great for the Serbian Government to be able to bring them to agree to so large a concession. The Serbians were still filled with the glow of their triple repulse of Austria; and for the moment the new danger seemed to have drawn off. The great European thunderstorm was now echoing far away in the mountains of Carpathia and the plains of Poland. It was difficult for the Serbians to realise at that moment that a time would come when security would be cheap at a great price.

In April there came another twist in the devious track of Balkan intrigue. M. Venizelos had tendered his first resignation, and Constantine was entering upon his first effort to build up an absolute monarchy in Athens. On April 15th the Crown Council made a sudden offer to bring Greece into the war on the side of the Allies. The Allies gravely suspected the honesty of this offer. They knew that Greece was already hand in glove with Germany; and there were strong reasons to believe that the Royalist Government could not be entrusted with Allied secrets. In any case, the Allies sent no reply; and it was not until Venizelos regained power that they resumed friendly negotiations with the Greek Government.

All through this time Mr. Lloyd George himself was resolute against having any dealings whatever with the King's party in Greece. He took the strong line that the Allies, as guarantors of the Greek constitution, should refuse to negotiate with any Government which existed in contradiction to the elementary principles of democratic constitutionalism.[71]

At long last (1917) this policy prevailed. That ancient and historic torch-bearer of freedom, Greece, swung round to our side. She ended by resisting the despotisms of the North as she resisted the despotisms of the East in olden days. King Constantine went into exile. M. Venizelos became the ruler at Athens. He threw the sword of Greece into the trembling scales of the great European struggle, and helped to decide the issue.

The end justified the hope to which Mr. Lloyd George clung through the darkest hours of Royal Greek apostasy.

But who shall say what might have happened if he had not, through the black years of 1915 and 1916, kept alive in Western Europe the flickering sparks of faith in Greece?

------

[64] On Sunday, August 26th, 1917, at Athens, M. Venizelos revealed the details of an earlier entente between Greece and the Allies, planned by him before the battle of the Marne. It was frustrated by King Constantine. The Greek White Paper since published fully confirms this.

[65] These were the main points. The actual conditions were very complex:

(a) That England should endeavour to bring about the collaboration of Bulgaria with Greece, in which case Greece would withdraw her opposition to Serbia ceding part of Macedonia to Bulgaria.

(b) If this condition could not be obtained, then the Powers should obtain the co-operation of Rumania, and the neutrality of Bulgaria.

(c) If not, then Greece must be assisted by a substantial British contingent, or a joint British and French contingent.

[66] This suggestion actually came from Sir John Stavridi, the Greek Consul-General.

[67] See the Dardanelles Report passim, 1917, Cd. 8490.

[68] See Dardanelles Commission First Report, p. 39. "It can scarcely be doubted that, had it not been for the Dardanelles Expedition, Bulgaria would have joined the Central Powers at a far earlier date than was actually the case. Mr. Asquith was strongly of this opinion in the extracts quoted from his evidence. 'Yes, I am certain of it,' he said to the Chairman.'" (Page 40.)

[69] The Greek White Book has revealed that an understanding existed between Bulgaria, the Central Powers, and Turkey ever since August, 1914.

[70] Extract from his evidence in the Dardanelles Report.

[71] The treachery revealed by the Greek White Paper has since shown the wisdom of this attitude. King Constantine, it is now known, was in close and constant communication with the German Emperor.

CHAPTER XVI

SERBIA

"We here highly resolve that these dead shall not have died in vain." —Abraham Lincoln, 1863.

Mr. Lloyd George now turned from the disappointments and tragedies of the Near East to look more closely into the situation at home.

The opening of 1915 was a season of hope in Great Britain. The great effort to force the Dardanelles filled the public mind with visions. That attempt was then most lyrically applauded by those who afterwards rushed to denounce it. The whole outlook was magically irradiated with the mirage of that golden promise.

Here was a quick cure for all our troubles.

Men dreamt of a speedy blow that would cut off the Central Powers from Turkey, and open to Russia an easy door to the West.

They thought little at that moment, and knew less, of the blows which Germany was preparing for Russia.

The story of the Dardanelles expedition has been fully told.[72] We all know the origin and history of that expedition, and can apportion with some fairness the proper spheres of blame and praise. Mr. Lloyd George took little active personal part in the planning and preparations for it, though he was a member of the War Council, and later in June, became a member of the Dardanelles Committee.[73] His own proposal had been frustrated by events. Here was an alternative, hatched by other brains, inspired by other hopes. It was a serious thing to oppose it outright. His attitude from the beginning was one of suspended judgment.

"Whatever you do, do thoroughly; if you do it at all, put your full strength into it" —that may be summed up as his constantly reiterated counsel in regard to the Dardanelles.

If this advice had been adopted perhaps even that ill-starred enterprise might have met with better fortune.

But meanwhile, on other fields of war a situation was developing even more menacing to Europe as a whole. The great Teutonic attack on Russia began to develop with terrible success in the early spring; and Mr. Lloyd George took from the first a most serious view of this tremendous onslaught.

In the middle of February vast new armies of Germans, prepared in the winter, advanced to the invasion of Courland, Poland, and Galicia. The Russian armies still in Eastern Prussia had been speedily driven back across the frontier in wholesale defeat; and the northern German armies began to advance on to Russian soil. In the centre of Eastern Europe the Germans advanced victoriously to within fifty miles of Warsaw before they met with a serious check. In the south the Austrians drove the Russians from Bukovina. The whole German-Austrian line was advanced throughout the length of Europe, from the Baltic Sea to the Carpathian Mountains; and the hosts of the Central Empires were preparing for that great dramatic thrust which in May drove the Russians clean out of Galicia.

Such was the situation which British statesmen had now to face. It was impossible to regard it with indifference.

Mr. Lloyd George refused to be deceived by any rosy hopes either in East or West. His own view was that a firm grasp of reality was the first step to success. Unless they looked facts in the face, they could not grapple with them.

He came to be regarded as the Cassandra of the war; but, as Lord Morley once remarked, the worst thing about Cassandra was that she proved to be in the right!

Surveying the prospects of the great war in Europe as a whole, Mr. Lloyd George was seriously concerned about several vital matters.

The most important of these was that, comparing the available military man-power on both sides in this great contest, the Entente Allies were at that moment hopelessly outnumbered.

Germany and Austria at that moment had under arms or preparing to be armed-according to the intelligence supplied to the Government-no less than 8,700,000 men. Turkey had 500,000; she was soon, indeed, to supply a far greater number of her population as mercenaries to Germany.

On the other hand were France, Great Britain, Russia, and Serbia. Italy had not yet come into the war; and America was still afar off. The trouble with Russia was that, though she had such an immense population, she had many exemptions and few rifles. France was always doing her very best; but her census figures spoke for themselves. Great Britain was doing wonders with her voluntary system. But the question now for the first time faced him full front-Would our voluntary system suffice to keep up our armies, much less to supply the still greater armies that might be required for victory?

He still, at that moment, clung to the voluntary system. He thought that the necessary men could be still obtained by the voluntary system if it were properly applied. His own idea at that moment was that the best method of obtaining these men along voluntary lines was to follow the quota system. He was in favour of letting each county and town know clearly what was the proper proportion of men for them to supply for the national need, and then to leave the rest to local pressure and local patriotism. He firmly believed that if, for instance, it was officially announced that a particular county ought to supply, say, 10,000 men, and if that county had hitherto supplied 6,000, the remaining 4,000 would be forced to come in by the strength of local pride.

That scheme was never really tried. For some reason or other, there were forces at work against the territorial system of recruiting ever since the beginning of the war; and thus one of the greatest springs of national energy remained untapped.

It was also his opinion that at that time the Dominions would send far larger forces of men if they were fully informed about the real facts of the situation, instead of being fed by news from agencies whose chief motive seemed to be to feed the popular vanity. That sensible policy was afterwards so strongly urged by Dominion statesmen that it was to some small extent adopted.

Such were broadly Mr. Lloyd George's views and feelings in February, 1915. He was still leaning to the Eastern field of war and looking out anxiously for any chance of resuming his Eastern plan if Greece should become more friendly or Bulgaria repent of her Teutonic affections. But in the British scheme of war the plan of breaking through in the West had now resumed its hold on military minds; and in March the new armies made their first great attempt in the attack known as the battle of Neuve Chapelle. The valour and heroism of our troops in that splendid effort broke against the tangled defences of the German hosts; and in April and March our armies were once more fighting for their bare existence in the second battle of Ypres. In May came Dunajec, the smashing climax to the onslaught of the Germans on the Russians in Galicia.

Tremendously occupied as he was through the spring and summer with the great national effort to supply our armies with adequate munitions, Mr. Lloyd George was never blind or indifferent to the general trend of what followed.

Events began to succeed one another with fearful rapidity. In May and June the Russians were cleared out of Galicia. Then began that great rush forward of the central German armies which swept over fortress after fortress "like castles of sand," and submerged all the fairest towns of Western Central Russia.[74]

To these disasters there were, indeed, compensations in other fields of war. On May 23rd Italy declared war against Austria. In July Botha conquered South-West Africa. In the West the British and French troops still held on against the overwhelming forces of Germany attempting to snatch the Channel coast with every devilish device of gas and flame.

But, on the whole, the balance was against the Allies. The fact that stared Mr. Lloyd George in the face, wherever he looked at the fields of war, was that the Allied armies were outnumbered by the stupendous and unexpected man-power of Central Europe.

It was this fact that led him in this autumn to give to the public the first intimation that he, hitherto a convinced voluntaryist, was now being converted, against his will, to compulsory military service. The intimation was given in the preface written to a collection of his early war speeches.[75]

In the burning words of that remarkable address to the nation he communicated the views which he had slowly formed from a close and prolonged study of the facts throughout the summer:

"I know what we are doing: our exertions are undoubtedly immense. But can we do more, either in men or material? Nothing but our best and utmost can pull us through. Are we now straining every nerve to make up for lost time? Are we getting all the men we shall want to put into the fighting line next year to enable us even to hold our own? Does every man who can help, whether by fighting or by providing material, understand clearly that ruin awaits remissness?"

Then came the dramatic climax:

"If the nation hesitates, when the need is clear, to take the necessary steps to call forth its manhood to defend honour and existence; if vital decisions are postponed until too late; if we neglect to make ready for all probable eventualities; if, in fact, we give ground for the accusation that we are slouching into disaster as if we were walking along the ordinary paths of peace without an enemy in sight-then I can see no hope. But if we sacrifice all we own, and all we like for our native land; if our preparations are characterised by grip, resolution, and a prompt readiness in every sphere-then victory is assured."

The meaning of this appeal was obvious. "To call forth its manhood," could only mean conscription for the war; and it was to that policy, indeed, that Mr. Lloyd George had been driven by what seemed to him the inevitable logic of the terrible events in the fields of war. In no other way, indeed, did he think that the effort could be sustained.

There was no man who had thrown himself more vigorously into the volunteer recruiting campaign; there was no man who had more sincerely believed in it. His speech to the young men at the City Temple on November 10th, 1914, is a splendid expression of that appeal. It is still the best attempt to argue with that extreme pacifist spirit which he has always treated with respect-with that imaginative sympathy which understands while it condemns.[76]

But now he had come-reluctantly but irrevocably-with the terrible honesty of a man up against facts-to the conclusion that the voluntary system would not suffice against this tornado. "You cannot haggle with an earthquake." Here was a thing that transcended all theories —a convulsion of nature itself.

Having reached this conclusion, he never veered. He stood by silent through all the experiments of those days-the "Derby scheme," the quarrel between the married and the single, the "starring" and "unstarring" —until slowly the whole of the Ministry swung round to his point of view. Assailed by old friends with a hurricane of abuse-maligned and misinterpreted by men who season peace with venom-he yet held on steadily to his view. There are many things one has to dare and endure for country and fatherland. Perhaps the hardest thing of all in this country is to profess a change of opinion.

"They say-let them say." He paid little attention to these assaults. More terrible things were absorbing his attention.

The failure of the purely naval attack on the Dardanelles on March 18th (1915) had been followed by the military preparations and landing on April 25th, and the subsequent great military offensive on the heights of Gallipoli. By the end of July that offensive had failed. At this point in the development of events-at the end of July-Mr. Lloyd George now definitely again urged on his colleagues in the Government to consider once more the plan of going to the assistance of Serbia as alternative to going further forward with the Gallipoli attack. At this time he was very busy with his munition campaign in the country. But on the few occasions when he was able to take part in the deliberations of the Dardanelles Committee his attitude always was-the Germans are going to break through Serbia as soon as they can; so either make certain of getting to Constantinople quickly, or consider whether you ought not to go to the assistance of Serbia with all the strength you can command. The forces on Gallipoli were obviously the nearest available for such a rescue. The alternative adopted of a renewed attack on Gallipoli by way of Suvla Bay in August only resulted in a more tragic and wasteful failure.

His forebodings in regard to Serbia were destined to be very quickly fulfilled, for in October (1915) began that dastardly combined attack on Serbia which Mr. Lloyd George had foreseen since the beginning of the year. The Germans had now finished for the moment with Russia. With deadly method they turned to their next victim; and now the Bulgarians from the south and the Teutons from the north closed on that unhappy little country.

Mr. Lloyd George witnessed this assault with an anguish of soul inevitable to one born and bred in a little nation himself. Even at this last hour he did his utmost to rescue Serbia from her fate. He racked his brains to devise some method of saving Serbia. He pressed the military authorities with a vehemence inconvenient in a world of steady routine and disciplined ideas. He agitated, argued, pleaded.

But by this time the facts were too strong even for him. Between us and Serbia lay a Royalist Greece now indifferent if not actually hostile, coldly resolved to abandon her pledged word. Rumania was still hesitating and fearful. Russia was for the moment exhausted. No help was near enough to hand to save the doomed victim.

So the British Government were compelled to stand by helpless while the very nation on whose account the war broke out was conquered and outraged, her armies scattered, her population enslaved, and her children scattered like sheep through the mountains.[77] No more tragic chapter is recorded in the annals of Europe.

But the mischief did not end there. Not only did the conquest of Serbia give to Germany the great link with the East for which she yearned, but it completely destroyed all our remaining chances of success on Gallipoli. The very enterprise which had already taken the place of the Serbian expedition became futile from the moment of the Serbian disaster. In the beginning of October the Turks had been running so seriously short of ammunition that success for our arms seemed near at hand. By the end of the month they were fully replenished. The enterprise became plainly impossible from the moment that Germany, having now, by the conquest of Serbia and the coming in of Bulgaria, achieved a direct route to Constantinople, could pour through as much ammunition and as many big guns as the Turks required for their defence.[78]

On December 19th began the withdrawal from that fatal peninsula, and on January 8th of the following year not a single British soldier remained on those bloodstained shores.

Is it not possible that the more chivalrous and vigorous action on behalf of Serbia for which Mr. Lloyd George had so importunately pressed might have been also the best policy for the prosperity of the Allies in the war as a whole?

---

[72] In two Reports, 1917 —Cd. 8490 6^d and Cmd. 371, 2^s (Part II). The second, dealing with the military operations, is very sensational, and has not received enough attention.

[73] The Dardanelles Committee, which took over the control of the war from the War Council on June 7th, 1915, consisted of eleven members of the Coalition Government. The War Council were all Liberals. That was superseded on November 3rd, 1915, by the War Committee, consisting of seven Ministers. Mr. Lloyd George was a member of all these Committees.

[74] Swallowing up Warsaw on August 4th, Ivangorod on August 5th, Siedlce on August 12th, Kovno on August 17th, Novo-Georgievsk on August 19th, Brest-Litovsk on August 25th, and Grodno on September 2nd.

[75] Through Terror to Triumph. Arranged by F. L. Stevenson, B.A. (Lond.) (Hodder & Stoughton.)

[76] "To precipitate ideals is to retard their advent....The surest method of establishing the reign of peace on earth is by making the way of the transgressor of the peace of nations too hard for the rulers of men to tread."

[77] Some 30,000 Serbian boys were sent across the mountains to the sea to escape from the invader. Less than half reached the sea.

[78] See Lord Kitchener's final telegram of November 22nd, 1915, which decided the War Cabinet to evacuate (p. 57 of Pt. II, the Final Report of the Dardanelles Commission).

———————————

CHAPTER XVII

MUNITIONS

"Like a rickety, clumsy machine, with a pin loose here, and a tooth broken there, and a makeshift somewhere else, in which the force of Hercules may be exhausted in a needless friction, and obscure hitches before the hands are got to move, so is our Executive, with the Treasury, the Horse Guards, the War Department, the Medical Department, all out of gear, but all required to move together before a result can be obtained. He will be stronger than Hercules who can get out of it the movement we require" —Colonel Lefroy's letter to Miss Florence Nightingale, Sir Edward Cook's Life of Miss Florence Nightingale, vol. i. pp. 322-3.

From the early days of the war Mr. Lloyd George had perceived that there were two great difficulties ahead of us-men and the arming of men-and that perhaps the greater of the two was the arming.[79] For the first year, at any rate, the question of men seemed to present little difficulty. England's manhood came flocking to the banner of Lord Kitchener. The great multitudes of free citizens who freely poured into the recruiting offices after the retreat from Mons, will always be one of the most splendid episodes in our history. The patience and valour-the good-humour and endurance-of those first armies of "Kitcheners" will always add an imperishable glory to the name of him who summoned them.

So far, indeed, "nought shall make us rue." England rested true to herself and her great cause.

But it was not enough to gather the legions. It was necessary also to arm them. Here it soon became clear that we were up against a new portent. The stupendous war equipment of the German armies, both in guns and in munitions, has since become a commonplace; at that time it was a wonder and a surprise. The War Office went into the war still thinking in terms of the Boer War, when machine-guns were a new miracle and shrapnel was the last word in shells. They found themselves faced with an army in which machine-guns had become a multitudinous commonplace and shrapnel was already the humble servant of the high-explosive shell.

This was clearly, from the first, a struggle of machinery. It was not an old-fashioned war. It was a war monstrously new —a fight against a people immensely modern and scientific, as high in skill as they were low in ruth, armed cap-à-pie with every device of destruction, sharpened to the finest edge on the whetstone of prepared war.

All this has since become a commonplace; it is Mr. Lloyd George's distinction that he perceived it clearly in the autumn of 1914. Then in the Cabinet he already insisted on the need for increased armaments. He preached in season and out of season the need for guns; and in the autumn of 1914 the Cabinet Committee, of which he was a member, forced the War Office to order 4,000 guns instead of 600 for the following year (1915).

But as the weeks passed a situation began to arise which threw even this provision into the shade of inadequacy. It became clear that we had to help in the munitioning of our Allies. There was France-early in the war she lost her richest industrial districts. With splendid promptitude she had organised her factories for the making of guns, shells, and rifles. But she required to be supplied with the raw materials now lacking to her.

A far graver need was soon to arise in Russia. The German victories of 1915 placed Germany in possession of 70 per cent of the Russian steel-producing area. Her millions from that time required arming, not merely for victory, but also, it soon became clear, even for defence.[80]

To meet this colossal situation Great Britain was but poorly provided. The Navy absorbed for her great needs the principal national engineering resources of the country. The only British military machine of munition-supply at the opening of the war was the Ordnance Department of the War Office. Nothing could exceed the devotion and zeal of the men at the head of that office. But it was hopelessly under-equipped for so great a call. It was wanting in staff, resources, and ideas. It was perilously detached from our great civilian industries. It found itself faced with unparalleled difficulties of material and labour. For with the opening of the war we were cut off from some of our most important raw ingredients for explosives; and the very fervour of our first great recruiting campaign, too little directed and restricted, denuded the possible workshops of war.

There were many crises in this situation. One of the gravest occurred in the late autumn of 1914, when we were faced with a complete inability to supply the army with explosives for the making of mines. How that situation was met by a group of civil servants and public men, and its first acuteness lessened by the formation of an Explosives Committee in the Board of Trade under Lord Moulton has already been revealed by Lord Moulton himself.[81] It is one of the great stories of the war.

But no such departmental devices could long suffice to meet the terrific call of the situation as a whole. As the weeks passed, it gradually became clear to Mr. Lloyd George that, if we were to be saved, a tremendous and radical change was required. This was nothing less than the calling to our aid in this war all those great manufacturing resources of the nation which had given us our ascendancy in peace.

The manufacturers, indeed, were quite willing to come. They needed no call. They were eager to help. They already clamoured at the door.

But the soldier is not suited by the traditions of his calling to work easily with the civilian. That very virtue of iron discipline which is the habit of war militated against the free play of mind essential to a new development of industry. There is a story of a great business man from the North of England who, after being summoned to the War Office for the transaction of business, was kept waiting for two hours, and then told that the officer in command had gone off for his lunch. He is said to have picked up his hat and said decisively: "Tell the General that if he wants me again he must send a battalion to fetch me." It was a fair reminder that there are limits to the power of mere military discipline.

Those who lived in the centre of things during the spring of 1915 will remember the flood of such narratives-many of them told to the House of Commons[82] —which came from the mouths of indignant and offended manufacturers. Offers were rejected which afterwards proved essential. Orders were given and then forgotten. Machinery was set up and then not used. There was devotion and zeal; but there was no adequate organisation to meet the demands of the present, and no proper foresight as to the needs of the future.

Lord Kitchener, indeed, had a deserved reputation for organising capacity; but that eminent man was hopelessly overwhelmed. It was the fault of those who expected too much of him-who first spoke of him as a god and finally treated him as a dog. Reluctantly giving up Egypt for the War Office, Lord Kitchener found himself in control of a ship unmanned. The splendid military staff gathered at the War Office had been scattered to all the fields of war. He found himself very much alone. He felt compelled to act as his own Chief of Staff, his own organiser of recruiting, his own controller of supplies. Among his great gifts he did not possess that of easy and swift delegation. He saw that the War Office required to be built up afresh; but he did not feel equal to building it up during a great war. The result was that he took too much on himself, and most lamentably diminished his own splendid utility in the process.

Such a method was certain to lead to neglect and delay in some of the chief functions of war. All were delayed and many were neglected. But where delay and neglect met in most disastrous combinations was in this matter of the supply of the munitions of war.

So grave did this defect become that it threatened our cause before long with irretrievable disaster. It was only a great effort of the whole nation, combined in one common impulse of energy, that saved the cause.

In that effort Mr. Lloyd George took a great and leading part.

His plea for guns in the autumn of 1914 was followed up by a visit to France, where he was enabled to obtain insight into the great effort of industrial reorganisation which had enabled France to rearm after the loss of the North, and the shock of the German invasion. He returned with a full report on this achievement, due to the great energy and splendid public spirit of that great Frenchman, M. Albert Thomas.

Mr. Lloyd George proposed to the Cabinet that Great Britain should follow in the steps of France. Mr. Asquith was quite willing; and a Cabinet Committee was set up with advisory powers to work out the details. The Committee sat at the War Office with Lord Kitchener in the chair. The matter was fully discussed. The War Office appeared to agree to adopt the French scheme. Weeks passed. Then it was discovered that little or no action had been taken. It was clear that it was the executive arm which was at fault.

The winter months passed, and there was little quickening of energy. Hundreds of thousands of the Kitchener recruits were without clothes, arms, rifles, or guns. Rumours and murmurs began to come from the front of the tremendous British losses from superior German guns.

In February a new danger became instantly vital. The news came from the East of Europe of the definite breakdown of the Russian armaments. Their gigantic armies threatened to become unarmed mobs.

In the West things were little better. During February and March fuller details began to reach London-of one British machine-gun against ten German; of four British shells against forty German. The suppression of the free and independent War Correspondent had cast a veil of silence over the realities of the war. The truth was struggling to come through; and not all the efforts of all the censors could entirely suffocate and strangle it. But it meant that any zealous Minister had to fight hard against a lethal atmosphere of secrecy that soon bred ignorance.

Against this atmosphere Mr. Lloyd George persistently battled; and in the early weeks of April he made a fresh appeal for further speeding up. The Prime Minister (Mr. Asquith) agreed. On April 13th (1915) he appointed a strong Munitions Committee, known as the Treasury Committee, consisting of Ministers, civil servants and experts, with Mr. Lloyd George in the chair.[83]

That Committee had no executive powers. It could only co-ordinate departments, and make suggestions. It was no more than a departmental Committee; but, in spite of this shortcoming it was able to give valuable advice, much of which was acted upon. It supplied new ideas. It was often able to meet special emergencies.

But from the very beginning this Committee suffered from one grave, paralysing defect: it could obtain no full or comprehensive view of the needs and demands of the war. Perhaps the chiefs of the War Office did not know themselves. In the hurry and bustle of war perhaps it is not incredible they had no leisure to take the larger and longer view. But in a long war that view was indispensable to action. The result of that ignorance, therefore, was fatal to this Committee. It never knew enough to act or decide with effect. Lord Kitchener may have had his reasons; but the fact stands out that he refrained from arming this important Munitions Committee of April and May, 1915, with the full knowledge necessary for real power.

At this point an astonishing thing occurred. The Western Army took the matter into their own hands.

There are many things that fighting men will endure-incredible tortures, surpassing those of the early martyrs. But there is one thing which always tries them beyond the limit: that is to be hit without the power of hitting back-to be shelled without being able to shell. Such was now (in April and May, 1915) the intolerable situation of the men under General French's command in France.[84] They decided that it was not their duty to accept this cruel fate without some effort to find a cure.

They found their applications misunderstood, ignored, postponed. They realised that Ministers were not allowed to know the truth. They gathered from his public utterance at New-castle on April 20th[85] that the truth was being concealed even from the Prime Minister (Mr. Asquith) himself. They perceived that the public were blind-folded. They determined to take steps to open their eyes.

With this design and object, the Headquarters Staff in France invited certain famous journalists and publicists to the front to witness for themselves the results of the lack of proper shells in the attack on the Aubers ridge.[86] Most of those visitors found themselves helpless in the grip of a double censorship-in France and in England. One of them, however, the famous military correspondent of the Times,[87] wrote his despatch on the spot and sent it through the censorship of the field of battle, severe indeed, but on this occasion, perhaps, a little more friendly. In this way, and thanks to the historic prestige of the great organ which published it, there appeared in the Times of May 14th, 1915, that famous message from the front, "mutilated and twice censored,"[88] which itself proved so powerful a petard.

"The want of an unlimited supply of high explosive was a fatal bar to our success"—that was the verdict of the Times correspondent; and it was confirmed by every observer and every soldier at the front, including the soldier members of the House of Commons. Once the word was uttered in public, the floodgates were opened. It was in vain that the Government tried to stem the torrent of evidence. Lord Kitchener rose on May 18th to make a statement in the House of Lords; but in that speech he showed that strange habit of the unexpected which baulked even his friends. For, instead of denying, he practically admitted the indictment, and for the first time stated in public what seemed to contradict the Newcastle utterance of the Prime Minister-that there had been "undoubtedly considerable delay in producing the material."

This was indeed a mild way of stating the true facts. These continued now to pour through from the front with all the indecency of truth emancipated. The order-paper of the House of Commons began to bristle with questions and threats of debate; and it was only on the plea of public emergency that the Government postponed crisis.

On the following day Mr. Lloyd George received information which more than confirmed the statement of the Times correspondent. He realised with amazement that the Munitions Committee had been kept in ignorance of essentials; that the mainspring had been missing from the watch. He determined to resign from a function so void of power; and on May 19th he wrote a letter announcing his decision, and giving his grave and weighty reasons. He refused to remain chairman of a Committee which had no real executive power.

The situation now moved rapidly.

On the afternoon of that day (May 19th) Mr. Asquith announced to the House of Commons that the Liberal Government which had been in power since 1910 had ceased to exist, and that he proposed to reconstruct the Government "on a broader personal and political basis." In other words, he had decided for Coalition.

It was a wise and prudent decision. The Opposition had full grasp of the situation at the front. They had not yet manœuvred for battle, but there was already forming in the minds of their leaders the conviction that they could no longer accept the responsibility of a silence which would inevitably spell complicity. If they were to continue silent they must share the government. The only alternative was the open scandal of a bitter party struggle, not without the possibility of grave injury to national interests.

But a Coalition Government alone was not enough. It was necessary to have some guarantee that the general calamitous shortage of munitions[89] should not continue. It is not the habit of England to send her youth unarmed to face her enemies. At all costs this grievous peril must cease.

But it was already clear to all parties that the War Office was far too heavily burdened to continue bearing this responsibility. There must be a division of function. Lord Kitchener must be left to raise the armies. Another office must take over the duty of arming and equipping them. From this conviction arose the idea of a new Department-the Ministry of Munitions-for which Mr. Lloyd George was already, by the unanimous voice of public opinion, declared elect.

So on May 25th, 1915, after seven years as Chancellor of the Exchequer, Mr. Lloyd George closed the door of the Treasury behind him and became the first British Minister of Munitions. It was a great adventure. He was leaving behind him the secure vantage of an old historic Department. He was entering upon a region unexplored, without map or compass, without precedent or guide.

[79] "What we stint in materials we squander in life; that is the one great lesson of munitions." —Mr. Lloyd George in the House of Commons, December 21st, 1915.

[80] The evidence in the Sukhomikoff trial has now brought out the immensity of this shortcoming, not then fully divulged to the British Government by the Russian governing power.

[81] See his evidence in the Mond libel action.

[82] See Debate of April 22nd, 1915. Mr. Bonar Law gave some striking instances.

[83] Among the other members of that Committee were Mr. Balfour, Mr. Montagu, Mr. George Booth, Sir Herbert Llewellyn Smith, Admiral Tudor, and General Von Donop. Mr. Lloyd George made on April 22nd, 1915, a statement in the House of Commons as to the work achieved by this Committee.

[84] See his statement to the Journal correspondent in September 1917.

[85] "I saw a statement the other day that the operations, not only of our Army, but of our Allies were being crippled, or at any rate hampered, by our failure to provide the necessary ammunition. There is not a word of truth in that statement." (Loud cheers.) Times report.

[86] See the full account in Lord French's "1914." His statements have not in substance been affected by the controversies which have raged round this book.

[87] Lieutenant-Colonel Charles A'Court Repington, C.M.G.

[88] See the Times leading article. But on May 18th Mr. Asquith said in the House of Commons that the despatch was censored in France and Mr. Tennant added that it never came before the British Censorship. The open official chagrin at its emergence into print is one of the most significant features of the whole episode.

[89] Of all munitions, not only explosives. It proved subsequently that the chief want was big guns for the high-explosive shells and that the smaller guns were better suited with shrapnel.

CHAPTER XVIII

THE NEW MINISTRY OF MUNITIONS

"Now all the youth of England is on fire,
  And silken dalliance in the wardrobe lies;
  Now thrive the armourers, and honour's thought
  Reigns solely in the breast of every man."
Henry V, Prologue to Act II.

The little group of men whom Mr. Lloyd George assembled round him at No. 6, Whitehall Gardens, during the Whit-week of 1915, certainly seemed to have no easy task before them. A new Ministry had been founded, and a Bill to define its functions was being drawn up. But the Ministry possessed neither buildings nor staff, neither furniture nor office paper. It stepped forth into the world bare as a new-born babe.[90]

Even when its functions had been defined by Act of Parliament there always hung about this enterprise an atmosphere of indefinable adventure. Its relations to other Departments, and especially to the War Office, were never precisely defined. It was always the parvenu of Ministries. Throughout the crises of 1915 and 1916 it carried with it the spirit of Esau, its hand against every man and every man's hand against it.

After all, that was precisely the kind of office for which Mr. Lloyd George was best fitted. He was ever impatient of precedents; here was a case where he had to make his own precedents. He always loved trespassing. Here was an office where every movement was practically a raid on the ground sacred to some other Department.

He was never in the least troubled by the restrictions of the situation. He soon found out one vital fact-that our supply of shells had sunk to 75,000. But he rapidly grasped that there were many other things required for success besides shells. There were, for instance, guns to fire them from-big guns such as were entirely lacking at that time. In June of 1915, finding that he still could obtain no sure or certain idea of what was needed at the front, he travelled to Boulogne, and met a little party of officers, many of them French, in a small café. The party consisted partly of Generals, and partly of regimental officers. He listened to all; for he wanted to know what was wanted in the firing-line as much as what was thought to be wanted at Headquarters. He closely questioned the French artillerists as to the number of guns they were using. General Du Cane[91] was there from our Headquarters' Staff; and he brought with him a full report of what guns were required according to their views.

Mr. Lloyd George began to realise that the need for big guns was the centre of the situation.

After his cross-examination was over, Mr. Lloyd George turned to General Du Cane:

"Don't you think you had better go back and revise your estimates?"

General Du Cane promptly agreed-he had himself been converted. He went back to Headquarters.

At midday there was a break in these urgent talks. M. Albert Thomas suggested that in the afternoon they ought to have a formal meeting to go into the whole subject.

"I am sorry," said Mr. Lloyd George, "but I must get back to England."

"Go back already?"

"Yes, already-there is not a moment to be lost. These big guns must be ordered."

He went back. A revived estimate of the munition requirements in France was sent to Whitehall. Mr. Lloyd George increased that estimate. He sent it across to Lord Kitchener. The great man, willing but doubtful of our resources, sent it back with a comment: "That will take three years."[92]

Mr. Lloyd George then called together all the heads of the armament firms. He laid the scheme before them. They viewed it with grave doubts. They produced laborious estimates-discussed-consulted their chiefs.

Mr. Lloyd George put aside all the papers.

"Gentlemen," he said, "this has to be done if the country is to be saved. You will do it!"

There was nothing more to be said. They went away to do it; and they did it.

The high officials responsible for financial control were a little disturbed at his way of conducting business. Later on, yet more guns were ordered, and official protests from other Departments were carried up to the highest quarters. But before a decision could be reached the orders had been given out, and the great guns-the guns that saved France and England-were on the way.[93]

That was characteristic of his way of using the new machinery of the new Ministry.

How this new Department of State was gradually built up; how picked men from all over the country, and from the Civil Service, were gathered to the side of the new Minister; how buildings were secured from day to day for the work of administration; how excessive hours were worked and excessive risks were run by old as well as young, and women as well as men, —this story has already been largely told in the Parliamentary statements of the Munition Ministers,[94] and it is one of the most romantic and thrilling chapters in the history of the war.

There are one or two features in the history of this movement which especially illustrate the characteristics of Mr. Lloyd George and his power of appeal to the public.

The first of these was the rally of the business men of England in response to his call. The British commercial classes were not, in the period before the war, particularly attached to Mr. Lloyd George. They had some "bones to pick" with him. But it must be said, to their eternal credit, that when they realised the need of their country the old hatchet was at once put underground. They came in hundreds to help him. Many of them came without price, leaving their own factories and workshops, putting aside their chance of personal profit, and content to live on such salaries as their business could afford them. It is true that many of them have risen to high honour in this service. It is well that it should be so.

Happily there is sufficient soul of good in things to justify sacrifice and even to reward it. It is no ill thing that many of these men have risen to high honour and blazoned their names on the roll of England's noblest servants.

But it was not only the commercial men that came forward voluntarily to answer the call. The Civil Servants also volunteered from all branches of the Service to undertake increased responsibility without additional gain. It was laid down from the beginning that none of those Civil Servants who came into the Munition Service should receive extra pay for extra work. Second division clerks raised to higher posts still continued to receive the old salaries; so great was the eagerness to save the country that men worked overtime without complaint, and there were in those early days many men who came suspiciously near to working night shifts as well as day.

It was precisely the combination of the best Civil Servants with the best commercial men that gave to the Ministry of Munitions such a marvellous touch of efficiency. Manufacturers coming up from the provinces were now pleasantly surprised to find a new swiftness of despatch in the conduct of their business. Every one brought into touch with the Ministry of Munitions found a new spirit which seemed to give a new hope for the government of this country. There was a certain thrill about the most common affairs within those walls. Every servant of the Ministry, down to the very boys and girls who carried the messages, seemed to feel that they were called to a high task for a great end. It was in this spirit that this great effort was undertaken and sustained throughout the years that followed. At the same time the country as a whole found itself provided at last with a capable machinery for using its services. Not only was the centre quickened and sharpened to new uses, but the whole of the United Kingdom was mapped out and in every district there sat a Committee who formed a careful estimate of the resources of that area.[95]

On the basis of that estimate there now began to grow up, as if by magic, that vast network of new war factories which saved the armies in France. The factories grew up chiefly near the iron and coal which provided the raw material of munitions and handy to the great supplies of skilled labour.[96]

But no adjustment could avoid a great upheaval of social life. For it was part of this great change that a vast mass of labour must be transferred from the industries of peace to the industries of war.

It was also part of the great stress of this crisis that the State must be sure of its labour and that it must be able to draw from that labour the utmost power of effort, sustained and continued through a prolonged period of time.

Here lay the necessity for a new War Labour policy, difficult and delicate to justify and administer, but indispensable for the safety of the country.

It was clearly impossible to guarantee the adequate war output of this vast aggregate of factories and workshops on the basis of the old peace conditions-with an uncertain supply of skilled labour shifting about from shop to shop along the ordinary channels of demand and supply. The habit of "stealing" labour by the offer of higher wages had already grown to so high a point in the early days of the war that the Munitions Committee had had to issue an order under the Defence of the Realm Act making it an offence to "entice."[97] Thus the peace freedom of movement had already been suspended. But now it was necessary to carry the restrictions further and to guarantee to the nation at war a hold on its workmen similar in kind, though not in degree, to the hold on its soldiers.

Mr. Lloyd George characteristically wished to make the bold appeal, and to say to the workmen: "Submit to the same discipline as your sons in the trenches. Place yourselves under the same law, with this only difference-that you are better-paid men."[98] But this proposal, when laid before the leaders of the Trade Unions, met with fierce opposition. The "conscription of labour," as it was called, was denounced as a "new slavery." Some degree of national consent to such a measure was plainly necessary. So that proposal was dropped, and the Ministry of Munitions set out to search for a new policy.

The policy finally agreed upon took shape in the first Munitions Act and the subsequent amending measures. Round those measures a great strife afterwards arose, and it may be worth while to say something as to their origin and justification.

It was absolutely necessary, if the armies were to be properly supplied with the immense mass of munitions required, that the workers should both consent to the limitation of their freedom of movement and should also suspend a number of those limitations and conditions of toil which had been won in the course of the long conflict between Capital and Labour.

It was desirable to come to a bargain; and with that view the Trade Unions were consulted at every point. If the Government must trust Labour, Labour must also trust the Government. Labour must have assurance that a temporary suspension of conditions should not prejudice the position in time of peace. That assurance had been already given, and was now formally embodied in the Munitions Act.[99]

On these broad lines had grown up this Concordat, which, with all its frictions and inevitable misunderstandings, still carried the country through the moments of gravest peril. The liberty of Labour was gravely restricted; but the great and sufficient reward for such a sacrifice to every patriotic workman always was the knowledge that brave lives were being saved and brave hearts sustained at the front. Another important thing was that the country was being saved also.

Certainly the restrictions were very formidable. No workman or workwoman could leave their employment in the war factory without a special "leaving certificate." All rules or customs restricting labour were suspended; no strikes were allowed; and all questions of wages and hours were to be settled by compulsory arbitration. To administer these rules Munition Tribunals were set up in every district; and they had powers of inflicting heavy fines. Such provisions must depend largely on the good faith and good-will of employers; and there must always be some who will not "play the game." Hence the chronic movements of revolt-the rise of the shop stewards, the engineers' strike, the war-weariness of so many industrial districts in the summer of 1917.

In the autumn of 1917 Mr. Winston Churchill, the new Minister of Munitions, found it possible to suspend the leaving certificate and to slacken some of these conditions. But there could be no doubt as to their necessity up to that time.

The sole and sufficient excuse for these grave restrictions of liberty was always the war, and the war alone. War is a terrible master; and wherever he raises his head, few escape his tyranny. All that can be said is that, with all their troubles, the sufferings of the men in the workshops were as grains in the balance against the sufferings of the men in the trenches.

But, even so, the work of the men alone was not enough to meet the need. Other sources of labour must be tapped. It was now necessary to call in the women to the aid of the men.

Mr. Lloyd George ventured on a bold appeal. He asked the women to come from their pleasures and their comforts; he asked them to save the lives of their brothers, their sweethearts, and their husbands. They came in multitudes. They filled the ranks, and they filled the shells.[100] They silenced their sourest critics, even in their own sex. They worked by day and they worked by night. They earned for themselves a new position in the State. They showed that women could be patriots themselves, as well as the wives and mothers of patriots. Not easily will England forget those splendid women of 1915-18.

As for Mr. Lloyd George himself, he worked as hard as any one in the ranks of this new Labour Army. He was here, there, and everywhere. All through the summer of 1915 he travelled over the country, appealing, stimulating, and even when necessary rebuking. He visited all the industrial centres. He spoke straight to the English working classes; and it was only their worst friends who resented his honesty. He told them to suspend their peace weaknesses in this supreme hour; and he told them, as John Stuart Mill told them once before, where their chief weakness lay. He set up a Drink Control Board, as well as Munition Tribunals; and all that was best and most loyal among the artisans acquiesced. Ça ira; the plan worked; the machine began to do its duty.

Nothing was left undone. To fill up the ranks, unskilled men were trained to do the work of skilled. The Board of Trade organised a special army of Munition Volunteers. In the autumn of 1915 there was a great effort, in conjunction with the War Office, to bring back from the front some thousands[101] of those numerous munition workers, iron-workers, and miners who had been allowed to recruit in the first fine flush of the recruiting enthusiasm in 1914.

Mr. Lloyd George gave his whole mind to this one question-the making of war material. He had, as we have seen, found the Army with only 75,000 shells in hand in June, 1915; when he left the Ministry in June, 1916, he had provided shells in millions. He himself mastered the technique of shell-making and gun-making; he visited the factories and studied the machinery; he listened to every complaint from the soldiers at the front; he investigated every defect.

The real secret, indeed, of his work was that he kept in touch with the armies at the Western Front, constantly visiting them, studying their needs on the spot, listening to the actual fighting men. Above all he studied the German inventions. After a short while, thanks to the labours of our young scientists from the Universities, he was able to provide our soldiers with gas-masks that enabled them to face unshaken the worst deviltry of the enemy, and with gas that was a fit reply to theirs. He provided our men with flame-throwers which made them a fair match when they faced the flame-throwers of the Teuton.

I remember his taking me, one day in 1915, to see his little collection of these horrible devices in the basement of the old Metropole Hotel. He showed me the model shells, mounting by slow gradations to a giant's height. He lingered halfway along this row of shells. He put his hand on one. "When I started the Ministry," he said, "our shells went only as high as this. The German shells went to the top of the range. Was that fair to our soldiers?" It was a vivid illustration of what they were achieving.

So this gigantic new organisation was built up, and gradually brought its full weight into the struggle. Its functions were constantly enlarging. By proved fitness to rule over one city this new Ministry soon achieved the right to rule over ten. From supplying it took to making, from making it took to designing, and to designing after its own ideas. The great net-work of its new factories gradually spread over the land. Greatly daring, it built; it housed; it fed. From a servant it became a master. In August, 1915, it took over from the War Office the Royal Factory at Woolwich; and so it became the supreme war-maker of the nation.

Meanwhile, the soldiers at the front grew more confident and serene. They felt the support of the great working nation behind them. They grew more confident of supremacy. They knew that even the women-kind were "doing their bit." In each great battle, as the shells swept over their heads, they felt a new power at work in their favour.[102] They "went over the top" with the knowledge that the mailed fist of Prussia was to be met with the iron hammer of England.

To this new feeling and the confidence born of it we may largely attribute the great victories of the Somme, the storming of the Vimy Ridge, and the smashing onslaught on Messines.

Many Englishmen, great and small, have a right to share in the glory of this great work. We must not forget those men who, before the great central crisis arose, battled alone against a sea of errors and failings in high places-great civil servants like Sir Hubert Llewellyn Smith, or great public servants like Lord Moulton. Such men do not labour in the limelight. We must remember their services.

Nor must we forget loyal political helpers like Dr. Addison, Mr. Lloyd George's first lieutenant at the Ministry, and Mr. Montagu, his successor.

But, when all is said and done, the man who did the deed was Mr. Lloyd George. Without his resolution and decision England would have fared badly in that dark hour. It was he who designed, directed, and completed this noble and stupendous endeavour. It was he who carried it through. It was he who, when others failed, armed and strengthened our armies. It is scarcely too much to say that it was he who, under Providence, saved England.

---

[90] See Dr. Addison's description (House of Commons, June 28th, 1917): "There was to be one aim, and one aim only-to obtain the goods and make delivery of them to the Army. No other interests and no considerations of leisure were to be entertained."

[91] Lieutenant-General Sir John Philip Du Cane, Major-General R.A., G.H.Q., 1915. Afterwards British representative with Marshal Foch.

[92] Similarly, to Lord French he said eight years (Journal interview, Sept. 1917).

[93] Mr. Montagu, in the House of Commons, on August 16th, 1916, said openly that "Mr. Lloyd George ordered far more guns than were thought by the War Office to be necessary, and yet received new requirements showing that he had not ordered enough."

[94] Mr. Lloyd George's statement of December 21st, 1915, Mr. Montagu's statement of August 16th, 1916, and Dr. Addison's statement of June 28th, 1917.

[95] Twelve areas: England and Wales, 8; Scotland, 2; Ireland, 2; 40 local Munition Committees in the engineering centres consisting of local business men. (Mr. Lloyd George, December 21st, 1915.)

[96] Within a year the labour employed on munitions had gone up from 1,635,000 to 2,250,000, and there were 32 national shell factories, 12 for projectiles, 6 for cartridges, etc. (Mr. Montagu, August 1915.)

[97] There had also been in March an agreement between the Government and the Trade Unions called the Treasury Agreement, and administered by a Labour Advisory Committee. The general line of that agreement was an understanding to suspend restrictive Trade Union practices in return for a promise to tax excess profits.

[98] He put this appeal very strongly in a speech to the engineers at Cardiff on June 11th, 1915.

[99] Clause 20 of the main Act: "This Act shall have effect only so long as the Office of Minister of Munitions and the Ministry of Munitions exist."

[100] At Woolwich alone the number of women workers rose from 125 to 25,000.

[101] 40,000 soldiers were brought back. In addition, there are 38,000 War Munition Volunteers, and 30,000 Army Reserve Munition Workers. (Dr. Addison's speech.)

[102] By August 1916 the high-explosive shells had been increased by 66 per cent.; there had been a 14-fold increase of machine-guns; and a 33-fold increase of bombs. Every month saw as many great guns manufactured as existed at the beginning of the war. (Mr. Montagu, August 1916.)

CHAPTER XIX

PREMIERSHIP

"Not once or twice in our rough island-story,
    The path of duty was the way to glory."
    Tennyson.

This great revival in the supply of munitions to Great Britain and her Allies began, early in 1916, to show its effects on the fortunes of the war.

There were some things that could not be retrieved-Serbia, Bulgaria, Kut. On the Western fields of war there was a steady stiffening, and the 1915 peril of collapse gradually passed away. During the spring of 1916 guns and shells were accumulated in great masses for a summer attack.

The new Military Service Act, too, now began to come into action; a steady supply of young men began to fill up the gaps in the armies at the front.

What could be done by men and munitions was being done; and at any rate it was no longer possible for the commanders and men to feel that they were not being properly supported by the civilians at home.

It was not only in regard to the British armies that this great uplift of power took place. The Russians, too, now found themselves being supplied with streams of guns and shells from Great Britain; and Brusiloff began to prepare for his great thrust forward.

Thus events moved forward to those great battles of July and August, 1916, when, by sheer force of gun-power, we captured positions thought to be impregnable, and brought about the dramatic withdrawal of the German armies towards the French frontiers in the spring of 1917.

But, in the meantime, Mr. Lloyd George himself had been called away to other and higher tasks. He is one of those men whom Nature seems to have marked out as pioneers; and there seems to be almost a law by which, when such men have accomplished one great task, another sphere calls for them. At the Ministry of Munitions he had now done his work-that work of starting, inspiring, and organising which is peculiarly his. Other men could now take up the task and keep it going; they could run the engine once it was devised and set running; happily, there are many such men in the world.

It was fated that a tragic event should make it necessary that Mr. Lloyd George should now himself move forward.

On June 5th, 1916, Lord Kitchener, always the head and forefront of England's military effort, the great Captain of those legions to whom he gave his own name, met an untimely end in H.M.S. Hampshire, off the western coast of Scotland. The splendid cruiser which carried his fortunes was met by a fierce gale; but his mission to Russia was urgent, and he was not the man to delay. The ship altered its course to the lee side of the Shetland Islands, and there it met with a mine cast adrift by the storm, and quickly foundered. Lord Kitchener was last seen on the quarter-deck meeting death as calmly as he had faced life.

Mr. Lloyd George was called to take Lord Kitchener's place, and passed in June, 1916, from the Ministry of Munitions to the War Office. The effect of this change was to increase his power of control over the war, and at the same time to deepen his responsibility.

He did not stay long enough in the War Office to obtain complete grip of the administrative machine, or to introduce the reforms which were so desirable in that office. But this period of power was marked by some of those bold and sweeping strokes which are so characteristic. In the autumn of 1916, on one of his periodical visits to the Western Front, he realised that the Army was on the eve of a tragical breakdown of communications. The French roads were becoming worn out with the strain of the heavy transport traffic. We had not enjoyed that immense relief from the structure of small railways which was common to our Allies and our enemies. He also grasped the fact that the fortunes of all future "offensives" were going to depend on swift and decisive concentrations of guns, shells, and men, only possible by means of railways. The railways then at our disposal in France were quite insufficient to carry the burden of vast armies as well as the local life of the countryside. He insisted, against great opposition, both from officials and Press, on placing the railways under the control of railway men. He persuaded Sir Douglas Haig to make Sir Eric Geddes a General at Headquarters in charge of transportation. Later on, Sir Eric Geddes was given charge of all transportations in the United Kingdom, as well as in the British zone in France; and he imposed on the British civilian population those restrictions of traffic which have been so cheerfully borne. All this made a huge difference, both in the smooth working of the army machine in France, and in the organisation of those swift, sudden springs forward which played so great a part in the final victory.

But greater events were soon to claim his attention.

He had not yet obtained full grip of the machinery at the War Office when there loomed up in the East another of those great tragedies of the little nations, which, like Stations of the Cross, marked the stages of this world-agony.

Rumania had always felt strong sympathy with the cause of the Entente Allies. In spite of various cross-currents, the tide of her feelings had set very steadily towards the cause of the Western democracies. But she had hitherto been restrained by a very wise prudence from rushing into a struggle with powerful Empires close at hand.

But now fortune seemed to be swinging over to the democracies. The Somme and Verdun seemed to be the obverse and the reverse sides of the same victorious shield. The Italians were moving forward. The Russians were sanguine, and pressed Rumania for her assistance.

So the Rumanian Government, on August 27th, took the great decision and declared war on Austria.

All the world knows the episodes in that tragic story-the premature Rumanian advance into Transylvania, the sudden, treacherous attack in the rear from Bulgaria-the quick, smashing blows of the gathered German armies-the passing of that fearful harrow of war over that beautiful, romantic land.

No one saw this coming cloud more rapidly than Mr. Lloyd George. Early in September he read through the designs of the German commanders. With his uncanny eye for a military situation, he seemed to know what Hindenburg was going to do before he did it. He noticed a weakening in the attack on Verdun. He realised in a moment that Bulgaria would not be moving if she were not sure of German help. He saw straight into the heart of the German eastern ambitions, and he realised that here they had an opportunity which on no account would they pass by.

He was full of a feverish desire to avert the blow, even at the eleventh hour. Could not anything still be done? There was Italy-she was at the doors of the East-there was Russia. Was it nothing to them who passed by-this crucifixion of a little nation? There was always something especially poignant in his emotions over these tragedies. He was not a man suited to the part of sitting by and doing nothing.

But Rumania was already beyond the reach of our help. When Serbia was lost, Rumania was cut off also from British aid. The British Fleet, as Lord Salisbury once shrewdly remarked, cannot operate in the Balkans. Russia, the only possible rescuer, proved a broken reed. She was already paralysed by the sleeping sickness of internal treachery.

So Rumania went under. But the event had a reverberating influence on Mr. Lloyd George's mind. It brought him to a decision which he had long been meditating.

He could no longer go on being responsible for these repeated failures without a supreme effort to make them cease.

He had for a long time past gravely doubted whether he would not be more capable of helping in the conduct of the war if he left the Government. He had often been on the verge of resigning-on munitions, on conscription, on the Serbian failure. He had a growing conviction that the only hope of winning the war was through the nation; and he wanted to guide and to inform the nation. He longed to be "unmuzzled"—to speak out what he knew, to speak for himself alone.

But it had always happened that before he took action his policy had won; and then it became practically impossible for him to resign. Ministers cannot resign on delay alone. Yet these constant delays were piling up against us a constantly accumulating debt. Or, as with the proud Roman and the ancient Sibyl, the reward was diminishing while the price was not less.

The Rumanian disaster brought Mr. Lloyd George to the parting of the ways. He must either reform the Government to better uses, or he must gain his freedom-on that issue he was clear.

Reflecting deeply on the mode and method of reform, he saw but one way out —a smaller and more efficient body, wholly devoted to the direction of the war. That had been his view for a long time past-and every event had confirmed it. What was wanted was unified, unsleeping control.

He decided at last to place this view definitely and decisively before Mr. Asquith, the Prime Minister.

He did so in a long conversation on the morning of Friday, December 1st, 1916.

This was the first phase in a crisis into which Mr. Lloyd George entered with the utmost reluctance. He was sincerely attached to Mr. Asquith. He had that regard for him which is often based on an entire difference of temperament. He fully recognised the greatness of those qualities which have given Mr. Asquith so strong a hold on the esteem and affections of his countrymen. He wished to continue the working partnership. He made in the course of these negotiations every conceivable suggestion which could make the changed conditions tolerable to the proper pride and self-respect of a man who had deserved so well of the nation.

But on the fundamental necessity for a change in the organisation for control of the war, he remained throughout as firm as adamant. There could be no compromise on that point. There are certain questions on which no man can compromise. One is the safety and honour of his own country.

He regarded that as involved in his proposal to reform the machinery of war-control.

He had come to the conclusion that a smaller and stronger authority was absolutely necessary for the prosperous conduct of the war. He also held, with equal strength of conviction, that no man could bear at the same time the double burden of parliamentary leadership and of the day-by-day task of Chairmanship of the new War Council, with its entirely full and detailed responsibility for the conduct of the war. Mr. Asquith was universally acknowledged as the supreme parliamentary leader of his generation. He was a great national figure-head. It seemed a fair and reasonable proposal that he should continue to lead the Commons and the country, and should allow one of his colleagues to become the Chairman of the new War Authority. Mr. Lloyd George did not name himself as Chairman of that body. Mr. Asquith first named him. But it soon became quite clear to both that he was the only fit and proper man to carry out his own scheme.

Mr. Lloyd George, as we all know, laid these views in writing before the Prime Minister, and discussed them with him very fully during the two following days.[103] He laid them in memoranda and in conversations. As the talk went on the new proposal varied now and again in detail, but it remained always the same in essence. Mr. Lloyd George never disputed the supreme control of the Prime Minister: he even agreed to the final control of the Cabinet-for he had not yet ventured so far as to propose a supreme War Cabinet.

It is quite clear that Mr. Lloyd George's proposal startled and alarmed Mr. Asquith. That great man is above all things a constitutionalist; profoundly impassioned for the traditions of

English freedom. Trained up in parliamentary habits, it seemed abhorrent to him that any function of supreme control in affairs should be divorced from that fount and centre of power. It was not for his own personal position, we may be sure, that he resisted Mr. Lloyd George's proposals. They clashed with all that was deepest in his nature. The heir and successor of Pym, Selden, and Pitt could not lightly acquiesce in any derogation to the authority of Parliament or Cabinet.

What Mr. Asquith did not see was that new needs call for new measures; and that the needs of a war such as this, unprecedented in extent and violence, may also necessitate remedies without precedent on the parchments of the English statute-books.

At one stage Mr. Asquith appears to have agreed with Mr. Lloyd George, and Mr. Lloyd George was for some time (on Saturday, December 2nd) under the impression that the matter was settled on the general lines of his policy. He did not fight for details. He was willing to discuss the membership of the Committee; but he remained firm on the principle. He had already determined to resign rather than fail to carry it out.[104] But at that moment there seemed no necessity for such a step.

At this stage, however, there stepped into the arena those busy friends who, since the days of Job, have never been a man's best counsellors. Energy breeds foes; and there were men who were inclined to ask the old question: "Who is this man that he should rule over us?" These men held up the arms of Mr. Asquith in his resistance to the policy laid down by Mr. Lloyd George.

On the other side there were also friends-friends of the Press, certainly not inspired by any amiable feelings towards Mr. Asquith. They belonged to a section which had always stood honestly and boldly for a more active prosecution of the war. It was certainly not the fault of Mr. Lloyd George that this Press had espoused his cause in all his great efforts for the nation; and it was preposterous to expect that he should reject their help. A member of a Coalition Ministry has no right to keep up old party prejudices in his dealings with the Press; and it has always been the role of Mr. Lloyd George to be accessible to the Press on both sides. It had happened, indeed, that only a few weeks before Mr. Lloyd George had had a sharp passage of arms with Lord Northcliffe over the question of communications on the Western Front; and certainly there was no working alliance between them. There was nothing more than a fortuitous temporary agreement in regard to the conduct of the war.

On Monday, December 4th, there appeared in the Times an article giving a very clear and accurate summary of the negotiations, supported by a "leader" rejoicing over the discomfiture of Mr. Asquith.[105] It is the inveterate habit of British statesmen to listen with sensitive ears to the oracles from Printing House Square; and Mr. Asquith was no exception to this rule. He treated this blow as a thunderbolt. He immediately, on the morning of Monday, December 4th, wrote to Mr. Lloyd George plainly intimating that if this was to be the sort of view taken of his agreement he could not go on.

When he received this letter Mr. Lloyd George had not seen the Times article. He knew nothing about it. He certainly did not inspire it. He was as surprised as Mr. Asquith when he read it. But he has always taken a tolerant view as to the activities of a democratic Press. He wrote back to Mr. Asquith a friendly letter deprecating any attention to press attacks of which he had himself had to endure so many, and strongly urging Mr. Asquith not to play into the hands of the Times. He-Mr. Lloyd George-wanted an agreement. The Times did not.

But it was too late. Mr. Asquith's friends urged him to act and not to submit to what seemed to him a deliberate attempt to destroy his personal prestige. So on the afternoon he resigned and ended his Government. He acted with absolute correctness. He received authority from the King at once to form a new Government; and he wrote at once to Mr. Lloyd George. He could, in his view, start now afresh, unhampered by the negotiations of Saturday and Sunday.

His first condition was that he himself, as Prime Minister, must be Chairman of the new War Committee.

The former plan was thus now definitely rejected, and a clear challenge was thrown down to Mr. Lloyd George-not a personal challenge, but a challenge of principle. For Mr. Asquith sincerely and honestly held that his was the proper way to control the conduct of the war.

It was, indeed, now for Mr. Lloyd George to decide, not whether he should resign-for he was no longer Minister-but whether he should join the new Ministry on these terms, which clashed absolutely with his own plans. It was plainly impossible that he should do so.

So, still with regret but always quite decisively, on December 5th he placed his office at the disposal of Mr. Asquith in the formation of his new Ministry.

He parted from Mr. Asquith with every expression of personal regret, and offered his complete support of the new Government for the prosecution of the war.

After that events moved rapidly. On the Sunday (December 3rd) the Tory rank and file had met and decided not to follow Mr. Lloyd George. But Mr. Bonar Law made it clear that in that case they could not count on his leadership. He and his friends in the old Ministry refused to join the new Ministry. That made it impossible for Mr. Asquith to succeed.

The next step was for the King to send for Mr. Bonar Law. But the old Liberals, the Labour Party, and the Irish Nationalists refused to serve under his Premiership. He did not possess a parliamentary majority. It was useless for Mr. Bonar Law to take office with a minority following in the House of Commons.

Mr. Lloyd George, indeed, urged Mr. Bonar Law to make the attempt, and offered to serve under him.

The King, with a splendid desire for reconciliation, called a conference at Buckingham Palace, and tried to form a new Coalition Ministry of all parties under Mr. Bonar Law. But the thing was impossible. Asquith and his friends stood out; Mr. Asquith refused the Woolsack. He was contending for what seemed to him a definite issue of parliamentary control, and we can scarcely blame him for refusing to be spirited off the arena of political conflict, or relegated to a gilded cage.

It only remained for the King to send for Mr. Lloyd George, for he was now the only possible Premier. It was clearly his duty to accept the call. It was not easy for him to form a Ministry. The rank and file of the Tories, still shadowed by Budget memories, shrank at first from the idea of serving under so fervent a Radical; but Mr. Bonar Law was determined to submit all political divisions to the supreme issue of the war; and most of the powerful men of the party followed his patriotic lead. Many of the leading Liberal ex-Ministers plainly intimated, through various channels, public and private, that they were anxious to stand aside[106]; but most of the capable young men willingly came along, recognising that at this crisis there was a greater thing involved than personal loyalty. The Labour Party at first stood aloof. There were long conferences at the War Office. But at last Mr. Lloyd George won them over by large and frank concessions both in policy and share of office.

Such is a simple narrative of the events which made Mr. Lloyd George Premier. Of course there were mean and unworthy insinuations-of course there were men who saw, in this great and dramatic clash of ideas, nothing but the mean and sordid conflict of personal ambitions, or the still more squalid combat of rival journals. There will always be men with their eyes fixed on the ground when great signs are appearing in the heavens.

But to those who have followed this story the event will seem to be inevitable. At the given moment Mr. Lloyd George took the post of leadership, but he only took that post because for at least a year he had already been the leader. Great wars always have electric effects. For the ruling of such thunder-storms there is required a certain temperament of storm. The plain fact is that Mr. Lloyd George possessed that temperament-and sooner or later he must have been called to direct the thunderbolts.

When he really had the power to shape the machine of war after his own ideas, Mr. Lloyd George put aside half-measures. He boldly shaped a new instrument of Government-the War Cabinet as we afterwards knew it. That Cabinet was a small body of experienced administrators, united by the one tie of zeal for their country, who gave their whole energies entirely to the conduct of the war. Except for brief holidays, they sat daily, and sometimes twice a day. Minutes were kept of their proceedings, although their speeches were not reported. When any Department was concerned, the Minister affected attended himself, and took part in the consultations. Thus the Foreign Minister was there when there was a discussion of foreign affairs, the Chancellor of the Exchequer on finance, and so on. The result was that the departmental chiefs were more free for their own administrative work, and less worried with the problems of other Departments. On the other hand, there grew up a new Civil Service attached to the War Cabinet, and a more active machinery for keeping the offices in touch.

It was confessedly a great experiment-but experiments are necessary for war. It was certain that that other instrument, the old Cabinet-already showing signs of weakness in days of peace-had broken down in war; for every revelation, from the Dardanelles to Mesopotamia, spoke eloquently of the failure, not so much of the men, as of that machine. It met too rarely: its proceedings were too cumbrous; there was a lack of concentration; there was a constant scattering and diversion of energies.

There is no room here for vain regrets over the past. There is no space left for old party feuds-and certainly not for personal issues. Both of these men are great, distinguished figures, divided only by small shadows of honest difference. Those shadows will pass; in the light of greater events they will appear trifles; and the common need will knit us together. The resolution for unity must prevail.

---

[103] See the correspondence published in Appendix B.

[104] He had taken rooms at St. James's Court.

[105] "The conversion has been swift, but Mr. Asquith has never been slow to note political tendencies when they become inevitable." —Leading article, Times, December 4th, 1916.

[106] Mr. Herbert Samuel was offered office, and refused. Mr. Montagu finally joined as Secretary for Ireland.

CHAPTERXX

THE SAVING OF ITALY

> "Many hot inroads
> They make into Italy."
> Antony and Cleopatra, Act I, Sc. iv.

At the opening of the year 1917 the general situation of the World-war in Europe offered fair promise for the cause of the Entente Allies. On the Western front the immense latent resources of the British Empire were now coming effectively into play and were creating an opportunity for a really serious and formidable offensive. Tremendously reinforced in men and munitions through the powers of the Munitions and Military Service Acts, our gigantic armies inspired every observer with immeasurable hopes of victory. The soldiers themselves were full of that and fresh sanguine spirit in which the valour of the British race has always expressed itself. France was now recovering from the grievous losses of men endured in the first two years of the war; and the new Generals, men of the younger school like Nivelle and Pétain, were looking forward with no less confidence than ourselves to the results of a new Western aggressive on a larger and more effective scale.

But the Western front was only a portion of that far-flung line of embattled hosts who were holding back the great Teutonic armies from desolating the fairest regions of Western and Southern Europe. Far away across the snowy barriers of the Alps and beyond the interval of neutral Switzerland the Italian armies lay in caves and trenches stretched from the eastern frontier of the Swiss Canton Ticino right across the eastern Alps down to the shores of the Adriatic Sea. On the west of this hazardous line the Italians still held the Austrian armies to the edges of the main Alpine ridge. On the east they had pressed them in a series of heroic onslaughts through the mountains and across the deep valley of the rushing Isonzo. They had captured the high and coveted city of Gorizia, and they were threatening the suburbs of Trieste. They seemed on the eve of momentous conquests. But the very achievements of their heroic valour, so splendid to the outward eye, concealed a perilous and precarious military position.

"No one," said Mr. Lloyd George later on at Paris, "can look at these frontier mountains without a thrill of respect for the gallantry that has stormed them in face of the entrenched legions of Austria." Certainly no one who, like the present writer, has escaladed those peaks in days of peace. There are no greater episodes in this war than those of that titanic, gigantesque conflict amid the mighty jagged precipices and the deep gloomy abysses of the Eastern Alps.[107]

But the greater the effort, the greater the exhaustion. It is written large in letters of fire and blood across the history of the World-war that any excess of human loss is in itself one of the gravest of military perils. Italy poured out her blood without stint. Alone among the Allied nations she possessed one organised party-the official Socialists-genuinely opposed to the war. Taking advantage of this weakness, the Germans had made a special effort to weaken her home front. The great industrial centres of the north of Italy-Turin and Milan-had been the objective of perhaps the most sustained effort of German peace propaganda. The missionaries of this strange crusade had crossed the Alps by every mountain path and had mixed themselves among the armies, scattering their poisoned leaflets among the tired troops. Thus every preparation had been made for an easier assault. Like Hannibal when he crossed the Alps in a greater campaign, they had melted the rocks with vinegar.

The military position, indeed, was not so strong as it looked. The right wing of the Italian army was lunging forward victoriously, while the centre and left were still entangled in the mountains. These things were not clear to observers in the west of Europe; but there were English visitors with the Italian armies who became uneasily aware of them.

In the absence of any unified control it was impossible to take any effective steps to avert the coming danger. The British military chiefs had their views about the position of the Italian army; many Italians themselves had their views. But though these views were platonically interchanged there was no machinery by which they could be compared and collated, or produce any real effect on the course of the campaign. In other words, there was no central power of vision or action-no active organism that was responsible for the war as a whole, right from the North Sea to the Adriatic. As Mr. Lloyd George afterwards pointed out in the House of Commons, "there was a sort of feeling that that front was not our business."[108]

This did not, indeed, prevent Mr. Lloyd George from using such opportunities as presented themselves for urging his views. In January of that year (1917) there was an important Conference at Rome between the Allied Premiers and Generals; and at that Conference the whole European situation was surveyed in one of the most candid and exhaustive discussions that had taken place up to that time. These conversations extended over the whole ground, from the political relations between Italy and her neighbouring Allies to the question of the proper strategy for the Italian frontier. Mr. Lloyd George boldly placed before that Conference his own views as to the proper campaign to be adopted in the war between Italy and Austria. He pointed out the grave dangers to which Italy was exposed; and his own characteristic remedy was a reinforced aggressive across the Eastern Alps into the plains of Austria. That proposal afterwards tentatively put forward in his Paris speech received much foolish ridicule from English critics. If those critics would follow the advice of the late Lord Salisbury, and study large maps, they would observe that the most vulnerable flank of the Central Powers was to be found precisely through that very Alpine door north of Trieste round which the battle was then raging. While Berlin is remote from the Teutonic frontiers, Vienna is dangerously exposed to attack from the south and east, and every student of European wars knows that the great captains of war, like Napoleon, have always availed themselves of that fact.

This proposal was a revival in a more modest form of Mr. Lloyd George's earlier scheme for seeking a military decision on the Eastern front; and subsequently in his Paris speech he stoutly maintained that if there had been in January 1917 a proper unified machinery for military debate and execution the history of that year (1917) might have been different.[109]

But at that time both the Premiers of the Allied nations and the Generals of the Allied armies were fighting the war in water-tight compartments. It was not yet realised that the Italian front was actually a back door to the West. It required more startling events to convince the Allies that if either side broke through the line at any point, East or West, the whole line would be in peril. Until those events occurred there was not enough political or military driving power behind any proposal for unified control.

So throughout those months from August to October 1917 the military control was practically left to each set of military chiefs in his own section of the war. The communications and consultations between them were casual and uncertain; and naturally each set played for their own hand. For, other things being equal, the first duty of a soldier is the care of his own army. In our country it seemed the wisest course for the War Cabinet to leave all important military decisions to the military chiefs. The previous Government, indeed, had fortified the Generals with an Order in Council which practically gave them strategic control. It was considered best for the time being to fall in with that arrangement. There was, indeed, no alternative. "Never," as Mr. Lloyd George said afterwards in the House of Commons, "never in the whole history of war in this country have soldiers got more consistent and more substantial backing from politicians than they have had this year (1917).... No soldiers in any war have had their strategical dispositions less interfered with by politicians. There has not been a single battalion, or a single gun, moved this year except with the advice of the General Staff-not one. There has not been a single attack ordered in any part of the battle-field by British troops except on the advice of the General Staff-not one. There has not been a single attack not ordered. The whole campaign of the year has been the result of the advice of soldiers."

If the sole control of war by military authority was to be put to a decisive test, the campaign of 1917 supplied a crucial instance.

The vital need revealed by that test on the Eastern front was unity of control. But the same need was even earlier revealed on the West also.

There the year opened with smiling auspices. The retreat of the Germans from the Somme Valley and the final abandonment of the Verdun attack seemed to give the greatest hope for a successful Allied move forward against the foe. As at Waterloo, the moment seemed to have come to cry "Up Guards and at them!" Nor can it be said that there was any hesitation or lack of utmost heroism in the attack when it was delivered. On the contrary those attacks of 1917 displayed British and French valour at their highest point. But the want of co-operative effort and unified control led to a great reduction of war profits in the final balance-sheet of the year's efforts.

Sir Douglas Haig has frankly taken the world into his confidence as to the incidents of divided counsel. In his published despatches on those great events he has spoken freely. Sir Douglas Haig himself, a discreet and moderate man, had entertained the highest hopes, and had even gone so far as to express them through public channels. He was sanguine of a complete break-through. General Nivelle, the French Commander-in-Chief, was almost equally hopeful. It is no small gain to great armies when their chieftains start out with such high expectations.

Whether those expectations would have been fulfilled if the efforts of the British and French armies had been backed by unified control it is now impossible to say. But it is quite certain that the want of unity placed every obstacle in the way of victory. There were, indeed, shadows of control-scattered, intermittent efforts to bring the great armies into some form of combined action. But these efforts lacked authority or decision. There was a military conference of Allied Generals at the end of 1916; there was even an agreement to make a combined attack in Flanders. But the decisions of that conference do not seem to have carried with them any permanent effect on the Allied war councils. Probably the swift movement of events made a mockery of such long-laid schemes. At any rate, we have the fact that General Nivelle made a separate attack in Champagne in the spring of the year, with the result that our armies had to delay their advance until that great effort was brought to a decision.

General Nivelle aimed at a great mark. He, too, aspired to break the German lines. He succeeded in part, but at a cost of life too great for France at that moment. General Nivelle had to pay the price. He ceased to be Commander-in-Chief of the French armies. His place was taken by General Pétain, with the understanding that he should adopt a less aggressive policy. The result was that the British attack was delayed, and when it took place was undertaken alone. It achieved great objects, but not so great as had been hoped. The August fighting round Lens-the September onslaughts of Haig's armies east and north of Ypres, the assault of Passchendaele-all these battles displayed the valour of British, Canadian, and Australian troops at their highest point.

But there was no break-through. At the critical moment the British armies were checked by the mud and rain of the Flanders autumn. Heroism was literally choked in slime. The cold and gloom of winter descended on those splendid British stormers before their great task could be achieved.

Such were the fruits of divided control.

It was fated that there should blaze out a sign in the heavens even more startlingly blood-red before the forces of national and army particularism could be safely and successfully defied.

On October 24th (1917) the Italian eastern front was suddenly shaken by a hammer-blow from the German central command. A new army under the redoubtable Mackensen, secretly assembled behind the screen of the mountain ridges, took over the attack from the nerveless Austrians.[110] This German force made a sudden assault under cover of mist against a weak point in the Italian line. They attacked and penetrated the Second Italian Army in the neighbourhood of Tolmino on the Upper Isonzo. Only one Italian regiment gave way, probably weakened by enemy influences. But at such a critical point one was enough. It was like a small hole in a great dyke. The flood of German invasion swept in, and soon began to submerge the plain of Venetia. During the following week the Austro-German armies advanced by forced marches from the north-east and captured Cividale and Udine. The heroic Third Italian Army, conquerors of Gorizia, held on to the line of the Isonzo for a time. But they were taken in the rear, and it was necessary to command a retreat. Those brave regiments-the Alpini and the Bersaglieri-suddenly fell back, many of them preferring annihilation to retirement. The whole host rallied on the line of the Tagliamento; but in the terrible confusion of the great surprise the Italians lost 300,000 men and 2,000 guns.

Italy was now faced with a fearful peril. It was already clear that the line of the Tagliamento could not be held; it was uncertain whether any other line could be held. For if the Germans and Austrians could attain mastery of the Alps to the north every one of those river lines of Venetia would be outflanked; the whole northern plain of Italy would be invaded; the exquisite prize of Venice and the great industrial cities of Turin and Milan would fall as victims to the spear of the enemy. Southern Italy would be cut off from the Western Allies; and, indeed, the whole peninsula would be in danger, and with it our own naval hold on the Mediterranean Sea. None of the Western Allies could be indifferent to the threat of such calamities.

Mr. Lloyd George determined in a moment that Britain could not stand by indifferent. He resolved at once that he would not be responsible for a repetition of the calamities which had overwhelmed Serbia and Rumania. The year 1917 should not close as 1915 and 1916 had closed-with the head of a kingdom on a charger presented to the German Herod.

But it was necessary to act instantly. There was not a moment to be lost. Mr. Lloyd George decided to go to Italy; and he resolved to go armed with new powers of central control for the conduct of the war. He had made up his mind that it was at last necessary to relieve the Generals of their divided responsibilities by establishing a definite organism of central control.

Before starting for Italy he prepared and passed through the British Cabinet a document drawing up in a series of resolutions the constitution of a new central council for the conduct of the war. With that in his pocket he started to meet the Allied Premiers and Generals at the little seaside town of Rapallo, a gem to the east of Genoa on the Italian Riviera.

At that meeting he passed the resolutions contained in that document almost without an alteration, so ready were the French and Italians now to consent to any scheme for increasing the power of central decision.[111]

That was the first step in setting up the Versailles Council.

From Rapallo Mr. Lloyd George proceeded to Turin and Milan, everywhere encouraging the Italians and promising them speedy aid. He went as far as Peschiera, where he met the young Italian King, whose heroic devotion to his armies has rightly earned him the fervent love of true Italy. Mr. Lloyd George discussed fully with him all the details of the assistance that should be sent. Then with all speed he proceeded to organise and expedite the arrival of British and French reinforcements. Within a few days French and British infantry and artillery were speeding through the Monte Cenis tunnel to Italy.

For the moment, indeed, there was no need to bring the new powers of the Rapallo Conference into force. It was, at any rate, clear to every mind at this crisis that the whole front was one. It was apparent to any one who glanced at the map of Europe that the conquest of Italy by Germany would shake the whole Allied combination. It was obvious to the French, at any rate, that it might bring Germany to the back door of France.

Faced with such possibilities, British and French Generals vied with one another in helping Italy. What divisions could be spared from the Western front were spared. The young men of Western Europe marched through the vineyards and maize-fields of those beautiful plains of Northern Italy in the waning autumn to the help of the Italian armies now pressed back to the Piave. The coming of this help put new heart into the Italians. As our British boys advanced through the little white villages between Milan and the front they were greeted as crusaders. They were met by cascades of flowers from the joyful villagers, now recovering from the terror of a cruel invasion. For it was known by the Italians that the Germans were sending even Turkish and Bulgarian soldiery to the invasion of the fair Italian provinces.

So sustained and fortified-with such a sense of comradeship behind and beside them-the Italian regiments rallied. Along the line of the Piave they put up that splendid resistance which redeemed the name of Italy and inspired their people with a new strength and unity. To the north, among the mountains, they were helped by French and English battalions, thus forging between the peoples of Italy and Western Europe new links imperishable and without price.

Certainly so far the principle of unified control was justified by its results.

---

[107] Signor Philippo Philippi has brought from this phase of the war a wonderful photographic record which will make its glories lasting.

[108] November 20th, 1917. In the same speech Mr. Lloyd George delicately expressed the fact that we were aware of the Italian peril but unable to find any effective expression for our views.

[109] "I should like to be able to read to you the statement submitted to the Conference in Rome in January (1917) about the perils and possibilities of the Italian front this year, so that you might judge it in the light of subsequent events. I feel confident that nothing could more convincingly demonstrate the opportunities which the Allies have lost through lack of combined thought and action" (November 12th, 1917).

[110] Ludendorff's War Memories, Vol. II, pp. 497-99. He reveals that the attack was undertaken to prevent the collapse of Austria Hungary.

[111] "In substance it was the document prepared here, discussed line by line in the Cabinet, and which I had in my pocket after the last Cabinet meeting which was held a few hours before I left" (November 20th, 1917. Mr. Lloyd George's speech in the House of Commons).

CHAPTER XXI

THE VERSAILLES COUNCIL

"Besides, he says, there are two councils held;
　And that may be determined at the one
　Which may make him and you to rue at the other."
Shakespeare's Richard III, Act III, Sc. ii.

Italy was saved for the time; but if it was to be saved for all time, and if other dangers were to be averted, it was not enough to pass resolutions at Allied Conferences. The proceedings at Rapallo must be followed up by more effective action.

Mr. Lloyd George has always the instinct in his heart that no public purpose can be thoroughly achieved without the help of the peoples concerned. He is above all things a "crowd-compeller." It was now his imperious instinct that he should appeal from a secret conference to the great peoples of Western Europe. It was his powerful conviction that he must take them into his counsel as to the reasons for a new centralisation of war-control —in short, that he must appeal over the heads of the Governments to the nations.

If the new Versailles Council was to be anything more than an Aulic assembly, forcibly-feeble, strenuously impotent, it was necessary to rally behind it all the great democratic forces of the Western world. It was urgent to give it a new authority derived directly from the peoples. If this was to be achieved the peoples must be given a franker explanation of the strategy of the war, of the reasons for failure, and the motives for a new policy.

These are the reasons why, quite deliberately, on the way home from Rapallo, on November 12th, 1917, Mr. Lloyd George made that remarkable speech at Paris which was perhaps the frankest utterance of the war.[112]

This Paris speech fluttered all the dovecots of Europe, and some of the eagles' nests as well. It seemed to come as a caprice, a child of sudden impulse, from the brain of the British Premier. And yet the speech was most carefully prepared; a copy of it was sent to the War Cabinet in time for correction in case of need; it was handed over for interpretation before being uttered.[113]

There was nothing sudden about it. For the speech represented the slowly matured results of two years of observation, the fruits of prolonged meditation on the events of the war.

The step towards unity which was the central point of the speech represented his profoundest conviction on the strategy of the war.

Ever since the beginning of the war, indeed, Mr. Lloyd George had been an international as well as a patriot. As in the war itself, so in the Alliances, he was always against half-measures. If we were to be true Allies of France and Russia-or later on of Italy and the United States-then we must always work with them hand in hand, take close counsel with them as friends, act always together, not as separate States but as parts of one common organisation; the real beginning of a new "League of Nations." From the very outset he had no use for national sectarianism; he could not understand the idea of a tepid alliance, a Laodicean friendship, timorous of mutual help, suspicious of common counsel, feeble in reciprocal aid.

His reading of history had taught him that this kind of suspicion, especially strong in island countries, had been the sleeping sickness, the wasting paralysis, of all former mixed European Alliances. It was just this same aloofness, this same separatist pursuit of national aims, that robbed Marlborough of the fruits of his victories. It was precisely the same want of common planning that melted all Pitt's alliances like wax before the fire of Napoleon's energy. In more recent days, it was the similar want of understanding between the British and French Generals that prolonged the Crimean War.

Now he determined to strike while the iron was white hot. The fire burned, and he spake with his tongue. While the events in Italy were still fresh in the memory of Europe he pointed the lesson in vivid and biting language. It was certainly the first time that such a speech had been uttered at such a half-private function-an official luncheon of the Premiers arranged to give him an interval of relaxation in his journey back to England. No wonder the orthodox were alarmed.

Frankly and roughly, like a man in a hurry who has no time for honeyed speech, Mr. Lloyd George gave to the world his own innermost reasons for pressing forward the machinery of central control.

For the Versailles Council was to be a real and not a shadow control. He made it clear that he intended it to possess a genuine authority over the national military staffs. Even so, his proposals did not go so far as America and France desired; for France already wished for a Generalissimo, and the United States, being too far from the war even to aim at exercising control, were frankly willing to delegate the entire military power to the men on the spot.

But, even so, Mr. Lloyd George's plan contained the heart of the matter. Every one engaged in the controversy was aware that, once the germ of unified control was established, it would grow. No local control could compete with it. On that main principle Mr. Lloyd George was quite clear and definite. He stated outright that he would not stay in office unless his plan was adopted. "Personally," he said, referring to the Rapallo decision, "I had made up my mind that, unless some change were effected, I could no longer remain responsible for a war direction doomed to disaster for the lack of unity."

Mr. Lloyd George was far too old a bird to have any doubt as to what troubles this speech would bring on his head. He was speaking, as he himself said, "with perhaps brutal frankness at the risk of misconception here and elsewhere,"—perhaps even, he admitted, at the risk of encouraging the enemy.

He knew all that. But he also knew that there are times when such risks have to be taken. There are moments when an electric shock is necessary if men are to be really aroused to the duty of change. Eyesight, they say, is sometimes restored by a flash of sudden light. The same method may remove blindness of other kinds.

The new Council, he said, had already started work. It must have the support of public opinion if it was to have any genuine power. There must be a new central strength to resist sectional and national influences. What they wanted for victory was not sham unity, but real.[114]

The Paris speech was followed by an outcry even greater perhaps than Mr. Lloyd George had expected. The clamours of offended tradition and convention filled the air of London, especially of the London clubs. The uproar lasted for a full week, and then it found voice in the House of Commons, where Mr. Lloyd George was subjected to a kind of impeachment by Mr. Asquith and the Opposition leaders.

"This animal is wicked," wrote the French fabulist; "it defends itself." Such seems to be the feeling behind much of the fury provoked by Mr. Lloyd George on such occasions. Such events must be taken with tranquillity. The mutual play of criticism and defence goes to form the strength of our public life, and Mr. Lloyd George is the last man to appeal for mercy. Speaking this time in the House of Commons on November 19th he apologised for nothing. He manfully stood his ground in defence of the policy of the Versailles Council.

He revealed the important fact that Lord Kitchener was the first war-chief who proposed closer co-operation between the Allies. Lord Kitchener made that suggestion as far back as January 1915. It was then far more difficult to carry out. But the disasters of 1917 had made it easier.

He made even a more startling revelation. It was that the same proposal had been made in July of that very year (1917), not by the statesmen, but by the soldiers at a meeting of the Commanders-in-Chief at which Sir William Robertson, General Cadorna, and General Foch had been all present. So it was not true, as suggested in so many quarters, that this was a case of civilians forcing an idea of their own upon reluctant soldiers.

Then Mr. Lloyd George passed to that spirited personal defence of his Paris speech which has since become famous. It was, in many respects, an apology which extended to his whole career. It was an explanation of his own favourite political methods.

Briefly put, it was that he deliberately made a disagreeable speech in order to arouse public opinion. It was not enough to pass resolutions. What he wanted was public support. To obtain that he had resolutely and in cold blood set out to give a shock to the public mind.

"It is not easy to rouse public opinion. I may know nothing about military strategy, but I do know something of political strategy. To get public opinion interested in a proposal and to convince the public of the desirability of it is an essential part of political strategy. That is why I did it. And it has done it."

Here is a precise statement of his favourite method-the method which he has constantly used from the moment of his early defiance of the magistrates in North Wales right up to that famous interview of the "Knock-out Blow." It may be called the application to politics of the military method of the "Counter-attack."

The proof of the pudding is, after all, in the eating. The result, for instance, of these two speeches-the Paris speech and the Commons defence-was so to familiarise and popularise the idea of central military control that we now read them with some surprise at their moderation. We feel some astonishment that such apologies should have had to be uttered for a system of unified control which afterwards became a commonplace of Allied strategy. The hammer-blows of fate proved even more effective than the power of words in the House of Commons. But we must remember that at the moment Mr. Lloyd George was beating up against the wind. He had great forces working against him both within Parliament and without. He had to face a remarkable alliance between military professional pride, national feeling, and party tactics. The triumph of these speeches is that such forces have proved so powerless in the upshot against the overwhelming case for unity of control.

But the struggle was now only transferred from the debating-chamber to the council-room. There Mr. Lloyd George was met with a very resolute opposition from a body of military opinion supported by a very able and pugnacious Press. The military opinion, at any rate, was as honest as it was stubborn. The power of great national traditions was linked to the strength of professional feeling. It was hard and painful to come into conflict with men like Sir William Robertson. But the issue had to be fought through; and no Government would have been worth its salt which allowed a great political and international issue to be decided by military opinion. Mr. Lloyd George was fighting for one of the oldest principles of the British Constitution when he asserted the final supremacy of civilian control.

Yet it was not remarkable that the debate on this issue should have puzzled the minds of many honest men. For it raised the old question-should not matters of war be left entirely to the soldiers? Those who maintain that view seemed to have a very strong weight of common sense on their side. For how should civilians know anything of war?

A simple child,
That lightly draws its breath,
And feels its life in every limb,
What should it know of death?

And is not the civilian a mere child in the fiery matters of war?

In any ordinary war it would seem to be the right policy for statesmen to hand purely military matters to the soldiers and keep negotiations for themselves. The business of the statesman would appear to be to stand by as a possible peace-maker; although there have been wars which have been not only skilfully conducted but also wisely concluded by soldiers. Lord Kitchener, for instance, was never greater than in the negotiations which ended the Boer War.

But this World-war was already seen to be no ordinary war. If the European side of the war alone had been confined to Flanders, then, as in the wars of Marlborough, both strategy and statesmanship might have been left to the same man; although in that conspicuous case it was the civilian statesman who had to intervene before peace could be achieved. But, with operations confined and aims defined, the part of the civilians often lightly limited to the choice of generals and the provision of armies.

Here, however, was a war in which operations could not be confined nor aims defined. Here was a struggle already (1917) limited to no country and to no continent; carried on in three elements-earth, sea, and air —a conflict enveloping a planet.

In Europe alone the battle-front stretched across the whole Continent from west to east; and Palestine and Mesopotamia belonged to the same front as Belgium.[115]

Such a war has multitudinous aspects. It has its politics as well as its strategy; its tactics of the council-room as well as its tactics of the field. Military decisions have often to be based on political considerations; the movements of armies are decided by the relations of the Allied countries. Even strategy itself is revolutionised; for in such a war strategy stakes many new forms-there is the strategy of the air as well as the strategy of the earth; the strategy of the sea as well as the strategy of air. There is the strategy of continents as well as the strategy of countries. But all through the one distinguishing feature of the whole war was that nowhere in any aspect could strategy be wholly divorced from statesmanship.

The Germans recognised this fact throughout. The direction of their attacks-east or west-was often decided by political motives. War offensives were mingled with peace offensives, and the art of Machiavel added to the art of Napoleon. The hell's broth at Berlin was cunningly brewed of the mingled herbs of war and peace. Perhaps it would have been as well if sometimes we had given to them the flattery which consists in imitation.

But in Great Britain there has always been a cruder division between the soldier and the politician. Just as the soldier is suppressed during times of peace so the statesman is allowed little say during times of war. We have yet to learn from our enemies that war is a form of politics, and that neither of the two activities of the State can be wholly divided from the other. The cry of "Hands off the war!" uttered to the statesman is equivalent to a cry of dismissal.

Mr. Lloyd George, at any rate, was not at all willing to accept this impotent conclusion. He was clear that if the soldiers were to conduct the whole strategy of the war they must be responsible for the politics of the war also. The only conclusion of that logic was a military dictatorship. But, to do them justice, none of the honest soldiers who contended with him nursed ambitions of that kind. The only end to the argument, therefore, was certain to be a vindication of the civil power. To win the war, the soldier and the statesman must work hand in hand. That was the sound and safe line of policy along which Mr. Lloyd George steadily worked.

He tried his best to win over those eminent soldiers who honestly held the other view and op-posed the Versailles Council on principle. Sir William Robertson was offered the high position of British representative in the Council. From reasons which did him nothing but credit-reasons of honest conviction-he refused the position and took instead the Eastern Command. An-other soldier, Sir Frederick Maurice (Director of Military Operations on the Army Council) carried his opposition further on retirement from the Council. He wrote a letter to the Press openly disputing the accuracy of certain statements made by the Prime Minister in the House of Commons. Mr. Lloyd George offered a Court of Judges to try the case; but, on Mr. Asquith preferring a Committee of the House of Commons, Mr. Lloyd George decided to vindicate his own accuracy before the House of Commons itself. The result of his defence was that he obtained an overwhelming majority as a vote of confidence in himself and his Government. But it was necessary for the Army Council to vindicate discipline; and Sir Frederick Maurice was retired on half-pay.

Painful as this incident was to all who had regard for an honourable and high-minded soldier, it was a necessary and salutary assertion of civilian control over military.

British opinion, at any rate, steadily supported Mr. Lloyd George. Events at the front soon bore out only too clearly the soundness of his views. It was noted that in the battle of St. Quentin the German armies stuck at the link between the British and the French forces with the sure instinct that there they would find the weakest point. The moral was only too obvious. Control must not be less united, but more. Without a protest from any responsible quarter in Great Britain the famous Frenchman, General Foch, was in 1918 appointed Generalissimo on the Western front.

Thus the policy of Rapallo triumphed, and the unity of control was attained.

---

[112] See his House of Commons defence (November 19th).

"But I was afraid of this. Here was a beautifully drafted document in which you had concerned a considerable number of men, including a distinguished soldier-for a member of the General Staff was one who was most helpful to me in drafting the document-prepared, carried by the Allies at two or three conferences. Nothing happens, simply an announcement in the papers that at least we had found some means of co-ordination. There has been too much of that. I made up my mind to take risks...."

[113] "I considered it carefully....If that speech was wrong I cannot plead any impulse. I cannot plead that it was something I said in the heat of the moment. I had considered it, and I did so for a deliberate purpose." (House of Commons Defence, November 19th).

[114] Paris speech. Times, November 13th, 1917. See report in The Great Crusade, pp. 151-62 (Hodder & Stoughton 1918).

[115] "We have gone on talking of the Eastern front and the Western front, and the Italian front, and the Salonika front, and the Egyptian front, and the Mesopotamia front, forgetting that there is but one front with many flanks; that with these colossal armies the battle-field is continental" (Mr. Lloyd George at Paris, November 12th).

CHAPTER XXII

VICTORY

> "O God! Thy arm was here;
> And not to us, but to Thy arm alone,
> Ascribe we all."
> Shakespeare's Henry V, Act IV, Sc. viii.

The last year of the Great War was undoubtedly the most critical and momentous year in the modern history of these islands. By an amazing combination of events, Western Europe was subject to a sudden revival of extreme peril exceeding in violence the menace of 1914. Looking back from the security of the present time (1920) it is easy to underrate the threat of that great attack by the Central Powers: and, indeed, in our present discussions there is an almost perilous oblivion of the dangers through which we have passed. But those who study the memoirs of the German War Leaders, which have poured out since the close of the war,[116] will realise the complete confidence of the German General Staff in the victory which seemed to lie ahead of them, as the natural climax to the series of smashing blows which they had delivered to their enemies during the two previous years (1916-17).

General Ludendorff finds the chief reason for the German defeat in the war spirit which had been aroused in England under the leadership of Mr. Lloyd George, and in France by the inspiration of M. Clemenceau. Neither of those leaders would admit that they alone could have achieved so great a triumph for liberty over the menace of militarism. It was the spirit of the peoples of France and Great Britain that really achieved resounding victory-the peoples who shrank from no sacrifice and faced every trial rather than accept defeat. I have in my memory the spectacle of a regiment of boys of eighteen and nineteen-London boys, freshly plucked from the counter and the van-whom I met one evening, at the height of the crisis in the spring of 1918, marching to be entrained from Norfolk to Northern France. "Shall we win the war?" shouted one half of them, and the other half replied with an echoing shout —"Yes!" Those youths had been cut off from all leave and were being plunged into the firing-line at a few hours' notice. They went singing to almost certain death. They were the fit crusaders of a race that never contemplated defeat; and no man who had such a people behind him could vainly boast of his own single achievements.

Yet leadership counts for much, and vainly do the masses struggle if those at the top weaken and faint. There is no greater misfortune that can befall a race than failure of valour and resolution in high places. It was because Mr. Lloyd George kept, in the utmost stress of those events, his courage undimmed and his spirit unshaken, that he has rightly earned so large a part in the credit of victory.

Another scene comes back to me from those dark days. I was standing in front of one of the large-scale maps at Downing Street, noting the point reached by the German legions in one of those tremendous and determined efforts to drive us into the sea during the April of 1918. There was the sound of a step behind us, and suddenly we turned to find the Prime Minister also observing the map with a close and concentrated gaze. We knew that things were serious, and that there were influences at the centre in favour of withdrawing our armies from France. But of all the company he was the serenest. "Serious? Yes!" he said. "But by no means desperate. Look here!" and he pointed to the north of Calais. "We can flood that area if necessary. Then, if they drive us south of Calais, we can still hold on. France is a large place, and it has many ports. Retire from France? No, we will stand by our Allies to the last!" And he went away singing, as undismayed as those boys whom I had seen marching to France. A worthy leader of a worthy nation!

On another day I remember him describing to me a visit he had paid to the fighting line at the most critical moment of that great peril. He spoke with flashing eyes. "We motored," he said, "from the coast right up to the fighting front, and we did not meet a single British soldier in flight. Not one had turned his back to the enemy, not one!" Yet during that time the German guns were enfilading our trenches lined with English boys, and the chance of survival in that defence without death or injury had been reduced almost to the point of zero.

What was the cause of this last and most perilous phase? It was the collapse of Russia, produced by the Bolshevist coup d'état in Petrograd on November 7th, 1917. On that day, Lenin achieved the purpose for which the Germans had given him his passports into Russia. He destroyed Kerensky, who combined revolution with national war, and he substituted a policy of international peace combined with civil war. Both edges of that policy were sharpened to the destruction of Russia as a war power, and on December 20th Mr. Lloyd George warned the House of Commons that the collapse of Russia, following on the Italian defeat, would require a new and still greater output of man-power by Great Britain. A Bill for that purpose was introduced into the House of Commons on January 14th, abolishing almost the last exemptions from military service. Events in Russia moved swiftly. On November 21st the Bolshevists made to the Germans a definite proposal for armistice, and peace negotiations began at Brest-Litovsk on December 2nd. The Bolshevists twice broke up the Constituent Assembly at Petrograd by force of arms. The Germans put forward peace terms of such severity that even the Bolshevists were dismayed, and Trotsky attempted to declare peace without signing the treaty. Thereupon the Germans advanced their armies into Russia, meeting with no resistance, and occupying Minsk in the north and Kieff in the south. Powerless in the face of this invasion, the Bolshevists signed the peace treaty on March 2nd, surrendering Lithuania, Finland, the Ukraine, Poland, and the Baltic Provinces, promising demobilisation of their armies and internment of their ships. Russia was out of the war. On March 5th the Germans followed this up by signing peace with Rumania, and on March 6th they signed peace with Finland. Their great armies in the East of Europe were now free to work their will on the West.

Ludendorff has told us that even then there was some debate among the German military chiefs between the policy of defence in the West and the policy of attack. But Mr. Lloyd George saw clearly that the Germans would be obliged to attack. They were compelled by the logic of the blockade. With all her feverish triumphs in the East of Europe, Germany was, at that moment, in a parlous plight. She was in the position of a besieged city. She had either to break out or to surrender. The fearful ravage which she perpetrated in Rumania and the Ukraine, and in the western provinces of Russia also, were really the measure of her need. Food and materials were more necessary for her at that moment than military triumphs, and she hastened to cash all her victories into material produce of one kind or another. Like a hungry tiger, she devoured her prey. But there were other beasts afoot in Eastern Europe at the same time, and we know now that the division of the loot caused extreme bitterness between Germany and Austria-Hungary, and that the resentment of the Ukraine forced Germany to keep troops in the East of Europe which might have struck the decisive blow in the West. Such is the Nemesis of greed.

But still Germany could realise immediately over 2,000,000 new fighting men for the grand sortie now planned on the Western Front, and Ludendorff has told us how quickly and strenuously he trained the troops for this gigantic effort. The blow came on March 21st, against the Third and Fourth British Armies between the Scarpe and the Oise. Forty German divisions attacked, and on the second day, the 22nd, there was a break-through west of St. Quentin. On the following days the British line had to withdraw nearly fifteen miles, back to the line of the Somme, losing prisoners all the way, but inflicting very heavy losses on the attacking division. The British line was broken, but not the British Army. During the following days the German divisions steadily poured through the gap, crossing the Somme, capturing Albert and Mezières, some 90,000 British prisoners, and over 1,300 guns.

The peril opened by this event both to France and the British Empire lasted for four months, and during that period there was scarcely a day on which the strain was relaxed. Colossal issues were at stake, and among the chief was whether the British Empire should survive. Mr. Lloyd

George rose to the height of the crisis at once, and kept on the summit until the close. Day by day he never relaxed his energy or his courage. He did not abate, in those dark days, one jot of heart or hope. There was no resource or reserve of national strength which he did not bring to bear. There was no device that he left untried. It is easy to speak of the hurricane and storm when you have reached harbour, but there is little doubt that, unless we had had a good captain on the bridge, the great ship "British Empire" would have foundered.

He envisaged the problem in two ways-strategy and numbers. He saw the Allied Forces faced by overwhelming myriads of Teuton troops, combined under one central command. To resist this assault he was more than ever of the opinion that the defenders also must be placed under one command, and he carried his faith to the full logic of his conclusion. In April he agreed to the appointment of General Foch as supreme Commander of the Allied Forces. It was a step involving great risks and great faith. Fortunately Sir Douglas (now Lord) Haig agreed with Mr. Lloyd George, and played the game to the full, like the great soldier he was. Otherwise the thing could not have been done. The trial came for the British when, as the crisis deepened, Marshal Foch began to exercise his full powers, and to withdraw from the direction of the coast great British forces which had been placed there in reserve for the protection of the British line and the security of the Channel.

Like all great commanders, Foch himself had to take risks and to meet the German concentrations by great concentrations on his own side. For this purpose he had to wield full power over both British and French Armies, and he exercised it to the full in the great battles of that summer. It was an anxious time for the British Government. But Mr. Lloyd George had taken the full measure of Foch as a soldier: he fully believed in him, and he went to the whole extent of his faith. A working arrangement was come to by which Mr. Lloyd George went over to meet Clemenceau and Foch at Paris periodically, and the supreme conduct of the war was now in the hands of these three men. So far for the strategy which governed the great battles of that summer.

Then for numbers. Mr. Lloyd George saw in a moment that, unless drastic and exceptional measures were taken the Allied Forces would simply be snowed under by the hosts of the enemy. To meet this danger the natural counter-measure was to throw across the Channel all the troops in England sufficiently trained to go into the shock of battle. For this purpose he was obliged to suspend all the usual age limits from active foreign service and to send across the Channel the great army of youths enlisted under the Conscription Act, and hitherto prepared only for home defence. These great forces streamed across in the months of April, May, and June, and did something to fill up the gaps in the line. But as the weeks went by Mr. Lloyd George perceived that the British reinforcements alone would be unequal to the great task. The Germans were still straining every nerve, and they were fighting against time. Our Government could not precisely tell how many reserves the Germans still possessed, or how many men they could spare from their Eastern Front. The Germans were working on the calculation that the Americans could not come across till 1919 or 1920, and their submarines were operating feverishly to keep up the alarm on the Atlantic Ocean. The Americans themselves were too far removed from the scene of danger to realise at once the greatness of the emergency. But they only required the S.O.S. signal. Mr. Lloyd George determined to give it.

One morning that spring he made up his mind.

"We have to get 500,000 Americans over in four months, at the rate of 125,000 a month. How can that be done?" That was the problem as he saw it and as he expressed it. He began to send a series of telegrams to President Wilson through Lord Reading, explaining to Mr. Wilson the peril and the need of instant help. President Wilson immediately grasped the crisis. Mr. Lloyd George organised the Navy and the Merchant Service for the work of transport on the British side of the Atlantic, and President Wilson did the same on his side. So began that great Armada of help from the New World. The American divisions poured across the Atlantic, overcrowded on their transports, packed almost to suffocation, but willing to suffer all things in the great crusade on which they were bent. The Americans, indeed, did far better than the

British Government had expected. They sent a million men. It was a magnificent performance, and must ever be remembered to the credit of that great nation.

Then President Wilson and Mr. Lloyd George, acting together, went one step further. When the American troops arrived many of them were instantly brigaded with the British and French forces, and so they learnt with the greatest rapidity possible all the craft and ruses necessary for modern warfare. They did their utmost to acquire in a few months all those new arts of destruction which it had taken Europe years to evolve. To achieve this, for the time they gave up America's great dream of a national army. But, after all, the greatest fact of all was their arrival.

Meanwhile, during these weeks of suspense and endeavour the German armies had struck again and again in the last desperate campaign for victory. Through April, May, and June the issue still hung in the balance.

The second great attack on April 4th, when twenty German divisions, advancing towards Amiens, attempted to divide the British Armies from the French. That attack came very near to success. We all know how the Germans arrived at positions from which they could bombard Amiens and paralyse the communications, and it is blazed on the records of fame how the armies of the British Empire-men from Australia and Canada-held the line at Villers-Brettoneux, and by their invincible blending of defence and attack kept the assailing German divisions from achieving their purpose.

A few days later a new attack developed, this time farther north, west of Lille. From the British point of view this was the most menacing attack of all. It was a determined attempt to drive the British armies into the sea. On April 10th Armentières was occupied and the bloodstained Ridge of Messines crossed. On the 15th Bailleul was taken, and on the 25th the attack came to a climax with the capture of Kemmel Hill under the eyes of the German Emperor. Yet the Germans could not gain the decision they require. The British troops gave ground, but always fought on. The line bent, but it did not break.

But, as the weeks went on, the British Government replied in stern deeds which the whole British people supported. Not only did the younger men stream across the Channel, but the older men lined up to take their places. It was on March 9th that Mr. Lloyd George introduced that last and tremendous Military Service Act, raising the age to fifty, with a reserve possibility of fifty-five, and threatening to extend conscription to Ireland. Such extreme measures became in the result unnecessary: but partly because the British people showed that they were possible.

Ludendorff has described to us the gradual waning of his hopes[117] in face of the unbroken resolution of the British people under Mr. Lloyd George, the swift dying off in the fire of battle of all their best troops, and the failing of human morale which took place under the stress of those costly onslaughts. There is no more dramatic story in history than his account of the way in which the revolutionary poison which the Germans had inoculated into Russia by the sending of Lenin returned back into the German Army and gradually destroyed by its discipline and undermined its desire for victory.[118] But there is another side to that story. Ludendorff describes, without apparently understanding the significance of his narrative, the way in which his troops, when they had captured a position, would spend the precious minutes in overhauling and devouring the stores of food which they found.[119] He seems to regard that as merely a sign of the weakening of military discipline. But the plain fact is that hunger has no respect for discipline; and it was hunger that was eating at the vitals of the German nation-hunger and want of all the essentials of war. The blockade was completing the work of our armies. For our prisoners found that the Germans were lacking in the most elementary medical necessities and that their transport had reached a point of decay which made it almost impossible for them properly to feed and maintain their armies.

Ludendorff blames the German nation for not supporting the German Army, but the fact is that this was not a war of armies, but a war of nations. The German Army was still capable of great deeds, but the German nation behind was stricken to the heart. Therefore, the strength of the Army, which drew its vitality from the nation, was rapidly waning even in those moments of victory.

With his instinctive insight for the real facts of the situation, Mr. Lloyd George saw that even in the darkest hour here was the governing issue-which nation could hold out the longest. So now he set himself, with all his great powers, to hearten and encourage both the peoples and the Armies in France and Great Britain. He kept travelling between London and Paris, attending the meetings of the Versailles Council, visiting the armies at the front, and exchanging cheerful messages between the fighting men and the civilians. On the day Bailleul was captured, April 15th, he boldly declared that we had lost "nothing vital." On May 3rd he returned from the Versailles Council with a message from the troops to the nation at home —"Be of good cheer. We are all right!"

But the crisis was by no means at an end. In May there came a third German attack, this time towards Paris, and before it was broken it had driven the British and French armies across the Aisne and the Marne and had come within almost thirty miles of Paris. Those were anxious days. But the lure of Paris was again to prove fatal to the German Army. Foch withdrew his armies only to prepare for a fiercer spring. "My left is driven back, and my right is driven back. I shall attack with my centre!" was his famous utterance. The Germans were drawn perilously on, until with a sudden smashing blow on July 18th Foch crumpled up the right side of the phalanx which they were driving towards Paris. Ludendorff tells us that, even after that unexpected defeat, the German Staff still cherished hopes of victory towards the north, although, to all outside observers, their aggressive powers seemed to be exhausted.

It was the attack on August 8th of the British and French troops together, aided by an army of tanks, storming the German lines east of Amiens, that came to Ludendorff as the final blow to his hopes. From that time onward, until November, is one long story of unbroken victory for the Allies. But it was victory dearly purchased by blood and endurance; for the German armies retired sullenly and inflicted heavy casualties.[120] We must not underrate the heroism of those months. It is no small thing that the armies endured to the end. It is clear, from the memoirs of the German chiefs, that they were still looking eagerly for any sign of weakness, and that the smallest symptom of war-weariness would have led to a renewal of German hopes. Mr. Lloyd George saw this clearly, and never to the end did he give way to boasting. "The worst is over," he said at Manchester on September 12th, "but the end is not yet."

We know now from Ludendorff that suggestions for an armistice were made by him to the German Government immediately after August 8th. But at first the civilian power, under Count Hertling, the German Chancellor, and his successor Hintze, was inclined to hold out. It was not until after the smashing up of Bulgaria on September 16th, ending with its surrender on the 30th, that Hintze resigned and gave place to Prince Max of Baden. It was now the turn of the German military chiefs to resist the civilians in their passion for surrender. For Ludendorff was in favour of a final rally, whilst Prince Max was resolute to make peace.

It was to President Wilson that Prince Max made his overtures for an armistice based on the Fourteen Points,[121] and the negotiations continued all through October. No one who lived through those days will forget the high, austere dignity of the American President's replies, which fell on the German Government and people with all the inexorable force of impartial justice. He insisted that the Germans should leave all invaded soil, that they should cease their barbarisms on land and sea, and that the terms of Armistice must be such as to make a renewal of hostilities impossible.[122]

President Wilson carried the correspondence with Prince Max as far as he could without being in control of the armies, and then he telegraphed the letters to the Governments of his Allies in Europe. Mr. Lloyd George at once saw the practical peril of the new situation. It was that the German military chiefs might use the Armistice for a recovery of strength, and Ludendorff's Memoirs show that he had full justification for that fear.[123] He resolved at once that the only safe armistice would be one of complete disarmament, and with that policy in his mind he went to Paris to meet M. Clemenceau and Marshal Foch. There at Versailles a full historic conference of all the Allies took place, and lasted a fortnight. The European Allies modified President Wilson's terms on certain essential points. Great Britain excluded the control of the seas from the sphere of negotiations, and France insisted on a wider interpretation of President Wilson's reparation demand. President Wilson agreed to both these modifications.

Then the Versailles Council passed to their immediate practical conditions. Marshal Foch insisted that the Germans must ask for an Armistice in the ordinary military way from himself, the Allied Commander. That being agreed, the terms were framed-and they were pretty drastic terms. The German armies must retire across the Rhine and must be demobilised. German guns and ships must be surrendered.[124] In fact, Germany must be rendered incapable of resuming the war. Only on those terms was an Armistice possible with an enemy who had given such dire proofs of ill-faith.

Faced with these terrible terms, Ludendorff made a last effort to rally Germany to a final war of defence. But he was too late. He himself had fatally weakened the German fighting power when he suggested negotiations in August. Then the civilians had protested. But now that they had been converted to peace, nothing could make Germany face the guns again. Their military strength suddenly collapsed. Turkey surrendered on October 31st, and Austria-Hungary on November 4th. The bell of doom had begun to toll.

On November 4th the German Government made a final effort to command their fleet on to the high seas. But the fleet mutinied, and from that mutiny a revolution began in Hamburg which soon spread over Germany. On November 7th the British troops entered Valenciennes: on the 8th Prince Max resigned and was succeeded by Herr Ebert. On the 9th the Kaiser abdicated and fled into Holland. On that day the German envoys were received by Foch at his headquarters and the new German Republic accepted the terms of Armistice. On the morning of the 11th the Canadians entered Mons, that little town where firing had opened more than four years before, and precisely at 11 o'clock on that very morning the Armistice began. There was a sudden stillness from the North Sea to the frontier of Switzerland.

"Germany is doomed!" cried Mr. Lloyd George, speaking at the Mansion House on November 9th; and he proved a true prophet.

The Allies had won the war....

---

[116] The Memoirs of Von Tirpitz and Falkenhayn, and last, but not least, the frank and outspoken War Memories of General Ludendorff.

[117] War Memories (Hutchinson & Co., London), Vol. II, pp. 613-4 for decline of morale, pp. 643-5 for effect of our propaganda.

[118] Vol. II, pp. 642-4, 767-9.

[119] Vol. II, p. 611.

[120] There were seven distinct great battles after August 8th-Bapaume, Epehy, two battles of Cambrai, Courtrai, Selle, and Valenciennes.

[121] See Appendix D for the Fourteen Points.

[122] American Note of October 23rd, 1918.

[123] Page 721. The armistice terms were to permit a "resumption of hostilities on our own borders."

[124] Five thousand guns and 30,000 machine-guns, 5,000 locomotives, 22 big ships, and 50 destroyers.

CHAPTER XXIII

THE PEACE CONFERENCE

"War or peace, or both at once."

Shakespeare's Henry IV, Act V, Sc. ii.

The colossal strain of the last year of the Great War left both Ministers and peoples of the conquering Allies in a state of profound exhaustion. So near had been the peril of defeat that for a time it was scarcely possible to realise the fact of victory. For the first two weeks after the Armistice of November 11th, 1918, London, Paris, and New York were given over to a delirium of rejoicing such as the world never before witnessed. Mr. Lloyd George, speaking from the windows of Downing Street on the day of the Armistice, told the people plainly that they had a right to rejoice. He rejoiced with them.

But gradually, as the days passed, the world woke to the fact that the Armistice was only the opening of a new phase in the crisis of change. The Armistice terms imposed on Germany by the Allies had left her prone and helpless. She could not resume the fighting. Both the Central Empires were beaten and broken. The Emperors and the Kings were in flight. But the world could not be left to live in a vacuum. Desolation is not peace. Europe was like a shattered puzzle which had to be pieced together again before humanity could resume its normal life. It was urgent that a Conference should be summoned speedily both to make peace and to settle the future governance of the world.

There were some necessary delays. President Wilson came swiftly to Europe; but before attending the Conference he wished to consult the Governments of the Allies and to visit their capitals. He arrived in Paris on December 13th, and visited both Rome and London. His presence was acclaimed everywhere by enthusiastic multitudes, possessed by a great hope that the New World had truly come to redress the balance of the Old.

There was also the British General Election, which Mr. Lloyd George deemed necessary to confirm and strengthen his position at the Conference as spokesman for Great Britain. No time was lost. The General Election was announced immediately after the Armistice. Nominations were taken on December 4th after a very brief election campaign; the polls were held on one day, December 14th, under the new electoral arrangements; and the results were declared on December 28th. The result was an overwhelming vote for Mr. Lloyd George as the British representative at the Conference, and as the mandatory of a strong and decisive peace.[125]

There was some preliminary debate as to the city that should be chosen for the Conference. President Wilson and Mr. Lloyd George were at first disposed to choose a neutral capital; but the claims of France were strong. She had borne the territorial brunt of the war. So it was agreed that the Conference should meet in Paris at first, with the reservation that they should afterwards shift to Geneva. But once the huge machine of counsel was settled in Paris it was found impossible to move it. In spite of the preponderant power thus given to the pressure of the French Press, it is difficult to see now how any other capital could have been chosen.

The burden of British responsibility was far too heavy for the Prime Minister to bear alone. He decided to share it, as far as possible, with his whole Ministry and Government; and the result was that the fashioning of the Peace by Great Britain was far less of a personal affair than in any other of the victorious countries. Mr. Lloyd George took with him to Paris, as joint delegates, Mr. Bonar Law, Mr. Balfour, Lord Milner, and Mr. Barnes. Mr. Bonar Law, being leader of the House of Commons, was soon compelled to return to his duties in England; but he flew over to Paris at every serious crisis in the discussions. Mr. Balfour and Mr. Barnes remained all the time, and performed great services. Lord Milner went over when colonial affairs required his counsel and decision; and Mr. Montagu attended for Indian matters. But Ministers from all Departments attended in Paris whenever their advice was required; on critical occasions Mr. Lloyd George summoned meetings of the War Cabinet so that his decisions might have the full weight of the Coalition behind them.[126]

But besides the men of Great Britain the men of the Dominions were there too. The whole weight of the British Empire was behind the decision of the British Delegations. Each Dominion sent two delegates, one of whom in every case was the Prime Minister. The British Empire Delegation sat every day, and considered every big decision; their secretary was a member of the Secretariat of the Peace Conference; powerful men like Mr. Hughes, Mr. Robert Borden and General Botha had their say through this channel; and thus the whole Empire was kept in touch. There was here the beginning of a new Imperial organisation.

Behind all these leaders stood the great body of British officials; cool, experienced, industrious, alert, no body of men in that great crisis served their country better.

The first meeting of the Conference was held on January 18th, 1919, at the Palace of Versailles, and was an impressive gathering of the representatives of all the thirty Allied Nations who had taken part in the defeat of Germany. But as soon as vital decisions were approached it became obvious that it would be necessary to narrow the Council-chamber and to throw a veil over their debates. There was much inflammable stuff lying about, explosive national hopes and greeds, incredible aspirations after greatness. There were Cæsars and Malvolios among the Powers, both great and little. If the discussions had been published, great popular emotions would have been roused, hatreds stimulated, passions excited. The Conference might not have lasted a week. No sane advocate of "open diplomacy" will ever exclude the right of private debate.

The world watched impatiently while the inner Council was gradually narrowed from ten to five, from five to four, and finally, after Italy's withdrawal, from four to three. There was something of a sneer in the adjective applied —"The Big Five," "The Big Four," and the "Big Three." And yet the narrowing of the number was absolutely necessary for decision. Slow as decision was, it would have been far slower in a larger Council. It was vital that those who debated should keep confidence, and should be able to decide. With ten it was found that no secrets could be kept. With four confidence was easier, and decisions were possible.

The defects of this narrowing of the Council-chamber are painfully obvious. The arguments which led to decisions were known only to a few. Minutes were kept by the Secretary, Sir Maurice Hankey, and were distributed to the ten, five, four or three. But the world outside was fed on gossip, and mostly malicious gossip. The great concourse of able writers who had journeyed to Paris from all countries looked up, but could not be adequately fed. They became angry and irritated. They spread their spleen against the Conference through a thousand conduits, daily and weekly, and ultimately through a vast and growing literature of discontent. It is notable that the books published about the Conference since its close have been almost unanimous in their bitter scorn and condemnation.[127]

The Peace Treaty emerged with few friends and many enemies. That is the chief danger to its vitality and permanence.

At the foot of the Falls of Niagara there eddies a gigantic whirlpool round which objects are driven in endless fury, the prey of conflicting currents, tossed to and fro by buffeting waves, now hurled to the surface and then sucked down into the depths by irresistible forces. In that whirlpool guidance is nearly impossible. Man himself becomes a helpless victim; only by yielding could he survive. Resistance to such powers only increases the peril.

So it was at Paris in 1919. The Great War had been the Falls of Niagara; the Conference was the whirlpool. In that tumult of waters it was a miracle to survive at all, much less to achieve mastery. Not since Phaethon strove to drive the horses of the sun had any human being faced a greater task than the three men who emerged as the leaders in this vast event-Mr. Lloyd George, President Wilson, and M. Clemenceau. No man who has looked closely into their work will be inclined to judge swiftly or harshly. It was a burden too great for human shoulders. After six months of it Mr. Lloyd George returned to London whitened and lined, looking to his friends as if ten years had been added to his age.

But he fared far better than his colleagues. President Wilson returned to collapse into a grave illness. M. Clemenceau, the invincible "Tiger," the "Young old Man," continues his intrepid existence-but now retired-with a bullet in his back. Botha returned to South Africa to die.

They all worked terribly hard, both by day and by night. They sat in council for two and a half hours in the mornings and two and a half hours again in the afternoons. They went out little into society. In the evenings they read their piles of documents or saw important witnesses.

Yet no one was satisfied. What is the reason?

The chief reason is that the Conference worked throughout by process of compromise: and compromise has no lovers. It was in the main a compromise between three points of view-the French, the American, and the British. Hateful to strenuous souls! To yield nothing and to gain everything is to them the only statesmanship. But let us remember the other side. The war was not won alone; the peace could not be made alone. The armies had to combine for victory; the peace had to be combined too. No Great Power could have a peace entirely of its own, either in material gain or ideal aims.

The American aim, as shaped by their remarkable President and voiced in his splendid oratory, was for a peace of final world-conciliation.[128] He held up the "banner of the ideal." The French aim was a peace of security. The British aim lay somewhere between the two, a practical peace combining conciliation and security, punishing Germany without crushing it, improving the world but not seeking all at once to achieve the Millennium.

Clemenceau was an honest nationalist. But he did not seek so much to exalt France as to depress Germany. The idea of Foch was to stand guard over Germany with a flaming sword. The aim of the French Chauvinists was to break Germany up and disable her permanently. Clemenceau did not share these extreme views. He rebuked Foch for the interview in which he claimed that Germany should retire beyond the Rhine. He was too much of a statesman to believe that a modern nation could be permanently crushed. But he sought to weaken her to the ground for the next fifty years; and then he hoped for security in the new Alliance with America and Great Britain.

The part that Mr. Lloyd George played at Paris during those strenuous months was often that of conciliator between these two points of view-the French and the American. Such a conciliator was wanted: for the clash could not be concealed. "President Wilson has Fourteen Points," mocked Clemenceau; "the good God was content with Ten." "Every morning," he said on another occasion, "I repeat to myself—'I believe in the League of Nations!' "[129] It was difficult to achieve harmony between such a spirit and the lofty faith and austere hopes of the great Crusader from across the seas.

Here came in Mr. Lloyd George's characteristic qualities-his genius for compromise, his twinkling good humour, his amazing capacity for finding a middle way between different points of view. Again and again, when matters seemed at a deadlock-on the Saar Valley, the Polish Corridor, or even the perplexing question of Fiume-Mr. Lloyd George achieved, or nearly achieved, a settlement. It is scarcely too much to say that without him the Conference would have inevitably broken down, and one of the other two would have flung out of the Conference like Signor Orlando.

But Mr. Lloyd George was not only a conciliator-not merely the middle figure. He had a very definite view of his own as to the right peace to aim at. He was the first to formulate a peace; the first to insist on a decision. He was out for a peace stern but just. On Dantzig he took the initiative for moderation. He insisted on a settlement that would not create a new Baltic question. He was against Poland annexing a city of Germans-against it also for the sake of Poland. "We must set up a Poland that can live," he would say. "If swollen by enemy populations she will explode from within. Dantzig is outside the real orbit of Poland. Make it International." President Wilson supported him; M. Clemenceau was persuaded; and Mr. Lloyd George got his way.

Poland had good friends at the Conference. Not only was it the policy of France to aggrandise Poland as a substitute for Russia, but President Wilson was enthusiastically pro-Polish. On the general issue Mr. Lloyd George was entirely with them. He wished Poland to flourish as a self-governing State, but not to enter on its existence by inflicting on others the crime of Partition from which it had so deeply suffered itself. For that reason, in the last stage, he took a strong solitary line on the demand for a plebiscite that came from Silesia. The whole British Cabinet supported him, and there again in the end he achieved his purpose.

But on other matters the combination varied: Mr. Lloyd George sometimes took a sterner line than the other two. He was always for the trial of the Kaiser, as a supreme lesson to rulers. President Wilson opposed; M. Clemenceau was indifferent; Venizelos was opposed. But Mr. Lloyd George insisted, and persuaded them to agree to London as the place of trial.

On the Rhine question and the Saar Valley he supported President Wilson in opposing the extreme French claims, and finally achieved the compromise inserted in the Peace Treaty.[130] He opposed the French proposals to separate the Rhine Provinces from Germany and occupy in permanence the bridge-heads. He looked far ahead. "See here," he said to the French, "you will create another Alsace-Lorraine: you will give Germany a great cause."

He saw in such proposals the certain seeds of future wars, and wars to which he could not summon the youth of Great Britain. For he kept clearly in view that, under the League of Nations settlement, we, as a contracting party, might be called upon (under Clause 10) to defend with arms any detail of the settlement. It was always his aim to keep British obligations within the limits of the powers of the British Empire.

He supported President Wilson in the difference with Italy over Fiume, and Clemenceau supported both. But he always hoped to effect a settlement by persuasion. When President Wilson had made up his mind to issue an appeal to the Italian nation, Mr. Lloyd George persuaded him to agree to a postponement of twenty-four hours. President Wilson kept precisely to his promise. But it unfortunately happened that, just as the twenty-four hours expired, delicate negotiations were proceeding between Orlando and Mr. Lloyd George, and there were still hopes of a settlement. The appeal was published in the afternoon papers of Paris, and its immediate effects were to offend the Italian delegates, throw them back on to the point of honour, and drive them out of the Peace Conference. President Wilson acted with his usual high and simple honesty; but in this case, at any rate, if the aim was peace, open diplomacy did not score a conspicuous triumph.

In regard to Russia, there also Mr. Lloyd George always craved for a settlement as part of the new peace of the world. This was not his second, but his first thought. He started instantly after the Armistice with the idea of a joint meeting between the Russian parties. His first proposal was that they should meet at Paris; and this was laid before the Allied Chiefs early in the Peace Conference, in a conversation held at the French Foreign Office on Tuesday, January 21st, 1919.[131] The French Premier objected to the presence of the Bolshevists of Paris as a danger to French society. Mr. Lloyd George then proposed Salonika or Lemnos, as easily accessible from Russia. It was as the afterthought of an official that the island of Prinkipos was suggested; perhaps it was a measure of the fear of Bolshevism already existing among the Governments of Western Europe. The appeal to the Russian parties was issued as a result of this meeting of January 21st. We all know how it failed. It withered from sheer lack of support. The Bolshevists refused to stop fighting. The Russian "loyalists," already divided from the Bolshevist rule by gulfs of hatred and terror, rejected the very idea of a meeting. The French official class, always very powerful, was openly hostile, and actively worked against the proposal. The propertied classes in Great Britain, supported by a powerful Press, denounced and ridiculed the whole policy. The time expired for the meeting; and the policy expired too.

Then in February came the Bullitt Mission originally devised as a "feeler" by Colonel House. Mr. Bullitt went to Russia and experienced one of those astounding conversions which the leading Bolshevists, by showing only their better side, seem capable of producing. The American Delegation asked Mr. Lloyd George to see Mr. Bullitt; and, with his usual accessibility, he invited the young American to breakfast. The proposal brought by Mr. Bullitt was not an offer from the Bolshevists, but the suggestion of an offer by the Allies —a very different affair.[132]

President Wilson himself refused to meet Mr. Bullitt, a course which seems to gather some justification from Mr. Bullitt's subsequent proceedings in America. But the proposals embodied in the Bolshevist memorandum were not such as, at this time at any rate, had any chance of serious consideration. The mere proposal to take the whole matter out of the hands of the Peace Conference was not calculated to conciliate that body.[133]

Then in April came the Nansen episode, which turned out, in Mr. Bullitt's adroit hands, to be yet another effort to renew the peace negotiations of February. The gulf still proved impassable. The Allies would not authorise Nansen to undertake his intrepid and humane adventure without the power to distribute food and control the Russian railways: and the Bolshevists would on no account agree to that course. Neither side trusted one another. A civil war was raging, and the issue was still undecided. Neither side would give way; and once more the time limit expired.[134]

Still eager to attain peace in Russia, and finding that the hope of conciliation was vain, Mr. Lloyd George now swung over to the policy of helping Admiral Koltchak and General Denikin on the condition of obtaining democratic and constitutional guarantees. The guarantees were given, and seemed favourable. Help was sent. But there was one point on which the "White" Russians would make no concessions-the independence of the Border States. We all know how since on that rock of adventures of the "White" Russians have shipwrecked; and so the hopes of the Allies have been disastrously thwarted. It seems at the present moment as if an immense mass of human suffering might have been averted if the original policy of Mr. Lloyd George in January-February of 1919 had received reasonable and friendly consideration in London and in Paris.

In regard to the League of Nations, Mr. Lloyd George was never the prime mover, but always a faithful follower of President Wilson. Thus it was that Mr. Lloyd George never framed a scheme, but took the schemes of others as the basis for his advice and counsel. He profoundly believed in the League of Nations as the only way out for the human race. But he had not a very deep faith in schemes or constitutions. His idea was rather, in the good old British way, to evolve a League from the Peace Conference. He had in mind the precedent of the Imperial Conference, and he believed that periodical meetings of the Peace Conference, gradually including nations at first excluded, would lead to a slow growth of understanding between nations now too ardent for sovereignty to be affected by any decisions from Paris or Geneva.

President Wilson brought to Paris a scheme which he had already worked out. He had based it on the Phillimore Report amended by Colonel House, and rewritten by himself.[135] He then read General Smuts's remarkable memorandum, and revised his scheme again. That scheme was considered at an early meeting of the Conference and referred to a League of Nations Committee. President Wilson himself sat on the Committee along with Mr. Lansing, thus giving up to the creation of the Covenant a large part of his great energies and genius. Lord Robert Cecil was placed on the Committee as the British Representative by Mr. Balfour, and we know what a great part he played. Lord Robert was in frequent consultation with Mr. Lloyd George, who always kept in close touch with the drafting of the Covenant, and made many suggestions. When the Covenant was in danger, he supported President Wilson on his return from America in his insistence that it should be made part of the Treaty. Still, Mr. Lloyd George perhaps never shook off his instinctive feeling that there was an element of unreality in the drafting of a set constitution for the League. He doubted whether the intense patriotism created by the war could at once be poured, glowing hot, into the mould of a new international discipline. The action of Italy, and still more of the United States itself, seems since to have given some confirmation to his view.

Throughout all these discussions Mr. Lloyd George and President Wilson remained close friends. They were really kindred spirits, with the difference that Mr. Lloyd George had a longer experience of politics and diplomacy in the rusé old Europe. But both came from Puritan stock, and the high idealism and noble integrity of President Wilson's character must have often recalled to Mr. Lloyd George that splendid uncle who had taught and nurtured him. Of their relationships it may be said, as of Carlyle and Sterling, that they always ended their discussions friends —"except in opinion not disagreeing."

No two honest men, indeed, could expect to agree on all the questions raised at this multifarious Conference. Take the problems of the Near East. There Mr. Lloyd George very strongly took the view that the Turks had forfeited the right to rule over Christians. He was always disposed to look to the great Prime Minister, Venizelos, as the prop of the Alliance in the Eastern Mediterranean. That made him lean to the Greeks. M. Clemenceau followed the traditional policy of the Quai D'Orsay in its leniency towards the Turks. President Wilson, perhaps influenced by the American professors of the Roberts College at Constantinople, was disposed to advocate clemency to Bulgaria. This is an instance of minor differences which never threatened cleavage, but harassed and delayed the proceedings of the Conference. For Mr. Lloyd George was never inclined to neglect the Near East. There was the home and cradle of those little nations in whose destiny he so profoundly believed.

There were crises in the Conference when he boldly acknowledged that he had been wrong. Such a moment came when, in April, he was challenged on the Indemnity question by a mandatory telegram from 200 members of Parliament. He returned and faced his critics with defiance. "A good Peace," he said, "is better than a good Press." He had discovered in Paris that it was vain to hope for the great indemnities from Germany which Great Britain deserved, and for which he himself had hoped. He faced Parliament with realities; and Parliament bowed to the facts.

Speaking broadly, Mr. Lloyd George and his colleagues followed throughout a sound British tradition. Instinctively they were, in 1919, pursuing in Paris the same policy that Wellington and Castlereagh pursued during 1815 in the Congress of Vienna, and the Second Treaty of Paris after the victory of Waterloo. Just as they prevented a triumphant Prussia from crushing France, so Mr. Lloyd George and President Wilson prevented a triumphant France from shattering Germany to atoms.[136]

On the human side, Mr. Lloyd George lived in Paris a simple and homely life. He occupied a modest flat in the 23 Rue Nitot, near the Arc de Triomphe, in the pleasant neighbourhood of the Champs Elysées. European observers were surprised at the contrast between the daily life of the British Prime Minister and the high state which surrounded the American President, who occupied the Villa Murat over the way. But when they criticised the posting of sentries both inside and outside the President's house, and when the French people objected to being forbidden to walk on the American side of their own beloved Parisian street, they perhaps forgot that President Wilson stood in the place of Royalty as the sovereign head of the country for which he spoke.

The French, with their genius for affability, preferred the easy ways of Mr. Lloyd George with his love for their café life and their restaurants, and his general sociability. He was often received in the cafés and theatres with an almost embarrassing friendliness and respect, and sometimes the audience would rise and sing "God Save the King." At one café in the Champs Elysées the orchestra knew so well his passion for the "Sambre et Meuse" march, that they would play it whenever he entered without waiting for his request. He was, as ever, kindly to the journalists, and would, whenever possible, take a cup of tea with them at the Hotel Majestic-humorously renamed "Megantic," after his daughter. On Saturdays it was the pleasant custom of the British exiles to hold dances at this hotel, and Mr. Lloyd George would often look in and watch the dancing. He loved to see his youngest daughter Megan and his son Gwylem enjoying themselves at these democratic dances, to which only an Arctic prudery could find any objection. On Sundays he would often go touring in his motor-car through the devastated areas of France, in company with the general who commanded that part of the battle-field. In this way he visited most of the Western Front and had the chief battles reconstructed for him. He paid a special visit to Verdun, penetrated the forts where the blood-stains are still on the walls, and lunched in the Citadelle. All these things made him popular in France.

On most week-days he refused to go out in the evenings, retiring early, but not always to rest. He kept to his habit of holding his hospitable and homely breakfasts. He would sometimes take a Sunday off for a motor-drive to Fontainebleau with his friends. On such occasions he would talk no politics, but would indulge that precious capacity of gay and happy recreation which has so often been his salvation.

The negotiations, after long delay, ended with a final speed-up. President Wilson, on his return from his visit to America in February, insisted on the inclusion of the League of Nations in the Peace Treaty, and there was a rapid process of redrafting. On May 6th the draft was completed, and it was presented at Versailles to the German Foreign Minister, Count Brockdorff-Rantzau on May 7th. There followed six weeks of parley with Germany, which led to some important modifications in regard to the Saar Valley, the Polish Corridor, and Silesia. During this final crisis Mr. Lloyd George played the part of a bold and fearless conciliator: and he tried in every permissible way to make the peace possible for Germany's acceptance. President Wilson, on the other hand, hardened, and took the view that he was pledged to support the Treaty as now framed. But Mr. Lloyd George gained some important points, and by softening the terms certainly added to the hope of future peace in Europe.

On June 22nd the German Assembly ratified the Treaty, and on June 29th it was signed at Versailles by the German envoys. Mr. Lloyd George returned to England and eloquently defended the Treaty before Parliament, which unanimously ratified it on July 3rd.

As far as Great Britain was concerned, Mr. Lloyd George had now achieved peace.

---

[125] For further particulars of the election see Chapter XXIV.

[126] President Wilson brought with him four delegates, including Secretary Lansing, Colonel House, and one Republican, Mr. Henry White. M. Clemenceau was supported by General Foch, M. Pichon, M. Tardieu, and M. Loucheur.

[127] See, for instance, Dr. Dillon's very able book The Peace Conference (Hutchinson & Co: London), Peace Making in Paris, by Sisley Huddleston (Fisher Unwin: London), The Peace in the Making, by H. Wilson Harris (The Swarthmore Press: London), and The Economic Consequences of the Peace, by John Maynard Keynes, C.B. (Macmillan & Co., London.)

[128] See Appendix D.

[129] Some of these reported speeches are even more mordant, as for instance —"President Wilson talks like the good Christ, but acts like Lloyd George."

[130] The Saar Valley was finally given to the League of Nations for fifteen years, giving the French the output of the mines. At the close of that period there is to be a plebiscite, but if the vote goes in favour of Germany the mines must be bought back by Germany from France.

[131] See pp. 1240-2 of the Bullitt evidence: "Hearings before the Committee on Foreign Relations, United States Senate," vol. ii. The minutes of the meeting are given. I give them in full in Appendix C in order to show Mr. Lloyd George's point of view at this time.

[132] See Mr. Bullitt's statement to the Committee of Foreign Relations, United States Senate. "The Soviets undertook to accept proposals if made by the Allies not later than April 10th, 1919" (Hearings before the Committee on Foreign Relations, vol. ii. p. 1248). The proposals were not written down by the Bolshevists but conveyed through Mr. Bullitt, who placed them on record.

[133] See Mr. Bullitt's evidence, Hearings Before the Committtee on Foreign Relations, United States Senate, vol. ii. p. 1246. Mr. Bullitt's account of the conditions prevailing in Russia did not, of course, tally with other and more responsible evidence.

[134] See Mr. Bullitt's evidence, Hearings Before the Committee on Foreign Relations, United States Senate, vol. ii. pp. 1264-71, for full details.

[135] See President Wilson's first scheme in the Bullitt evidence. At the end of it nothing remained but a few clauses (Hearings before the Committee on Foreign Relations, United States Senate, vol. ii).

[136] In framing the Second Treaty of Paris signed on November 20th, 1815, it was with the utmost difficulty that Wellington and Castlereagh prevented the Prussian and Austrian representatives from annexing Alsace-Lorraine.

CHAPTER XXIV

THE NEW WORLD

"With malice towards none, with charity for all, with firmness in the right, as God gives us to see the right, let us strive on to finish the work we are in: to bind up the nation's wounds; to care for him who shall have borne the battle, and for his widow and his orphan; to do all which may achieve and cherish a just and lasting peace, among ourselves and with all nations."

Abraham Lincoln, March 4th, 1865.

"I don't envy the men who have to govern the world after the war," said M. Clemenceau to Mr. Lloyd George on one occasion in Paris during the Peace Conference. His instinct proved true. For indeed the world, both abroad and in these islands, has proved far less tractable since the guns have ceased to fire. There has been less killing, but more quarrelling. Above all, there has been a great increase of civil contention within the nations, from the extreme of civil savagery that has swept over Russia to the more moderate party contentions which have divided and weakened American effort, and which have, to some extent, distracted this country.

From the very beginning Mr. Lloyd George foresaw these troubles, and decisively made up his mind that, for his part, he would work to prolong the national unity achieved during the war. Since November 11th, 1918, he never swerved from his belief that the country could not afford the margin of effort necessary for party contention. Unity has seemed to him as necessary for recovery from the strife as it was for the strife itself.

For, consider the situation as it presented itself to the statesmen on the morrow of the Armistice. In every great belligerent European country trade had been entirely dislocated by the strain of the war. Ploughshares had literally been turned into swords. Vast workshops had been diverted to war. Huge populations of men and women had been shifted to munition centres. Now gigantic armies of soldiers and workers had to be demobilised, and over the whole situation hung the peril of unemployment. All the countries were exhausted, physically and mentally; it is not too much to say they were suffering from a modified form of shell-shock. In every great community there were suppressed labour difficulties, the accumulation of grievances that had been held back from expression during the four years of war. Then, underground in both France and Great Britain, there were the fanatics of Bolshevism, working like moles at the roots of society and ready to take advantage of every possible emergency to forward their terrific designs. In England the very police had been shaken in their discipline.

Against such dangers it seemed to Mr. Lloyd George that all reasonable men should combine and follow the road midway between "the falsehood of extremes." He was himself sometimes tempted, in some moods, to agree with the enemies who suggested that his work was done. Both for him and M. Clemenceau the achievement of victory seemed to mark the fitting consummation of their careers. But if such moods came, they soon passed. For retirement was impossible. It was not a time when any patriot could stand aside. The storm was coming, and it was necessary to ride it. The thought of retirement never seriously presented itself to his active and combative mind.

The first step was to secure a new mandate from the country for the work that lay before him. So he decided on a General Election.[137]

He had every excuse for this step in the situation of Parliament at that moment. The old Parliament which saw us through the war had lasted for eight years, although its statutory existence had been limited by itself to five years under the Parliament Act of 1911. Five times the War Parliament prolonged its own life, a process quite justifiable during the stress of that mighty struggle, but approaching almost to a scandal once active fighting had ceased. That Parliament lived longer than any of its forerunners in the past century, and, having been elected long before the war, was notably in many respects out of touch and tune with the war feeling of the country. Many of its members had been called upon to resign by their constituents, and by their attitude during the war had gravely belied the patriotic unity of the country. That was not all. A great measure of suffrage reform, far and away the most extensive since the Reform Act of 1831, had been passed into law in February, 1918. The new register had been completed by October 1st and contained two and a half times as many electors as the register compiled before the war. For the first time women had the vote, and the same right had been extended to soldiers on active service, to sailors, merchantmen, and fishermen on the sea, besides a vast population of new home voters. These were the people who had won the war. It seemed only fair and just that they should have a voice in the peace.

It has always been the fixed constitutional rule in this country that when a new Reform Act has created a large class of new voters the old Parliament becomes obsolete. That was the rule pursued in 1831, 1868, and 1885, and there seemed the more and not the less reason why at this crisis the country's fate it should be pursued in 1918. Nor can we be in any doubt that if Mr. Lloyd George had pursued the alternative policy of prolonging the life of the old Parliament he would have been equally blamed.

Mr. Lloyd George desired to carry through the General Election with as little party contention as was possible, and therefore informal approaches were made to the Independent Liberals during the autumn with a view to bringing them back into the Coalition. Those negotiations broke down, not on any material difference of political opinion, but mainly on the question of the date of the General Election. Mr. Lloyd George refused to adopt, as a governing political principle, this new reluctance to appeal to a new electorate. With regret he found himself compelled to agree to a division in the Liberal Party between those who befriended the Government and those who opposed it, and it is notable that he carried with him the great majority of the old party. Many of the Coalition Liberals found, when they went down to their constituencies, that their Liberal Associations supported them with a practically unanimous vote. The provinces were less factious than the London Clubs.

The Labour Party decided to leave the Coalition, to which they had adhered since December, 1916, and to fight the election as a body independent of all other parties. But even Labour did not leave the Coalition as a whole party, for in the process they became divided into several sections, and some of the ablest members of the Labour Party, including Mr. G. N. Barnes and Mr. G. H. Roberts, remained with the Government. The surprising lack of leadership in the Labour Party since the General Election, in spite of their notable victories at the polls, has been largely due to this division of forces, and to the fact that several members, such as Mr. Clynes and Mr. Brace, now acting as Independent leaders, were at heart in favour of remaining within the Government. The Labour Party, like the Independent Liberals, have also paid penalty for the spirit of faction.

Deserted by the bulk of the Labour Party, and by the old leaders of the Liberal Party, Mr. Lloyd George had to form his Coalition out of the combination of those Liberals who remained faithful to him, and the undivided forces of the Unionist Party. He and Mr. Bonar Law issued a joint manifesto, and letters passed between them which defined the Coalition policy. It was necessarily a policy displeasing to both extreme wings. For it is the essence of a coalition that nobody can get all his own way. At home, as abroad, Mr. Lloyd George had to compromise. For, after all, it is the first duty of a Coalition to coalesce. The justification of such a policy of compromise on matters of grave civil moment was indeed to be found only in the gravity of the civil emergency. It was not from one party only that Mr. Lloyd George asked the sacrifice, and it is not by one party only that he has since been attacked.[138]

The General Election took place on December 14th and Mr. Lloyd George was returned to power with a majority of 249 over all the independent groups. For the 602 seats in Great Britain no less than 478 official Coalition candidates were elected, while the suicidal policy of the Sinn Feiners resulted in the practical elimination of the Irish Party as a parliamentary force. Most of the leading Independent Liberals were defeated, and the Coalition was returned with a powerful and overwhelming mandate to carry out its stated policy both at home and abroad.

Parliament met to take the oath on February 3rd, 1919, and was opened by the King for business on Tuesday, February 11th. It was emphatically a war-born Parliament, but there were also signs of the New World which had emerged from the war. Only 365 of the old members had been re-elected. Labour stood out as the strongest party in opposition, and its parliamentary leaders took their places on the Front Opposition Bench.[139] The opening took place under ominous signs of civil strife. The unrest of labour, restrained by patriotic motives during the war, had already broken out into open flame. A general strike on the Underground Railways held London in a grip of paralysis, made harder by a bitter February frost. Mr. Lloyd George attended Parliament before going to the Peace Conference in order to utter a grave warning against the dangers of those social strifes. "This trouble," he said, "is impeding peace; and peace is the first necessity." He warned the country against certain symptoms of anarchy new to British movements; and he had grave reason for so doing. But, at the same time, his attitude towards the real grievances of Labour was always sympathetic and open-minded. His own life had taught him too well the reality of those fears which enshroud the workman's existence: the dread of unemployment; the precariousness of wage; and, above all, that fearful evil of over-crowding which had been so seriously aggravated by the war. He promised full investigation, and within a few days he called together at the Central Hall, Westminster, a Labour Conference between employers and employed, to whom he addressed himself in an earnest and persuasive speech. All through the labour troubles of this year Mr. Lloyd George pursued the same consistent policy. He was firm against anarchy, and yet open to reason in regard to all real complaints. He had his ears open to the call of the new order. But he dreaded the complete smashup of the old society before the new was ready, and the events in Russia faced him as a glaring red light. But he stood firm against coercion and repression as the only cure for unrest, and he saved his Government from pursuing the policy which, after Waterloo, led to the tragic anti-climax of Peterloo.

But there were many impatient men in the world in 1919, and the English mind was apt to demand payment in immediate cash for all Mr. Lloyd George's sanguine perorations. The Tube Strike in London was followed almost instantly by a great crisis in the mine-fields. The miners rejected the first Cabinet offer, and instantly went to ballot on the question of a general strike. The rank and file voted for the strike by a majority of six to one.[140] The Government replied by offering a Royal Commission, which the miners accepted after a candid debate between them and Mr. Lloyd George, which was certainly a new development of open diplomacy in civil affairs. Mr. Justice Sankey was appointed as Chairman of the Commission, and, after a hot debate in the House of Commons on February 25th, the Government promised that the Commission should report on the question of wages and hours by March 20th. On those conditions the miners agreed to appoint representatives to the Royal Commission and to present evidence.

Promptly on March 20th Mr. Justice Sankey's Commission reported, recommending an increase of two shillings a day in wages and an immediate seven-hour day, to be reduced to six hours in 1921. The revelations before the Commission as to the housing and conditions of labour among the mining population made it easy for the Government to meet the miners. They instantly granted them both these concessions, and the strike was postponed. But the question of nationalisation of the mines was held over, to become a widening political issue between the Government and Labour during the rest of the year.

The Labour crisis died down for the moment, and did not recur in an acute form until later in the year (October) when the railwaymen, whose needs had perhaps been too little regarded in the stress of the mining crisis, precipitated a struggle by a sudden and almost universal strike. For a few days the situation looked extremely grave, and there is no doubt that there were extreme forces working on both sides in the direction of civil war. But after a short period of natural impatience with the conduct of the railwaymen, Mr. Lloyd George steadied himself back to his old combination of firmness and concession. On the side of the strikers, both the miners and transport workers were in favour of moderation, and, in the end, the moderate forces won. The threatened revolution was averted by a quite ordinary compromise on hours and wages.

The whole crisis ended with a friendly and even enthusiastic meeting of both parties —a sort of "sing-song" —in the domestic atmosphere of 10, Downing Street. It was a striking exhibition of Mr. Lloyd George's characteristic gifts of control and conciliation.

Like Columbus's settlement with the egg, this performance seemed easy enough when it was achieved. But we must remember that Mr. Lloyd George stood between two forces both equally violent. On the one side there were the Direct Actionists, the "parlour Bolshevists" of the trade unions, fascinated by M. Sorrel's[141] opiate dream of dominating the modern State through its complex organisation of food and transport. The thing seemed so easy: and it would have been easy if Mr. Lloyd George had not, for months before the strike, prepared to prevent it. The motor-lorries that supplied London with milk were not organised in a day. They were part of a perfectly legitimate counter-stroke prepared by the Government when they realised the extent of the plot to hold up the national life. But on the extreme wing of the Government's side there was an equally violent section who cried, "Let's fight it out to the end! Let's smash Trade Unionism! Now's the time to put Labour in the cart!" —elegant phrases, which we all heard in those days. To this temper Mr. Lloyd George was vitally opposed. He was out to fight Bolshevism and "Direct Actionism," but not Trade Unionism. Happily, in this middle policy he was met half-way by several far-sighted leaders of trade unions, notably Mr. J. H. Thomas, who, while resolutely upholding the rights of the railwaymen, refused to surrender to the revolutionaries. On the Friday Mr. Lloyd George came to the conclusion that he, too, must resist his own extremists and go half-way to meet the trades union moderates. We all remember how, under this new policy of conciliation, the terrors of that critical week passed away like mists before the wind, and Sunday brought us a sudden and welcome peace. It was the triumph of the middle point of view, the old method of British common sense which refuses to burn the house in order to build it better.

Mr. Lloyd George was now called to Paris for the great work of European settlement, and the task of reconstruction was left to his Ministers at home. From February to May Mr. Bonar Law led the House of Commons and practically acted as Home Prime Minister. He began to develop the programme of reconstruction promised by the Government at the time of the General Election. On February 26th Mr. Shortt introduced a measure to which Mr. Lloyd George had given a great deal of thought and attention-the Ministry of Transport Bill, constituting a bold claim on behalf of the State to supreme control of railways, canals, tramways, roads, harbours, docks, and electric supply. On March 17th Sir Eric Geddes ably defended the Bill and gained a second reading without a division.

It was scarcely to be expected that so great a change should take place without resistance from the vested interests asked to submit to control. In the course of the discussions that ensued various claims of the State had to be modified and some withdrawn, especially in regard to the docks and roads. But in the end a powerful measure was passed on to the Statute Book, and already, with the firmer grip over transport and traffic which the Ministry of Transport is able to exercise, the country is feeling the tremendous advantages of this measure. It is safe to say that no Party Government could have carried so big a measure with so little debate within a year of the ending of the war.

After Transport, Housing —a far more difficult question. The difficulties and troubles which beset the Government throughout 1918 on this critical question have become notorious to all men. Dr. Addison took the first step by introducing, on April 7th, a Housing Bill which was certainly stronger than any hitherto placed before Parliament. Mr. Lloyd George, before going to Paris, had taken an active part in pressing this measure. He had ruthlessly forced a peerage on Mr. Hayes Fisher and had thus seriously shaken the old-time resistance of the Local Government Board. The main policy of the new Housing Act, as Dr. Addison framed and passed it through Parliament, was to throw the burden of housing on to the local authorities. The local authorities have not proved equal to the task. The strong wind which was blowing at the centre had not yet reached Slocum-in-Pogis and Little Puddleworth. The financial credit of the smaller local authorities was not equal to the new burden, and they were not powerful enough to face the great vested interests which control the raw material. Some of the great municipalities acted with a larger mind, but the small towns and rural districts held back. There was much talk and few houses. The result was that at the end of the year the Government had to make a fresh appeal to the private interests, adding a bait rising to £150 for every house built. Certainly no good-will was absent either on the part of the Government or the central departments. But this task of 1919 is handed on to 1920, and may require a vaster combination of energy and good will than has yet been brought to bear on it. What seemed to be wanted was that Mr. Lloyd George should bring to bear on this question some of the high patriotic enthusiasm which combined employers and workmen to face the Munition crisis of 1915. He, took the first step in this process by meeting the building trades in December, 1919.

After these greatest questions there came a series of minor measures to round off the Government's social policy. The Ministry of Health Bill, introduced in February and passed during the Session, concentrated all the authorities responsible for public health into one great department, which will gradually function as a new centre for the preventive and curative measures suggested by the advance of medical science. The Land Acquisition Act, in spite of the criticism brought to bear on it, is already of immense value in enabling the new housing authorities to acquire land. It is now safe to say that the trouble of the land is the least of the questions involved in the matter of housing. The Land Settlement Act, passed to help place ex-soldiers on the land, quickened and extended the facilities for acquiring land for settlers either on small holdings or allotments. The Extension of Rents Act, passed in March, prolonged to one year after the war the freedom from a rise in rent granted to small householders, and the margin of rents covered by the Act was considerably raised in the course of the debate.[142] The Industrial Courts Act set up an industrial tribunal for the settlement of disputes, and, providing good-will gathers round it, may, in the end, give to us a good working substitute for compulsory arbitration. Towards the end of the Session Parliament passed a bold measure granting yet a further step in the extension of self-government to India, and in one day it generously increased the grants to old age pensioners. Mr. Lloyd George ended the Session by sketching in outline the bases of a new Irish settlement. Not a bad record for a Parliament which has been denounced in all the terms of the political vocabulary as reactionary, illiberal, profiteering, and even corrupt!

Thus since the Armistice, in domestic crises as in foreign, Mr. Lloyd George has continued to be for this country the central figure of hope and hate. He keeps his old faculty of commanding the interest of men. Now, as in the boyish scrimmages of his youth, his flying colours draw others on. For the moment (1920) he strives for peace and unity in civil endeavour. But that is not because his eye is dimmed or his combative strength abated. He is by nature a partisan leader, and it has cost him no small effort to continue in his present part. The defensive on two fronts is not his characteristic role. His instinct is still for the heart of the battle: there, at any rate, his spirit is not aged. If party warfare should become once more the best thing for the country, he will not shrink from enlisting again in that service. But events have thrown on him the mantle of national leadership, and it is a great responsibility to descend again into the party arena. That is not his present reading of a statesman's duty in these difficult days. His mind is rather filled with another vision-the vision of a State deliberately consenting to sink faction in the cause of a larger purpose-of a community which, with all its passion for the healthy strife of party, can tell when to forego that strife, and can scent the danger from afar. It is the old vision of a house not divided against itself, but working together all parties and all classes, for the common good. Is it to fade into the light of common day? That is the question-the vital question-before us all.

Perhaps the habit of party passion, the love of party contention, is too deeply rooted in this island people. Perhaps the gulf between the classes has already become too wide to be bridged. There are signs and omens pointing that way. But, if so, let us not be too certain that this party habit, because it is our habit, is necessarily a virtue. Remember Rome and Carthage. Rome united, and Carthage divided. Rome stood, and Carthage fell.

At any rate, here is this other vision-the vision of a Britain that stands together, shoulder to shoulder, "foursquare to all the winds that blow," a Britain that does not wound itself, and therefore does not rue. To "be of the same mind one towards another" may be a vain hope and a dream that fades; but, at any rate, it is not ignoble.

It is for this faith that Mr. Lloyd George now stands before the world, as a national leader of this great and victorious British folk, now slowly groping its way out of the shadow of death into the way of peace.

---

[137] See Chapter XXIII, second page.

[138] By a section in all parties. For instance, the Morning Post, the Daily News, and the Daily Herald, are all equally vigorous in this combined attack.

[139] Sixty-three Labour members were returned out of some 300 Candidates.

[140] For the strike 611,998; against, 104,997.

[141] The founder of the French Syndicalist movement. See his book Reflexions sur la Violence.

[142] From £50 per annum to £70 in London, £60 in Scotland and £55 in the counties.

CHAPTER XXV

THE MAN

"He, though thus endued with a sense
    And faculty of storm and turbulence,
    Is yet a Soul whose master-bias leans
    To home-felt pleasures and to gentle scenes."
    Wordsworth's The Happy Warrior.

That element of tranquillity which Mr. Lloyd George enjoys in his own home-that "happy fireside clime" which to him is always truly —

"The pathos and sublime
Of human life" —

perhaps accounts for the serenity of his outlook on public life.

That serenity is never more conspicuous than in seasons of hurricane. Like some ships, he rides steadiest in rough seas. When people around him are most disturbed, he is often the most calm.

There is doubtless an element in his nature which rejoices in conflict and storm. I remember once finding him in his private room at the House of Commons when it was urgent to bring him word that Scotland Yard reported the intention of certain persons to take his life. His response was to strike up a verse of a great Welsh hymn which passed beyond my scope of understanding; but it was clear, from the flash of the eye, that it was a song of rejoicing. "Well," I said, "aren't you at all disturbed?" "No," he said, "with the world in storm I rejoice. I love all this smashing of windows and tumult of nations. I remember the saying of a great Welsh preacher: 'Such disturbances of the world always mean some great movement in the realms above' —a reflection on earth of some heavenly strife. I believe that is true." I did not attempt to argue with this mood; but this sympathy with unrest explains much in his career, and most of all his skill in riding through tempests and mastering storms. For it is at such moments that he is at his best. Nothing seems to frighten or appall him. When the hearts of others are dismayed he is touched with a new emotion. It is a kind of exaltation, which seems to work in some kind of harmony with that universal spirit which rides the storm and works through the whirlwind.

It is these moods which have most confused his critics and distorted their judgment of him. Those who know Mr. Lloyd George only on one side of his nature have always expected to see him fall over some political precipice. His zeal, in their opinion, would eat him up. He would just run the hot course of so many furious political firebrands. Some rash and hasty blunder would occur, and he would flare out into the darkness.

Yet this disaster has never occurred. And why? Because behind all those flashes of spirit there has been a steady pursuing purpose; discreet, cautious, shrewd. "Whenever Mr. Lloyd George seems most rash," said to me an old friend of his who has seen him in many situations, "I always know that there is a cold, shrewd calculation behind it."

It was a true judgment. For, with his great power of words, he combines a tremendous sense of facts. If he finds himself on the wrong course, he will often hark back. If he has erred in speech he will apologise. After the most vehement attack he will make friends with his victim. It is this combination of the slow qualities with the swift-of judgment with daring, of mercy with rigour, of slow reflection with swift attack, of the zeal of the Cambrian with the shrewdness of the Fleming-that marks him off from so many of his race. For it is not so much the emphasis of one quality as the combination of several contrasted qualities that goes to make human greatness.

Like all great stalkers and trappers, Mr. Lloyd George is very difficult to follow. He has often doubled on his tracks whilst his faithful disciples are still walking straight into the danger. He talks so freely and frankly that his paths seem to be those wherein wayfarers, though fools, may not err. But with all that frankness he really keeps his own counsel and forms his own decisions. That is why so many simple people are so surprised-and sometimes even a little hurt-to find that, after they have given him the very best of their advice, he has just gone on his own way.

Mr. Lloyd George by no means despises the tactics of public appeal. If necessary, he will use even the theatrical in order to impress the public mind. Soon after the Birmingham riot, at the height of the Boer War, his friends opened the Daily Express to find that there was a scheme afoot to do him violence at a meeting to be held in Bristol that evening. They wired a warning to the organisers of the meeting at Bristol. They need not have troubled; for whatever danger faced him was of Mr. Lloyd George's own fashioning. He had deliberately gone to the office of the Daily Express, advertised the place of the meeting, announced his intention to denounce the war, and practically challenged them to kill him. The organisers at Bristol had done their best to conceal the meeting. This was his way of correcting the discretion of his own friends.

This was immediately after that reverberating event at Birmingham, when he in fact nearly lost his life. Late on that stormy evening he rang me up in the Daily News office from Birmingham. He wished me to go and inform his wife at Wandsworth that he was safe. "But," I said, "what I am to tell her? Where are you?" "That I cannot divulge," he said in a laughing voice. "At present I am a member of the Birmingham Police Force" —and he gave me his number. Through the telephone I could hear the tinkling of cups. "Well," I said, "you are having a good supper." "Yes," he said, "we are making merry, and the mob are making merry outside. We are both happy!" It was perhaps characteristic of the calmness of his domestic life that, on reaching Wandsworth late that night, I found the house closed and the whole family fast asleep. Mrs. Lloyd George happily had not heard of the danger through which he was passing at Birmingham.

Then, as now, this habit of courage was always his supreme public characteristic. "Of all qualities in public life," he said to me once, "courage is the rarest." From the earliest episodes of his career, from that day when he defied the Bench in North Wales, here-in his courage-has always been the conscious centre of his power. He has always believed that if you want to destroy a popular idol you must learn to face it and to fight it-to put it to open shame-if necessary, to insult it. Fear rules the minds of men; and against fear courage alone prevails. This was always the moving faith at the back of all his great campaigns, whether of peace or of war. It was with this weapon that he has fought both Governments at home and Prussians abroad. It was the element of policy that underlay that frank directness of speech which offended the cultured classes of England so profoundly at the time of his Budget campaign.

For he convinced himself that modern public speakers had got into the habit of referring too politely to great national evils. He believed that the most effective weapon to use against these evils was to revive some of the lost frankness of our forefathers. His great aim was to prove that it was safe to speak as plainly about a duke as about an ordinary citizen. He had known in his young days how cowed men could be, how fearful of shadows, how frightened by ghosts. The thing he had most admired about Mr. Chamberlain was his plainness of speech. It was his deliberate policy to revive that habit. Mr. Lloyd George's oratory of the year 1911 was the direct successor of Mr. Chamberlain's during the years between 1886 and 1893.

As to the abuse he encountered, he counted that as a political gain. He was fond of the story of the workman who had heard a political agent expressing terror at the fury of a certain class. "Bless my heart!" said the workman, "we never thinks you mean business until they squeals." So it was with the avalanches of calumny which fell upon Mr. Lloyd George between 1911 and 1914. He knew that it was the penalty of challenging the powers in high places. It showed that his proposals really "meant business." "Their abuse," says Sir Fretful Plagiary in The Critic, "is the best panegyric." So Mr. Lloyd George ploughed the road to fame through the abuse of those years.

Yet all the time he suffered. He has a heart very sensitive to the affections of the people. He was puzzled at the way men hated him. It was not the danger of it he minded; for he would scarcely allow the Scotland Yard men to protect him. It was the pain of it. He frankly hates dislike; his nature craves the sun; he is at his best among friends. "I cannot imagine why they detest me so," he said one day during that time. "I seem to be the best hated man in England." The reply was obvious. "If one half of England hates you too much, then surely the other half loves you too absurdly." He was instantly all smiles. "That is perfectly true," he cried-and put the melancholy thoughts aside.

During the struggle over the Licensing Bill of 1908 he received numerous postcards written in what was intended to be blood, but looked suspiciously like red ink. These documents generally threatened him with instant death, probably combined with torture —"something lingering, with boiling oil." They came, or professed to come, from enraged publicans fearful for their livelihood. These postcards got curiously on his nerves. "I don't mind so much being killed," he said one day, "but I should hate being killed by a publican." There seemed to him something curiously unsatisfactory in such a way of going out.

But in general he has taken little heed of threats. It was only with great difficulty that the Attorney-General could persuade him to sanction a prosecution in the famous case of the poisoned arrow conspiracy. He was always in favour of leniency to the Suffragettes. It is not merely that he hates excessive punishment. His haunting sense of humour seems to be offended by the idea that he is taking up so much room in the world. He dislikes the attendance of detectives almost as much as Mr. Gladstone did. "Can you possibly tell me where Mr. Lloyd George is going?" was the frequent cry of those unhappy followers of Mr. Lloyd George to his friends in those perilous days of civil strife. "He is always giving us the slip," was their complaint. Sitting one day on one of those little green chairs in the Green Park for which the Londoner pays his obol —a favourite seat of his in those days of peace-at the end of a long talk he sighed and looked grave. He inclined his head towards a shabby-looking individual who was smoking a pipe and sitting not far off under a tree reading a newspaper with apparent indifference to the whole world around him. "There is my guardian angel!" said Mr. Lloyd George.

It is not only in facing hostile audiences that he has displayed his courage. He has never hesitated to tell his friends the truth. He has that gift of leadership which consists of making followers do something which they do not want to do. He has put aside all fear of those great influences which overshadow English public life-birth, money, prestige, caste. He represents in high places a new freedom from all those bogies-almost the realisation of Robbie Burns's dream:

"For a' that, an' a' that,
    It's coming yet for a' that,
That man to man, the world o'er,
    Shall brithers be for a' that."

Not in his most vehement Limehouse days did he say anything stronger than the Scotch ploughman said in his famous song:

"Ye see yon birkie ca'd a lord,
    Wha struts, an' stares, an' a' that;
Tho' hundreds worship at his word,
    He's but a coof for a' that."

Mr. Lloyd George, in fact, always tests man by what is in him; not by the guinea stamp, or by the pedigree. Why should he not? Birth! What birth can there be higher than that of a Welshman? —"The oldest race in these islands." Money? "I can always get money for a cause; there is no difficulty about money." That has always been his view; and who can wonder that such should be the belief of a man who has made millionaires subscribe for their own taxation!

Of prestige he is perhaps more fearful. He was tremendously impressed with Oxford when he stayed in that town for some days on his visit to the Palmerston Club during the Boer War. "I am glad I never came here," he said. "I should never have recovered from the influence of this place; it would have been with me all my life." He was indeed strongly gripped by Oxford and its "dreaming towers." After two days of it he was, for the moment, half subdued. "Ah!" he said, "how the past holds you here." All of which shows what a mistake our forefathers made when they excluded the Nonconformists from our ancient universities.

It is indeed quite a mistake to suppose that Mr. Lloyd George is dead to the voices of the past. There is no greater delusion than to regard him as an unlettered man. If the best education is to turn a boy loose in a library, then he has enjoyed to the full that form of schooling. He started life with the training of a lawyer, which he always claims to be the best mental discipline to which a human mind can be subjected. Those laborious explorations of French and the classics through which he passed with his "Uncle Lloyd" as companion, were certainly not less useful as a training than the fugitive crammings of the average University undergraduate. At any rate, he learnt to read for himself; and to absorb what he read. Since those early days he has been a wide reader in all his spare time. He knows his English historians better than most Englishmen. He can hold his own with most classical scholars in discussions on ancient history. Perhaps, indeed, Rome holds him most of all the countries. He knows his Mommsen well, and he spent the long convalescence from the throat illness that came to him after the Budget in reading some of the latest Italian historians of ancient Rome. He emerged from that illness a formidable expert in later Roman history, especially in the land laws of the Gracchi. In fact, he has most of the outfit of the scholar except the scholar's pride.

Parallels from history are dangerous; but they always haunt the mind of a well-read imaginative man. Mr. Lloyd George is very fond of them. One evening in 1908, when we were sitting in the Orangerie at Stuttgart, in a pause of the German tour of that year, the conversation began to turn on the possibilities of a war between Britain and Germany. The parallel of Rome and Carthage came like a flash from Mr. Lloyd George; it brought from him one of those far-reaching forecasts which, in other days, would have earned him the mantle of a prophet. "There is the same commercial rivalry," he said, "the same sea jealousy, the same abiding quarrel between the soldier and the merchant, the warrior and the shopkeeper, the civilisation that has arrived and the civilisation that is still struggling to arrive." He paused, and then he added: "I wonder if we shall be as unprepared as Carthage; I wonder if we shall be as torn by faction?"

It is curious to look back now on that conversation, in that comfortable, well-lighted garden-the pride of that old German town-with the vault of stars above us, and the murmur of a great city around us. We thought no more of it at the time. But now it comes back.

In his games, Mr. Lloyd George is a keen sportsman. Golfers, as a class, have the seriousness of religious devotees. But no man could pursue the little white ball round a course with a steadier concentration than Mr. Lloyd George. No player could be keener on victory. "Golf is like life," he loves to say, "you never quite make up for losing a hole." His game has much improved in recent years; though he never claims to be a champion. He has not again repeated the achievement of "holing out in one." That was at Cannes in the far-off, merry days before the Great War. It had the beauty of the unexpected. He drove off: and lo and behold! the ball disappeared. The caddies hunted everywhere; and it was just being pronounced a "lost ball," when a sharp youth looked into the hole, and there the ball was quietly reposing!

It is usual on these occasions to present the caddy with a bottle of whisky. Mr. Lloyd George gave the lad five francs; and of course there were candid friends who said that the caddy had put the ball in the hole. There are always critics, even on the golf-course.

His worst enemies cannot accuse Mr. Lloyd George of "side"; so there are some who say that he has not enough. He is, in fact, the simplest of men, fond of being surrounded with friends, and very faithful to the humble friends of his youth. He is curiously unconscious of his own position in the world. To one who congratulated him on his elevation to the Premiership he merely replied, "Oh! I had forgotten that!" And I believe that he had.

This simplicity makes him very thorough. He knows his own ignorance. When he was Chancellor of the Exchequer he went to Somerset House and went carefully through the whole system of the old land taxes and their working. When he was guiding his Budget through the House of Commons he had a daily meeting of the Treasury experts, with whom he discussed every detail. That is always his method-to learn all he can from others. He is a great listener, and learns rather by the ear than by the eye.

He is very considerate for his secretaries and his staff; but he works them hard. He has no place for "slackers." When he first went to the Treasury, he astounded that august Department by beginning work at ten o'clock. They soon caught the habit, for later on they slaved for him in a way that astonished the onlooker. He can make others work because he works himself.

At one time he took a great interest in the organisation of the Civil Service. On first becoming a Minister, he was astonished to discover the rigidity of the division between the First and Second Classes of the Civil Service. He wished the system to be more fluid. Once he was struck by the ability of a certain civil servant, and he wished to place him in a position of trust. "It is impossible!" was the reply; "he is only a second division clerk." Mr. Lloyd George looked up with a flash of whimsical indignation. "Why!" he replied, "I am only a second division clerk myself!"

Whenever one tries to discover the secret of his power over men, one comes back to that supreme gift of his-the gift of the silver tongue-the power of public speech. That is, after all, the thing that has made him supreme over men. To hear him at his best one must hear him on a public platform, addressing a great public audience. There are few fireworks, no shouting, no declaiming. He opens easily, in a soft, quiet voice: he always works up to his effects. There are "purple patches" now and again; but the bulk of it seems almost conversational, and is often broken by colloquial phases —"Can you hear at the back there?" "Ah! well, you must listen if you want me to speak to you." He is almost always very soon on good terms with his audience; it is only by shouting him down that his enemies can prevent that. He is never angry on a public platform; he seems always quite at home, as if it was his real natural element. He can be scathing at times-withering, scornful, contemptuous. But that mood rarely lasts long. He generally returns swiftly to his gentler moods-persuasion, appeal, emotion. He almost always prepares a careful peroration, generally a memorised piece of prose poetry, very often drawn from some great phase of nature-from the hills or the sea. Then his speeches end on the high note; and his audiences go home with a sense of having been uplifted.

There they are right-for it is precisely his power as a speaker to uplift the hearts of men. He has his own moods. But from those he carefully selects the very best, and gives them to the world. No public man can do more.

MRS. LLOYD GEORGE

DAVID LLOYD GEORGE AS A YOUNG MAN

CHAPTER XXVI

HIGHWAYS AND BYWAYS

"Jog, jog on, the foot-path way,
  And merrily hent the stile-a:
  A merry heart goes all the day,
  Your sad tires in a mile-a."
  Autolycus in Shakespeare's
  The Winter's Tale, Act IV, Sc. ii.

But, on the whole, it is the future rather than the past that rules the mind of David Lloyd George.

To him the future has always been an unexplored miracle-ever in travail with some new birth. To him, behind the veil of the coming time, there always lies a possibility of some event such as the world has never known-of some creation such as the world has never seen. He has moods when he seems "fey" with his belief. "I am out to abolish slums," he cried one evening, in 1912, walking across London upon a winter's night beneath a starless sky. He meant it. His bitterest enemy could not have laughed at that utterance if he had heard it.

In such moods he was at that time (1908-12) indeed "The little Brother of the poor." He was filled with a certain storming passion of pity, so powerful that it seemed to destroy all obstacles-to bridge all difficulties. All the accumulated memories of his own childhood-all the recollections of the poor cottagers among whom he had been brought up, all their sufferings and pains, all their oppressions and tragedies, seemed to be moving behind him like some great tide and driving him on. I remember his explaining once his own consciousness of the mark which such an upbringing left on a man's life. He was talking about the East End Settlement movement, and of its attempt to bring the leisured classes nearer to the workers. He was a little doubtful. "It is a gulf which can never be bridged," he said. "You people can never understand what it is to be really hungry or out of work. The difference lies in security. The poor man is always in danger, and he always knows it."

It was such a knowledge that inspired him with his enthusiasm for Old Age Pensions and for his Insurance Schemes. It was just this security that he wanted to give to the life of the poor. And yet he has never been a sentimentalist over their troubles. He looks at them, so to speak, from the inside. The sentimentalism of the philanthropic middle classes rather annoys him. What he always craves for the poor is justice, and not charity. In the days of the Insurance Act he was sincerely afraid of creating a dependent working class. He was surprised when he received so little help in his contributory policy. "I will never try to be good again," he said laughingly one day. "They call me a demagogue, and next time I will really be one." Such was his chaff.

In conversation he first expressed the idea of social insurance by a parallel from the Canadian farmer who insures his wheat against early winter frosts. That was the image in which he expressed his sense of the vast power of the modern State to build up a properly organised system of individual security. Having once conceived this idea, the various benefits came to him in waves of compassion-sickness, invalidity, maternity, consumption. He worked all these benefits out from his own experience of the sorrows of the poor. "I want to make the little stranger welcome," he said one day, talking about the maternity benefit. "It is horrible to think that he should come trailing clouds of trouble instead of 'clouds of glory.' " The story of the consumptive benefits is interesting. He had not felt the need of this benefit until one night he read through a very powerful medical work describing the ravages of consumption in modern Britain. The extent of the evil at once fully dawned on him. He came down in the morning with his mind fully made up. He went straight to the Treasury, called together his experts, told them to put aside £1,500,000 to fight consumption,[143] and so created that famous sanatorium benefit which is still proving only the first step towards removing a gigantic evil.

He faced all these familiar troubles of modern life with a "divine discontent" new to modern men. We all knew these things; but most of us had become so familiar with them that our anger was blunted. Our reforming temper had grown tired and stale. But this Welshman approached the matter with some of the ardour of the revivalist. He would not accept the ordinary excuses; he believed these evils to be curable. Fresh from the Welsh hills, he flamed with a new surprise at the power of poverty over modern civilisation. He showed some of the ingenuous dismay of a surprised Gotama emerging from his garden. He realised that private efforts had been tried and found inadequate. What he saw with a flash was that the State alone could cope with the evils produced by the State; the Government must become the parent and no longer the stepmother of its own children.

Once he realised this idea he was eager to carry it into effect. He was passing from one great effort to another-from the Insurance Act to the Land Campaign-when the Great War burst upon him. Then the very elements of civilisation had to be defended against an even greater peril.

It is recorded that the rebuilders of the Temple had to build every one with "his sword girded by his side."[144] There must have been times when they had to lay down the trowel entirely and work with the sword alone. Such a time came to Mr. Lloyd George in 1914; the trowel was only laid down. Now it is being taken up again.

What struck the observer most in his achievements during those years (1908-14) was his daring and originality. Plenty of clever English minds had been working on these problems ever since 1886. But how little had been done! How long we had had to wait for Pensions and Insurance! How strangely academic and remote were all those University and West End speculations on these problems! How quarrelsome were the philanthropists! How divided were the English Labour leaders! Then from outside came this zealous Welsh Crusader, and while all these people were still talking he proceeded to act. When the world had recovered from its surprise most of the persons concerned turned round and attacked Mr. Lloyd George. However right he might be in his aim, there was always sure to be something wrong with his methods. This attitude frankly puzzled him. "Why! they talk as if I was trespassing," he used to say. "Is charity, then, a form of property? Is kindness a monopoly?" The attitude of the doctors especially surprised him. "I have made a discovery," he said one day with a twinkle in his eye. "I have discovered that disease is a vested interest!"

Throughout all these struggles over social reform Mr. Lloyd George tempered his enthusiasm with a very even sense of political tactics. He knew well that, to carry England with him, he must always have a great political party at his back. There were times when this was not easy. Neither of the great political party machines in this country is exactly impassioned for new ideas. It is rather typical of the faithful party man to view a new proposal with actual dislike. "Why not leave it all alone?" is a common attitude with all parties.

Then there is the value of a grievance. There is even a type of party man who actually regrets to see his cause succeed. "If we pass the Bill we shall lose the cry!" you hear him say. "Mr. Lloyd George is passing too many Acts of Parliament," was the common complaint of the period among the very faithful.

To this type of man the Budget of 1909-10 was rather a distracting affair. They were always trying to "dilute" it. The Insurance Bill, too, would certainly have been thrown over if Mr. Lloyd George had not staked his fortunes on it; and, as to the Land Campaign, that was viewed with open disfavour in the same quarters. For every party has its priesthood; and in politics, as in religion, all priesthoods are conservative.

But, in spite of all this trouble within the party, Mr. Lloyd George was always resolute not to quarrel with the machine. One of his fixed principles was —"Keep the party machine on your side." He was certainly not a typical party man-far from it. He regarded the party as the instrument and the cause as the end; whereas the typical party view is that the cause is the instrument and the party the end. But he knew the power of the machine; he often quoted

Mr. Chamberlain as an instance showing that in the end the machine won. "Mr. Chamberlain fought both of the machines in turn," he used to say, "and, in the end, both combined against him and beat him." Roosevelt was another case which impressed him deeply. "Ah!" he commented, when that great man was beaten so decisively in 1913, "Roosevelt ought not to have quarrelled with the machine."

On these grounds he has often accepted the second best in policy.

He has often allowed himself to be convinced against his will. After the defeat of the Education Bill in 1906, for instance, he was as eager to go back to the country as Mr. Gladstone after the Lords' rejection of Home Rule in 1893. Both these great fighters felt instinctively that a party which accepts a defeat asks to be defeated again until it is finally smashed. You cannot expect a country to vote for ever for a party that accepts defeat as its proper portion. But in this case, as in others, rather than quarrel with his party, he acquiesced in the decision to go on.

Still, he was glad when the split with the Lords became irrevocable. It happened that I had the fortune of announcing to him the resolution of the Lords to throw out the Budget. It was down at Lord Renders beautiful house near Guildford, where Mr. Lloyd George was staying for the last time with that faithful Nestor of Welsh Liberalism. Mr. Lloyd George had been very anxious. He knew that the wiser Unionist leaders in the Lords had been in favour of accepting his Bill. He was afraid that the Lords were going to refuse battle on grounds so favourable to their assailants. When I told him the news his face shone. "The Lord," he cried, "has delivered them into our hands!"

In the same way, he has always been very slow to take the step of resignation from high political office. How often have his friends-generally a man's worst advisers-urged him to resign over some failure to gain his own way! But he well knows that there is nothing more difficult in politics than the art of resigning opportunely. You must have a great issue and you must have your people behind you. "You cannot be always resigning," was one of his favourite sayings during the critical years of 1909-12. It is true that he often came near it, but he would generally compromise the matter and pass on. He was equally against Cabinets resigning in a hurry. After the second General Election of 1910 there was a meeting when the Liberal Cabinet, wearied out with a long struggle, was on the verge of resignation. Every member who spoke at this fateful meeting had favoured resignation. Mr. Lloyd George felt strongly opposed to it, but he was almost silenced by the unanimity of his colleagues. At last he scribbled a line and threw it across to Mr. Winston Churchill. "I feel strongly against resignation," he wrote. "What do you think?" Mr. Winston Churchill scribbled below: "If you feel against it, speak against it." Mr. Lloyd George spoke against it, and spoke so persuasively that the idea of resignation was dropped.

Even on fundamental issues he would often accept personal defeat for the time. He had to decide whether to go out into the wilderness or to work with men to whom he was attached, and with whose ideas he broadly and profoundly sympathised. When the draft of the new Home Rule Bill was before the Cabinet in 1910 he moved to exclude Protestant Ulster. He made the longest speech he had ever addressed to a Cabinet on that issue. He prophesied what was certainly coming-the resistance of Ulster; the refusal of Protestant England to join in coercing her; the hesitation of the Government to carry out their Act. He was in favour of telling the Irish Party straightaway that the Government of 1910 was not strong enough to include Ulster in the Home Rule Bill. He would have left the Irish Party to accept or reject the Bill as it would have then stood. He himself believed that in such a case Ulster would come in during the parliamentary discussions on the Bill. He was defeated in his proposal. Being defeated, he loyally stood by the Cabinet and steadily supported the Bill. It was not until long afterwards, when he himself became Prime Minister and responsible for policy, that he revealed to the world in that dramatic speech which drove the Irish Party out of the House, the fact that he had always been in favour of the exclusion of Ulster.

In literature and art Mr. Lloyd George does not pretend to be among the elect. He gives himself no airs and has no pretensions. He is just himself. He states, without parley, his own genuine opinions on books and pictures; and, as that is the rarest habit in the world, it is always interesting. Nine out of ten literary and artistic judgments are reflections or echoes-repeated at second-hand from some bolder speaker, or even vaguely salvaged from the dim abysses of memory. The most refreshing thing in the world, therefore, is an honest, fresh, and original judgment. It is characteristic of Mr. Lloyd George that he never hesitates to give that in any company.

In literature he votes with both hands for Byron, perhaps because Byron is the poet of liberty, and also because that great writer, with all his faults, has the quality of daring. But he boldly contends that the Welsh are among the greatest of modern poets; and he will recite their verses at large, even to English friends, in order to confirm his claim.

In prose, he is devoted to George Meredith.

In music, he places Handel first among his heroes. There, again, in great works like the Messiah, he seems to discover some quality of sublimity which elates and inspires him.

But there, again, his living passion is really nationalist and based on national affections. The only music that profoundly moves him-touches his soul-is the music of the old Welsh hymns and folk-songs. Not long ago he spoke up boldly for the music and literature of his own nation before all the world.[145] There he voiced his own deepest conviction on these matters. The music and songs of his own people strike the deepest chord in his nature.

In religion his outlook always seems to be broadly Christian rather than sectarian. Brought up in his uncle's creed of the "Disciples of Christ," which is really an attempt to hark back to the purity of the early Gospel teaching, he has an inherited hatred for dogmas. He is very fond of such parables as those of the Good Samaritan, which he instinctively regards as the best comment on the claims of priestcraft.

He has a profound interest in all forms of Christianity. There was a time, many years ago, when he was fond of going the round of the Churches. He would also listen in the old days with the closest interest to the discourses of the Salvationist preachers on Wandsworth Common; and he would often contribute to their collections, and talk to their officers. And yet, at the other extreme, he has always had a curious admiration for Roman Catholicism. He would sometimes argue that the Methodist discipline in Wales was founded on the Catholic model. I remember going with him into a London Catholic Church where he listened with rapt attention to the chanting of the Latin psalms. There was something in the roll of the language which penetrated and held him. But he was always a great listener. He would never complain at the length of a sermon. When at Brighton he would take his friends to listen to the preaching of a young Nonconformist minister at whose feet he sat with whole-hearted admiration. He would always argue that the standard of preaching among the Nonconformists had steadily risen and was now higher than among the Anglicans. He attributed that fact very largely to post-graduate colleges like Mansfield. He was a great admirer of Principal Fairbairn, and would listen to that great man's hour-long discourses without moving an eyelid.

Wit is his most sparkling characteristic; and there are few companies of talkers among whom he is not the wittiest. His laugh will change the mood of the gravest men, just as his smile has been known to affect the attitude of immense multitudes. And yet wit is not his greatest gift. I should place higher that power of insight into deep truths which he will display in sympathetic company. Generally the theme of this insight will be politics; and there is no subject which he is more swift to illuminate with telling phrase. In these moods he will seem to be looking at all parties, and even at himself, from the outside. It is an extraordinary gift of detachment, literary and artistic in its nature, and peculiarly rare in a party politician. It goes with a Celtic love of whimsical paradox, like the talk of a man at his ease, a little disturbing to the strait sect of the faithful party men.

But it will not always be politics that his mind plays on in this manner. In moments of relaxation he will take a wider range. Sometimes it will be this very subject of religion, which is never very far absent from his thoughts. "Christianity," he said to me once, "is like a gold-mine. We are always imagining that it is exhausted, and that no more gold can come out of it. Then humanity digs a little deeper, and it always comes across a fresh seam." He always seems to be digging a little deeper himself.

His judgments of great men who came before are always just a little inclined to severity, perhaps as a rebound from the snobbery of history. Looking round at that great gallery of the Englishmen of Napoleonic days which adorns the breakfast-room at 10, Downing Street-Pitt, Wellington, Nelson, Fox, Burke-he said once: "None of them were very great-the greatest of them all was the man in the little frame in the corner-the man they honoured least-the Irishman, Edmund Burke." Perhaps it was the orator and the thinker in Burke that drew him. Or perhaps, even more, the Celt.

But it would be unfair to take him too seriously in these judgments. He is above all things a conversationalist in regard to all such matters. It is only in politics that he would ask to be taken as an expert. There he works very gravely and arduously. It is sometimes said that he does not read much. When he can, indeed, he prefers, like many very busy men, to acquire knowledge by the ear; and he likes to meet men who know, and to learn from them. But he can read widely and deeply when he thinks it necessary. He will read steadily through great Blue-books when he is preparing a parliamentary case; and when he was preparing for the Insurance Act he studied deeply and widely the whole literature of English social conditions, and in the parliamentary debates he displayed astonishing mastery.

He is a great newspaper reader. It is his habit to read practically the chief daily newspapers in bed in the morning before he comes down to breakfast; and it is somewhat disconcerting for his breakfast guests to discover that he already knows all the news of the day. He never reads either a newspaper or a letter at any meal. He talks and attends to his guests, as every civilised host should do.

"He always speaks to me as if I were the only person in the world," said one who met him rarely, and was opposed to him in politics. That utterance explains, perhaps, better than any other the secret of his social power. He has a profound sense of equality, and will treat the humblest human being as courteously as the highest. He is always very popular with humble people who serve him, such as hall-porters or maid-servants.

Not, indeed, that he suffers from that inverted snobbery which puts its boots on drawing-room sofas and reserves its insolence for crowned heads. It is well known that King George V and Mr. Lloyd George are sincere friends, and bound by mutual respect and admiration. The friendship began after the death of the King's father, and has deepened ever since. They have much in common-habits of arduous industry, the love of home and family, the passion for simple things. In private he constantly expresses his deep esteem and regard for the King as a man and a father. He is thoroughly at home in that happy domestic atmosphere of the present Court.

He is a splendid travelling companion; he loves the novelty and stimulus of foreign touring. He likes the friendly open-air life of foreign capitals; and he is never tired of exploring new cities. They come back now as radiant memories-those travels over Europe which we took together in earlier, peaceful days-in France and the Tyrol, over plains and mountains, through villages and cities.

One experience comes vividly back. We were staying in a little Tyrolese village named Vent. Some of us, being mountain climbers by election, had set off at 3 a.m., the climber's hour, to mount a high snow-peak, the Similaun. We returned in the afternoon to find that Mr. Lloyd George had disappeared from the inn.

He returned later and told us his experience. He had tired of his reading, looked up at the glistening peaks and decided that he, too, could and would climb mountains. He had taken his stick, set off alone, and proceeded to attack the nearest peak, without ice-axe or guide. He surmounted a rock-ridge, crossed a glacier, and reached a distant height. None of us could comprehend how he managed to return alive.

There it is again, in small matters as in big-this note of daring, of refusal to accept defeat, of assertive invincibility. It is the key-note of his character. In every study of David Lloyd George it pursues you everywhere and all the time.

There never was a time in human history when such a quality was more needed. Frowning heights lie behind and in front of-roaring cataracts of catastrophe-gleaming peaks of suffering and sacrifice-frozen glaciers of death, seamed and crevassed with agony. May he help us to win through!

---

[143] As a capital sum for building, in addition to £1,000,000 a year for maintenance out of the Insurance Fund. Even these sums have proved quite inadequate.

[144] Nehemiah IV, 8.

[145] At the Welsh Eisteddfod of 1917.

CHAPTER XXVII

THROUGH FOREIGN EYES

> Praise enough
> To fill the ambition of a private man,
> That Chatham's language was his mother tongue
> And Wolfe's great name compatriot with his own.
> Cowper.

Travelling about the world before the Great War, no one could fail to notice that the name of Mr. Lloyd George had already become an ensign. Men had begun to apply it to that particular type of statesman, becoming happily less rare, who take risks on behalf of the "common people." It had become a way of classifying a statesman to speak of him as "Our Lloyd George." This was especially the case with little nations. In Norway, for instance, during the winter of 1913-14, I found that that remarkable social reformer, Mr. Castberg, was generally spoken of as the "Norwegian Lloyd George"; and on meeting him I was surprised to find how closely he was modelling his policy on that of the British statesman. His chief aspiration was to meet Mr. Lloyd George and discuss with him his own schemes for simplifying and enlarging Norwegian social insurance and reforming their land system.

This was but one example of a very general tendency. There was another remarkable fact. Those who met and talked with Socialists either in France or in Germany during 1912-14, must have been astonished to discover that, in speaking of Great Britain, their thoughts were concerned not with any British Socialist leader, but almost always with Mr. Lloyd George. The reason of this was simple, but illuminating. European Socialism had for half a century been hand-cuffed to an impracticable idealism. Here was a man who achieved things. He might be an opportunist and a compromiser. Well, then, there was something to be said for opportunism and compromise. For the great thing was that, while all the idealists were still dreaming, this man was awake and doing.[146]

Apart from the Socialists, there was one European statesman who, long before the war, already realised Mr. Lloyd George as a possible European force. That was the great Cretan Greek, M. Venizelos. The instinctive mutual regard and respect of these two men is one of the most remarkable things in latter-day politics. There was telepathy in it. Across the length of Europe they seemed to have caught some message from one another even before they were acquainted. It was Mr. Lloyd George who especially urged on the Greek Government that M. Venizelos should come to the London Conference of 1912. It was on that visit that they met at the house of a friend and had a long conversation. They found much in common —a common hope for the little nations, a common belief in the unity and federation of the Balkan States as the one hope of the Near East.

It was after this that M. Venizelos said to a friend —"Mr. Lloyd George will save Europe."

It was only gradually that Mr. Lloyd George emerged in Western Europe as a commanding figure in the world war. It was the French who first among European nations discovered him as a European. This was partly, no doubt, from some instinctive sympathy between the Gaul and the Celt; for very large numbers of Frenchmen-the Bretons-are actually still Celtic-even Welsh-both in thought and language.

It was also that Mr. Lloyd George, in his great munitions campaign, took so many ideas from the French and realised in a moment, across the gulf of language, the extraordinary swiftness and power of the French mind, their amazing courage and capacity in enterprise and organisation. We have seen how, early in the war, he sat at the feet of the French Socialist Minister, M. Albert

Thomas; and how, at the Boulogne Conference of June, 1915, he learned from the French gunners. It would be foolish to pretend that Mr. Lloyd George talks French very well. But he has learnt to understand their spoken language when it is uttered by masters like M. Briand and M. Thomas.

But it was not till 1916 that Mr. Lloyd George stood out to the French with a bright, particular light of his own. Amid the doubts and hesitations of their own politicians they caught a glimpse of a man across the Channel who dared to lead-who ventured to tell the people the unpleasant truths, and to direct them to unpleasant duties.

"A speaker full of free and generous inspiration," says M. Georges Leygues in the Evènement of July 7th, 1916, greeting his appointment to the Ministry of War, "he never fails in his perception of realities, and he goes straight to the fact. Passionate interpreter of the soul of his people, which he knows so well in all its phases-living incarnation of the ardent Welsh race, he enjoys a real ascendency over the masses. He can make them understand and accept the length of the effort necessary to shake that which most offends the proud people of the West-that boastful and brutal barrack-yard spirit under which the German military caste designed to bring the free mind of the world."

In December, 1916, during the great ministerial crisis which led to the Lloyd George Premiership, these French writers saw far more clearly than the journalists of London what was at stake. In London, on both sides, the writers and politicians were too much absorbed in the personal and party issue-they regarded it too much as a conflict of newspaper "combines." In France, on the other hand, the journalists all realised that the difference turned round great issues-great questions of method in the conduct of the war. Here is what that great journal, Le Temps, wrote on December 7th, 1917:

"The English ministerial crisis is just a conflict, at an acute stage, of two principles and methods of government. One represents the normal maintenance of traditions, or rather of conventions, which have stood the proof of long administration-the ordinary march of the governmental machine. According to this view, that machine can give us its full value, if only all its wheels are strengthened without being modified. The other view holds that there must be new simplifications of the machinery. The driving power must be organised and concentrated in one control-and that a control of energy. The time of good intentions has passed. This is no longer an affair of 'Wait and see.' Mr. Lloyd George takes his stand clearly and simply on the side of decisive action."

The Temps was not alone. Philippe Millet, writing in L'Œuvre on the same day, showed that he had a glimpse of the same issue:

"It is necessary to look beyond the conflict of persons. Then one discovers a practically unanimous desire to constitute at last a true War Government. What England has in her mind is the formation of a sort of Committee of Public Safety."

England, he perceived, had become more revolutionary than France.

"Conscription had made a greater change in England because it was in itself a revolution. Beginning later than ourselves, the English have taken on the habit of changing their political organisation at great speed and as fast as the war compels them; and their acquired pace is probably in this stage superior to ours. It is in England rather than in France that one sees at this moment the spirit of Carnot reviving."

Here surely was a very profound political observation. With the same keenness of insight M. Clemenceau, writing on July 1st, 1917, in L'Homme Enchaîné, saw in Mr. Lloyd George a great political experimentalist adapting his course always to the actual events of the war:

"The English Prime Minister is, above all things, a man of action-one of those who, under the active impulse of living thought, apply themselves to one task only-and that is to bring order and method into the plans and resolves which come to them from a rigorous scrutiny of realities."

Other French journalists, still seeing these incidents more clearly from across the water, rejoiced at the change on the broadest possible lines. "The state of war," wrote M. Gustave Téry, "demands that all deliberations should be brief and decisions prompt. Now how can they possibly be so, if all power is exercised by two dozen Ministers who pass half their time in discussion and the other half in deploring their impotence?" Gustave Hervé was even more outspoken in La Victoire (December 7th, 1916):

"Roughly the veils are torn aside in all the allied countries; and from Petrograd to Paris, from London to Rome, the whole world turns anxiously towards their Governments, crying, 'We want leaders!'

"Lloyd George has been the first in our great countries of the West to hear the cry of the people."

M. Fitzmaurice, in the Figaro, foresaw how the crisis would end:

"Perhaps he will not have the support of all his colleagues of to-day, some of whom are precisely those whose delays and decisions he was arraigning, and from whose hands he wished to take the War Council; but he will have with him all the men of action of all the parties who recognise in him a true leader because they have seen him at work and they know that they can count on him. He will have with him all the English people and all the Allies."

The Matin on the same day (December 7th) analysed the position as follows:

"In reality the conflict which divides the English political world is nothing new in the history of peoples. In moments of great gravity, even of less gravity than the present time, there has often been felt this imperious necessity to trust the management of affairs to men of energy. Even revolutions have arisen, in England itself, and several times, from the discontent created by Ministers who were excellent in moments of calm but feeble in serious crises."

The Journal wrote thus:

"One element dominates the situation. It Is the preponderating position of Mr. Lloyd George. No Prime Minister could govern to-day without asking not so much for his collaboration as for his directions. Lloyd George is the soul of England at war, and the principal combative arm of Great Britain. Why keep him then in the second political place? The brain that conceives ought also to be the will that directs."

It is, indeed, a remarkable proof of the interest taken by Frenchmen to-day in the personality of Mr. Lloyd George that perhaps the best of all the shorter sketches of his career has been written by M. Paul Louis Hervier and published by that enterprising magazine, Je Sais Tout, in its issue of April 15th, 1917.

To-day, indeed, it is scarcely too much to say that in France Mr. Lloyd George is the best known and loved of all European statesmen-not even excluding the statesmen of France itself.

Or turn to another splendid European Ally-Italy. There, too, Mr. Lloyd George is well appreciated as a leader in the Entente Alliance. Here is a passage from the Secolo in December, 1916:

Once more we see Lloyd George, the watchful, the innovator, the inaugurator of new ideas. He has known how, in the country classic for its individualism, to strengthen and enlarge the sphere of State action. His first political experiments from 1906 to 1914 were all directed to destroy the laissez-faire system, and to substitute for it the direct and co-ordinated action of the State, especially when the action of the State attacked the privileges of the rich classes. To-day Lloyd George seeks to bring into being a veritable "War Socialism."

The Giornale d'Italia took the same line:

In comparison with the preceding administration, the new Government is distinguished for its firmness of decision. England takes another step along the path of warlike evolution....Lloyd George's power is the power of a warrior, who is determined to subordinate every private interest, that the interest of the whole nation may prevail....He voices the conscience of the whole British Empire, which fully realises that every barrier must be overturned, every obstacle overcome, that stands in the way of the development of those resources for war without which it is impossible to beat the enemy.

The Idea Nazionale echoed the same view:

There is a new feeling among the Governments of the Entente —a new determination to conquer "without the aid of time." The old Governments were characterised by their conviction that time was a substantial ally. This constituted an element of weakness. The speech of Lloyd George, however, is an authentic interpretation of the signs of the times....

In an interview with the Morning Post in December, 1916, that remarkable Italian, Signor Bissolato, expressed these views:

"You ask me what I think of Lloyd George? That is tantamount to asking me what I think of England. It is rare in history that a nation has found itself as perfectly identified with one man as England is to-day with Lloyd George. The world, enemies and friends included, stands amazed by the energy Lloyd George displays in dealing with the huge difficulties that the war has raised. But few know that in the energy of this one man is apparent the energy of the whole English nation. What is particularly fortunate is his decisive arrival to power at this juncture. I say this because if a nation at such critical times as these does not find the man who is destined to lead it, it runs the danger of remaining like the giant who cannot find a weapon to fight with in a conflict which is to decide his fate....England's good fortune in having found Lloyd George is the good fortune of the whole Entente."

Let us cross from Europe to our new and splendid Ally, the United States. There the career of Mr. Lloyd George has always been followed with the closest interest. There was a touch of enterprise —a salt savour-about his Budget that took the fancy of a country always in love with daring. The quick and observant journalists who watch affairs in England on behalf of the American democracy were already warning their people that Mr. Lloyd George was putting them out of date. In a very remarkable sketch of Mr. Lloyd George's land proposals sent to the American Press in April of 1912 by Mr. James Creelman, he told them that England was on the verge of a revolution that would make America look old-fashioned.

"These are stirring and epoch-making times in Old England.

"The old and powerful order of things is about to pass away."

And in his bright American way he depicted the English aristocracy crying out:

"Oh! for a way to get rid of the grey-eyed, smiling little Welsh demon who sits at the Imperial Treasury planning new taxes on wealth and land; who puts evil ideas of social justice into the head of the calm, keen, adroit Prime Minister and all the rest of the Cabinet, and who has bewitched the once humble and contented British people until they no longer reverence or respect orthodoxy or the nobility and upper classes!"

Mr. Lloyd George has always been fully as interesting to the leading men of America. When they visit England, it is he whom they most desire to see and to meet. President Wilson looks at the world with a slower, calmer gaze, and arrives at his conclusions very much more gradually.

But President Roosevelt always held Mr. Lloyd George in a fierce admiration, not unmingled with envy for his success in carrying with him a militant democracy. Mr. Roosevelt wrote shortly before his death as follows to a public man in his country:

"Give my heartiest regards to Lloyd George. Do tell him I admire him immensely. I have always fundamentally agreed with his social programme, but I wish it supplemented by Lord Roberts's external programme. Nevertheless, my agreement with him in programme is small compared with the fact that I so greatly admire the character he is now showing in this great crisis. It is often true that the only way to render great services is by willingness on the part of the statesman to lose his future, or, at any rate, his present position in political life, just exactly as the soldier may have to pay with his physical life in order to render service in battle."

As to our own far-flung Empire, there never has been much doubt about their views in regard to Mr. Lloyd George.

There are enough Welshmen in Canada to see to that Dominion. Sir Wilfrid Laurier, in a letter of introduction written a year before his death, wrote:

"Mr. M. is one of your most ardent admirers; and if you do not know it let me tell you that their number in this country is legion."

There he certainly spoke the truth.

Sir Richard Flavelle, the famous Canadian financier, was present in London during the great financial crisis. On returning to Canada, in a speech at Ottawa on September 26th, 1916, he spoke as follows:

"During those days the men who met the Chancellor (Mr. Lloyd George) in Committee were struck with one or two personal characteristics. One of the noted ones was the man's self-effacement. He sought for no glory for himself. He sought for no recognition for himself. One of the early evidences of the measure which he had taken of the situation was found, by the gentlemen who waited upon him, that Mr. Austen Chamberlain sat by his side. He crossed over to the other side of the House, and he said —'I need your assistance.' "

Less expected than the praise of Canada is the admiration of India. Mr. Lloyd George has never visited India, and he would not claim any special knowledge of India. But India is the country of the poor man; and the poor man all over the world has heard in his speeches a new call of hope. To him Mr. Lloyd George seems a light in great darkness, the glimmering of a new dawn. Writing before the war, the Indian Patriot said:

"Of all the statesmen at the head of affairs in England to-day no one exercises the imagination of India so much as Mr. Lloyd George. He is not known as 'Mr.' here, but has gone over to the ranks of greatness, and is called simply 'Lloyd George.' His force and his earnestness always appeal to the imagination. His speech is carefully read and treasured up. The cry of India is —'When shall we have a Lloyd George over here?' and the story of his pensions for the old, his insurance for the sick has become a legend from the West.

"When will he come as our Viceroy?" is what a poor man asked the writer. And he was disappointed to be told that he may not come at all. 'But then Mr. Lloyd George has many followers, and any one of them, trained as he is, may come!' And here was consolation!"

"They all love him, and are ready to lay down life for him; and all because he has done so much for the poor." That is the verdict of India, where kindness to the poor is a first call on all religions, and not a pious aspiration controlled by the Poor Law.

Then there are the little "Neutrals." They ought, by all the rules, to have seen the best of the game. There is a remarkable article in the Journal de Genève of May 15th, 1917, which seems to embody the judgment of the most cautious and level-headed of all the neutral observers of the war:

"Mr. Lloyd George has been called 'the Prime Minister of Europe.' There is truth in that utterance. Of all the statesmen who exercise to-day an influence over the destinies of the world, Mr. Lloyd George is the most attractive, the most personal, the most wilful, the most audacious. More than all the others, he sees the future and prepares for it.

"He has two talents which complete his outfit. He knows how to will, and he knows how to speak."

Finally, there is one tribute that comes from abroad to Mr. Lloyd George which certainly ought not to be omitted from this survey:

Of all British statesmen, he was, during the war, the best abused in the enemy Press.

----

[146] A remarkable instance of this comes to hand. Prince Kropotkin, in addressing the Moscow Conference (August 1917), told the Russian Socialists that there was more Socialism in Mr. Lloyd George's speeches than in all their dreams.

APPENDIX A

Principal Dates in Mr. Lloyd George's Life

Birth of David Lloyd George	January 17, 1863.
Death of his father	June 7, 1864.
Is taken to Llanystundwy	August, 1864.
Enters the village school	1869.
Passes Law Preliminary	1877.
Enters solicitor's office at Portmadoc	1878.
Family moves to Criccieth	May 1880.
Visits Houses of Parliament	November 1881.
Speech on Egyptian War at Portmadoc	November 1882.
Passes Law Finals	1884.
Starts practice at Criccieth	1884.
Starts practice at Portmadoc	1885.
Speaks at Michael Davitt's meeting	1886.
Llanfrothen case	1888.
Marries Miss Maggie Owen	January 24, 1888.
Adopted as Liberal candidate in Carnarvon Boroughs	December 1888.
Elected Alderman for Carnarvonshire County Council	1889.
Returned M.P. at By-election (majority, 18)	April 10, 1890.
Fight over Clergy Discipline Bill	1892.
Second election (majority, 196)	July 8, 1892.
Revolt over Welsh Disestablishment Bill	1895.
Third election (General Election—majority, 194)	1895.
Opposes Agricultural Rating Bill	1896.
Opposes Voluntary Schools Bill	1897.
Opposes Tithes Bill	1899.
Speaks against South African War	October 27, 1899.
Opposes South African War	1900.
Fourth election at Carnarvon Boroughs (majority, 296)	October 6, 1900.
Mobbed at Birmingham	December 18, 1901.
Fights Education Bill	1902.

Welsh Education Revolt	1903.
Defies Schools Coercion Act	1904.
President of the Board of Trade	1905.
Fifth election at Carnarvon Boroughs (majority, 1224)	1906.
Settles Railway Strike	1907.
Becomes Chancellor of the Exchequer	April 12, 1908.
Passes Old Age Pensions Act	July 1908.
Visits Germany	August 1908.
Introduces Budget	April 29, 1909.
Thrown out by Lords	November, 1909.
Sixth election at Carnarvon Boroughs (majority, 1,078)	January 1910.
Passes Budget	April 28, 1910.
Becomes member of Party Conference	June-November 1910.
Seventh election at Carnarvon Boroughs (majority, 1,208)	December 1910.
Introduces Insurance Bill	May 4, 1911.
Carries Insurance Bill	December 1911.
Land Campaign	1912-1913.
Great War opens	August 4, 1914.
Becomes Premier	December 1916.
Armistice	November 11, 1918.
General Election	December 14, 1918.
Peace Conference opens	January 18, 1919.
Peace ratified by Parliament	July 21st, 1919.
Peace ratified at Versailles	January 10, 1920.

APPENDIXB THE CRISIS OF DECEMBER, 1916

The Correspondence between Mr. Asquith and Mr. Lloyd George

Memorandum of Mr. Lloyd George to Prime Minister, December 1st, 1916.

War Office, Whitehall, S.W.

1. That the War Committee consist of three members-two of whom must be the First Lord of the Admiralty and the Secretary of State for War, who should have in their offices deputies capable of attending to and deciding all departmental business-and a third Minister without portfolio. One of the three to be Chairman.

2. That the War Committee shall have full powers, subject to the supreme control of the Prime Minister, to direct all questions connected with the war.

3. The Prime Minister, in his discretion, to have the power to refer any question to the Cabinet.

4. Unless the Cabinet, in reference by the Prime Minister, reverses decision of the War Cabinet, that decision to be carried out by the Department concerned.

5. The War Committee to have the power to invite any Minister and to summon the expert advisers and officers of any Department to its meetings.

10 Downing Street, Whitehall, S.W.

January 1st, 1916.

Secret

My dear Lloyd George,

I have now had time to reflect on our conversation this morning, and to study your memorandum.

Though I do not altogether share your dark estimate and forecast of the situation, actual and perspective, I am in complete agreement that we have reached a critical situation in the war, and that our methods of procedure, with the experience which we have gained during the last few months, call for reconsideration and revision.

The two main defects of the War Committee, which has done excellent work, are:

(1) That its numbers are too large.

(2) That there is delay, evasion, and often obstruction on the part of the Departments in giving effect to its decisions.

I might with good reason add (3) that it is often kept in ignorance by the Departments of information, essential and even vital, of a technical kind, upon the problems that come before it: and (4) that it is overcharged with duties, many of which might well be relegated to subordinate bodies.

The result is that I am clearly of opinion that the War Committee should be reconstituted, and its relation to and authority over the Departments be more clearly defined and more effectively asserted.

I come now to your specific proposals.

In my opinion, whatever changes are made in the composition and functions of the War Committee, the Prime Minister must be its Chairman. He cannot be relegated to the position of an arbiter in the background or a referee to the Cabinet.

In regard to its composition, I agree that the War Secretary and the First Lord of the Admiralty are necessary members. I am inclined to add to the same category the Minister of Munitions. There should be another member, either without portfolio or charged only with comparatively light departmental duties. One of the members should be appointed Vice-Chairman.

I purposely do not in this letter discuss the delicate and difficult question of personnel.

The Committee should, as far as possible, sit de die diem, and have full power to see that its decisions (subject to appeal to the Cabinet) are carried out promptly and effectively by the Departments.

The reconstitution of the War Committee should be accompanied by the setting up of a Committee of National Organisation, to deal with the purely domestic side of war problems. It should have executive powers within its own domain.

The Cabinet would in all cases have ultimate authority.

Yours very sincerely,

(Sd.) H. H. Asquith.

10 Downing Street, S.W.

December 4th, 1916.

Secret

My dear Lloyd George,

Such productions as the first leading article in to-day's Times, showing the infinite possibilities for misunderstanding and misrepresentation of such an arrangement as we considered yesterday, make me at least doubtful as to its feasibility. Unless the impression is at once corrected that I am being relegated to the position of an irresponsible spectator of the war, I cannot possibly go on.

The suggested arrangement was to the following effect. The Prime Minister to have supreme and effective control of War Policy.

The agenda of the War Committee will be submitted to him; its Chairman will report to him daily; he can direct it to consider particular topics or proposals; and all its conclusions will be subject to his approval or veto. He can, of course, at his own discretion attend meetings of the Committee.

Yours sincerely,

(Sd.) H. H. Asquith.

War Office, Whitehall, S.W.

December 4th, 1916.

My Dear Prime Minister,

I have not seen the Times' article. But I hope you will not attach undue importance to these effusions. I have had these misrepresentations to put up with for months. Northcliffe frankly wants a smash. Derby and I do not. Northcliffe would like to make this and any other rearrangement under your Premiership impossible. Derby and I attach great importance to your retaining your present position-effectively. I cannot restrain, or, I fear, influence Northcliffe. I fully accept in letter and in spirit your summary of the suggested arrangement-subject, of course, to personnel.

Ever sincerely,

(Sd.) D. Lloyd George.

10 Downing Street, Whitehall, S.W.

December 4th, 1916

Secret

My dear Lloyd George,

Thank you for your letter of this morning.

The King gave me to-day authority to ask and accept the resignation of all my colleagues, and to form a new Government on such lines as I should submit to him. I start therefore with a clean slate.

The first question which I have to consider is the constitution of the new War Committee.

After full consideration of the matter in all its aspects, I have come decidedly to the conclusion that it is not possible that such a Committee could be made workable and effective without the Prime Minister as its Chairman. I quite agree that it will be necessary for him, in view of the other calls upon his time and energy, to delegate from time to time the Chairmanship to another Minister as representative and locum tenens; but (if he is to retain the authority, which corresponds to his responsibility as Prime Minister) he must continue to be, as he always has been, its permanent President. I am satisfied, on reflection, that any other arrangement (such as, for instance, the one which I indicated to you in my letter of to-day) would be found in experience impracticable and incompatible with the retention of the Prime Minister's final and supreme control.

The other question, which you have raised, relates to the personnel of the Committee. Here again, after deliberate consideration, I find myself unable to agree with some of your suggestions. I think we both agree that the First Lord of the Admiralty must, of necessity, be a member of the Committee.

I cannot (as I told you yesterday) be a party to any suggestion that Mr. Balfour should be displaced. The technical side of the Board of Admiralty has been reconstituted, with Sir John Jellicoe as First Sea Lord. I believe Mr. Balfour to be, under existing conditions, the necessary head of the Board.

I must add that Sir Edward Carson (for whom personally and in every other way I have the greatest regard) is not, from the only point of view which is significant to me (namely, the most effective prosecution of the war) the man best qualified among my colleagues present or past to be a member of the War Committee.

I have only to say, in conclusion, that I am strongly of opinion that the War Committee (without any disparagement of the existing Committee, which in my judgment is a most efficient body, and has done and is doing invaluable work) ought to be reduced in number: so that it can sit more frequently, and overtake more easily the daily problems with which it has to deal. But in any reconstruction of the Committee, such as I have, and have for some time past had in view, the governing consideration to my mind is the special capacity of the men who are to sit on it for the work which it has to do.

That is a question which I must reserve for myself to decide.

Yours very sincerely,

(Sd.) H. H. Asquith.

December 5th, 1916.

My dear Prime Minister,

I received your letter with some surprise.

On Friday I made proposals which involved not merely your retention of the Premiership, but the supreme control of the war, whilst the executive functions, subject to that supreme control, were left to others. I thought you then received these suggestions favourably. In fact, you yourself proposed that I should be the Chairman of this Executive Committee, although, as you know, I never put forward that demand. On Saturday you wrote me a letter in which you completely went back on that proposition. You sent for me on Sunday, and put before me other proposals; these proposals you embodied in a letter written on Monday:

"The Prime Minister to have supreme and effective control of war policy.

"The agenda of the War Committee will be submitted to him; its Chairman will report to him daily; he can direct it to consider particular topics or proposals; and all its conclusions will be subject to his approval or veto. He can, of course, at his own discretion, attend meetings of the Committee."

These proposals safeguarded your position and power as Prime Minister in every particular. I immediately wrote you accepting them "in letter and in spirit." It is true that on Sunday I expressed views as to the constitution of the Committee, but these were for discussion. To-day you have gone back on your own proposals.

I have striven my utmost to cure the obvious defects of the War Committee without over-throwing the Government. As you are aware, on several occasions during the last two years I have deemed it my duty to express profound dissatisfaction with the Government's method of conducting the war. Many a time, with the road to victory open in front of us, we have delayed and hesitated whilst the enemy were erecting barriers that finally checked the approach. There has been delay, hesitation, lack of forethought and vision. I have endeavoured repeatedly to warn

the Government of the dangers, both verbally and in written memoranda and letters, which I
crave your leave now to publish if my action is challenged; but I have either failed to secure
decisions or I have secured them when it is too late to avert the evils. The latest illustration is
our lamentable failure to give timely support to Roumania.

I have more than once asked to be released from my responsibility for a policy with which I
was in thorough disagreement, but at your urgent personal request, I remained in the Government. I realise that when the country is in the peril of a great war, Ministers have not the same
freedom to resign on disagreement. At the same time I have always felt-and felt deeply-that
I was in a false position, inasmuch as I could never defend in a whole-hearted manner the
action of a Government of which I was a member. We have thrown away opportunity after
opportunity, and I am convinced, after deep and anxious reflection, that it is my duty to leave
the Government in order to inform the people of the real condition of affairs, and to give them
an opportunity, before it is too late, to save their native land from a disaster which is inevitable
if the present methods are longer persisted in. As all delay is fatal in war, I place my office
without further parley at your disposal.

It is with great personal regret that I have come to this conclusion. In spite of mean and
unworthy insinuations to the contrary-insinuations which I fear are always inevitable in the
case of men who hold prominent but not primary positions in any administration —I have felt
a strong personal attachment to you as my Chief. As you yourself said on Sunday, we have
acted together for ten years and never a quarrel, although we have had many a grave difference
on questions of policy. You have treated me with great courtesy and kindness: for all that I
thank you. Nothing would have induced me to part now except an overwhelming sense that
the course of action which has been pursued has put the country-and not merely the country,
but throughout the world, the principles for which you and I have always stood throughout our
political lives-in the greatest peril that has ever overtaken them.

As I am fully conscious of the importance of preserving national unity, I propose to give
your Government complete support in the vigorous prosecution of the war; but unity without
action is nothing but futile carnage, and I cannot be responsible for that. Vigour and vision
are the supreme need of this hour.

Yours sincerely,

(Sd.) D. Lloyd George.

10 Downing Street, S.W.

December 5th, 1916.

Private

My dear Lloyd George,

I need not tell you that I have read your letter of to-day with much regret.

I do not comment upon it for the moment, except to say that I cannot wholly accept your
account of what passed between us in regard to my connection with the War Committee.

In particular, you have omitted to quote the first and most material part of my letter of
yesterday.

Yours very sincerely,

(Sd.) H. H. Asquith.

In the meantime, I feel sure that you will see the obvious necessity, in the public interest, of
not publishing, at this moment, any part of our correspondence.

War Office, S.W.

December 5th, 1916.

My dear Prime Minister,

I cannot announce my resignation without assigning the reason. Your request that I should
not publish the correspondence that led up to and necessitated it places me therefore in an embarrassing and unfair position. I must give reasons for the grave step I have taken. If you forbid
publication of the correspondence, do you object to my stating in another form my version of
the causes that led to my resigning?

Yours sincerely,

(Sd.) D. Lloyd George.

As to the first part of your letter, the publication of the letter would cover the whole ground.

10 Downing Street, S.W.

December 5th, 1916.

My dear Lloyd George,

It may make a difference to you (in reply to your last letter) if I tell you at once that I have tendered my resignation to the King. In any case, I should deprecate in the public interest the publication in its present form at this moment of your letter to me of this morning.

Of course, I have neither the power nor the wish to prevent your stating in some other form the causes which led you to take the step which you have taken.

Yours very sincerely,

(Sd.) H. H. Asquith.

APPENDIXC THE PEACE CONFERENCE

Bullitt Exhibit No. 14

McD. I.C. 114. Secretaries' notes of a conversation held in M. Pichon's room, at the Quai D'Orsay, on Tuesday, January 21st, 1919, at 15 hours (3 p.m.).

Present:

United States of America. —President Wilson, Mr. R. Lansing, Mr. A. H. Frazier, Colonel U. S. Grant, Mr. L. Harrison.

British Empire. —The Right Hon. D. Lloyd George, the Right Hon. A. J. Balfour, Lieut.-Col. Sir M. P. A. Hankey, K.C.B., Major A. M. Caccia, M.V.O., Mr. E. Phipps.

France. —M. Clemenceau, M. Pichon, M. Dutasta, H. Berthelot, Captain A. Potier.

Italy. —Signor Orlando, H. E. Baron Sonnino, Count Aldrovandi, Major A. Jones.

Japan. —Baron Makino, H. E. M. Matsui, M. Saburi.

Interpreter. —Prof. P. J. Mantoux.

M. Clemenceau said they had met together to decide what could be done in Russia under present circumstances.

President Wilson said that, in order to have something definite to discuss, he wished to take advantage of a suggestion made by Mr. Lloyd George, and to propose a modification of the British proposal. He wished to suggest that the various organised groups in Russia should be asked to send representatives, not to Paris, but to some other place, such as Salonika, convenient of approach, there to meet such representatives as might be appointed by the Allies, in order to see if they could draw up a programme upon which agreement could be reached.

Mr. Lloyd George pointed out that the advantage of this would be that they could be brought there from Russia through the Black Sea without passing through other countries.

M. Sonnino said that some of the representatives of the various Governments were already here in Paris, for example, M. Sazonoff. Why should not these be heard?

President Wilson expressed the view that the various parties should not be heard separately. It would be very desirable to get all these representatives in one place, and still better, all in one room, in order to obtain a close comparison of views.

Mr. Balfour said that a further objection to M. Sonnino's plan was that if M. Sazonoff was heard in Paris it would be difficult to hear the others in Paris also, and M. Clemenceau objected strongly to having some of these representatives in Paris.

M. Sonnino explained that all the Russian parties had some representatives here, except the Soviets, whom they did not wish to hear.

Mr. Lloyd George remarked that the Bolshevists were the very people some of them wished to hear.

M. Sonnino continuing, said that they had heard M. Litvinoff's statements that morning.

(That was the statement that Litvinoff had made to Buckler, which the President had read to the council of ten that morning.)

The Allies were now fighting against the Bolshevists, who were their enemies, and therefore they were not obliged to hear them with the others.

Mr. Balfour remarked that the essence of President Wilson's proposal was that the parties must all be heard at one and the same time.

Mr. Lloyd George expressed the view that the acceptance of M. Sonnino's proposals would amount to their hearing a string of people, all of whom held the same opinion, and all of whom would strike the same note. But they would not hear the people who at the present moment were actually controlling European Russia. In deference to M. Clemenceau's views they had put forward this new proposal. He thought it would be quite safe to bring the Bolshevist representatives to Salonika, or perhaps to Lemnos. It was absolutely necessary to endeavour to make peace. The report read by President Wilson that morning went to show that the Bolshevists were not convinced of the error of their ways, but they apparently realised the folly of their present methods. Therefore they were endeavouring to come to terms.

President Wilson asked to be permitted to urge one aspect of the case. As M. Sonnino had implied, they were all repelled by Bolshevism, and for that reason they had placed armed men in opposition to them. One of the things that was clear in the Russian situation was that, by opposing Bolshevism with arms, they were in reality serving the cause of Bolshevism. The Allies were making it possible for the Bolsheviks to argue that Imperialistic and Capitalistic Governments were endeavouring to exploit the country and to give the land back to the landlords, and so bring about a reaction. If it could be shown that this was not true, and that the Allies were prepared to deal with the rulers of Russia, much of the moral force of this argument would disappear. The allegations that the Allies were against the people, and wanted to control their affairs, provided the argument which enabled them to raise armies. If, on the other hand, the Allies could swallow their pride and the natural repulsion which they felt for the Bolshevists, and see the representatives of all organised groups in one place, he thought it would bring about a marked reaction against Bolshevism.

M. Clemenceau said that in principle he did not favour conversation with the Bolshevists, not because they were criminals, but because we would be raising them to our level by saying that they were worthy of entering into conversation with us. The Bolshevist danger was very great at the present moment. It had invaded the Baltic provinces and Poland, and that very morning they received bad news regarding its spread to Buda-Pesth and Vienna. Italy, also, was in danger. The danger was probably greater there than in France. If Bolshevism, after spreading to Germany, were to traverse Austria and Hungary, and so reach Italy, Europe would be faced with a very great danger. Therefore, something must be done against Bolshevism. When listening to the document presented by President Wilson that morning, he had been struck by the cleverness with which the Bolshevists were attempting to lay a trap for the Allies. When the Bolshevists first came into power, a breach was made with the Capitalist Government on questions of principle, but now they offered funds and concessions as a basis for treating with them. He need not say how valueless their promises were, but, if they were listened to, the Bolshevists would go back to their people and say, "We offered them great principles of justice, and the Allies would have nothing to do with us. Now we offer money, and they are ready to make peace."

He admitted his remarks did not offer a solution. The great misfortune was that the Allies were in need of a speedy solution. After four years of war, and the losses and sufferings they had incurred, their populations could stand no more. Russia also was in need of immediate peace. But its necessary evolution must take time. The signing of the world's peace could not await Russia's final avatar. Had time been available, he would suggest waiting, for eventually sound men representing common sense would come to the top. But when would that be? He could make no forecast. Therefore they must press for an early solution.

To sum up, had he been acting by himself, he would temporise and erect barriers to prevent Bolshevism from spreading. But he was not alone, and in the presence of his colleagues he felt compelled to make some concession, as it was essential that there should not be even the appearance of disagreement amongst them. The concession came easier after hearing President Wilson's suggestions. He thought they should make a very clear and convincing appeal to all reasonable peoples, emphatically stating that they did not wish in any way to interfere in the internal affairs of Russia, and especially that they had no intention of restoring Czardom. The object of the Allies being to hasten the creation of a strong Government, they proposed to call together representatives of all parties to a conference. He would beg President Wilson to draft a paper, fully explaining the position of the Allies to the whole world, including the Russians and the Germans.

Mr. Lloyd George agreed, and gave notice that he wished to withdraw his own motion in favour of President Wilson's.

Mr. Balfour said that he understood that all these people were to be asked on an equality. On these terms he thought the Bolshevists would refuse, and by their refusal they would put themselves in a very bad position.

M. Sonnino said that he did not agree that the Bolshevists would not come. He thought they would be the first to come, because they would be eager to put themselves on an equality with the others. He would remind his colleagues that, before the Peace of Brest-Litovsk was signed, the Bolshevists promised all sorts of things, such as to refrain from propaganda, but since that peace had been concluded they had broken all their promises, their one idea being to spread revolution in all other countries. His idea was to collect together all the anti-Bolshevist parties, and help them to make a strong Government, provided they pledged themselves not to serve the forces of reaction, and especially not to touch the land question, thereby depriving the Bolshevists of their strongest argument. Should they take these pledges, he would be prepared to help them.

Mr. Lloyd George enquired how this help would be given.

M. Sonnino replied that help would be given with soldiers to a reasonable degree or by supplying arms, food and money. For instance, Poland asked for weapons, and munitions; the Ukraine asked for weapons. All the Allies wanted was to establish a strong Government. The reason that no strong Government at present existed was that no party could risk taking the offensive against Bolshevism without the assistance of the Allies. He would enquire how the parties of order could possibly succeed without the assistance of the Allies. President Wilson had said that they should put aside all pride in the matter. He would point out that for Italy, and probably for France also, as M. Clemenceau had stated, it was in reality a question of self-defence. He thought that even a partial recognition of the Bolshevists would strengthen their position, and, speaking for himself, he thought that Bolshevism was already a serious danger in his country.

Mr. Lloyd George said he wished to put one or two practical questions to M. Sonnino. The British Empire now had some 15,000 to 20,000 men in Russia. M. de Scavenius had estimated that some 150,000 additional men would be required, in order to keep the anti-Bolshevist Governments from dissolution. And General Franchet d'Esperey also insisted on the necessity of Allied assistance. Now Canada had decided to withdraw her troops, because the Canadian soldiers would not agree to stay and fight against the Russians. Similar trouble had also occurred amongst the other Allied troops. And he felt certain that, if the British tried to send any more troops there, there would be mutiny.

M. Sonnino suggested that volunteers might be called for.

Mr. Lloyd George, continuing, said that it would be impossible to raise 150,000 in that way. He asked, however, what contributions America, Italy, and France would make towards the raising of this army.

President Wilson and M. Clemenceau each said none.

M. Orlando agreed that Italy could make no further contributions.

Mr. Lloyd George said that the Bolshevists had an army of 300,000 men, who would, before long, be good soldiers, and to fight them at least 400,000 Russian soldiers would be required. Who would feed, equip, and pay them? Would Italy, or America, or France do so? If they were unable to do that, what would be the good of fighting Bolshevism? It could not be crushed by speeches. He sincerely trusted that they would accept President Wilson's proposal as it now stood.

M. Orlando agreed that the question was a very difficult one for the reasons that had been fully given. He agreed that Bolshevism constituted a grave danger to all Europe. To prevent a contagious epidemic from spreading, the sanitarians set up a cordon sanitaire. If similar measures could be taken against Bolshevism, in order to prevent its spreading, it might be overcome, since to isolate it meant vanquishing it. Italy was now passing through a period of depression, due to war weariness. But Bolshevists could never triumph there, unless they found a favourable medium, such as might be produced either by a profound patriotic disappointment in their expectations as to the rewards of the war, or by an economic crisis. Either might lead to revolution, which was equivalent to Bolshevism. Therefore, he would insist that all possible measures should be taken to set up this cordon. Next, he suggested the consideration of repressive measures. He thought two methods were possible: either the use of physical force or the use of moral force. He thought Mr. Lloyd George's objection to the use of physical force unanswerable. The occupation of Russia meant the employment of troops for an indefinite period of time. This meant an apparent prolongation of the war. There remained the use of moral force. He agreed with M. Clemenceau that no country could continue in anarchy, and that an end must eventually come; but they could not wait-they could not proceed to make peace and ignore Russia. Therefore, Mr. Lloyd George's proposal, with the modifications introduced after careful consideration by President Wilson and M. Clemenceau, gave a possible solution. It did not involve entering into negotiations with the Bolshevists; the proposal was merely an attempt to bring together all the parties in Russia with a view to finding a way out of the present difficulty. He was prepared, therefore, to support it.

President Wilson asked for the views of his Japanese colleagues.

Baron Makino said that after carefully considering the various points of view put forward, he had no objections to make regarding the conclusions reached. He thought that was the best solution under the circumstances. He wished, however, to enquire what attitude would be taken by the representatives of the Allied Powers if the Bolshevists accepted the invitation to the meeting, and there insisted upon their principles. He thought they should under no circumstances countenance Bolshevist ideas. The conditions in Siberia east of the Baikal had greatly improved. The objects which had necessitated the despatch of troops to that region had been attained. Bolshevism was no longer aggressive, though it might still persist in a latent form. In conclusion, he wished to support the proposal before the meeting.

President Wilson expressed the view that the emissaries of the Allied Powers should not be authorised to adopt any definite attitude towards Bolshevism. They should merely report back to their Governments the conditions found.

Mr. Lloyd George asked that that question be further considered. He thought the emissaries of the Allied Powers should be able to establish an agreement if they were able to find a solution. For instance, if they succeeded in reaching an agreement on the subject of the organisation of a Constituent Assembly, they should be authorised to accept such a compromise without the delay of a reference to the Governments.

President Wilson suggested that the emissaries might be furnished with a body of instructions.

Mr. Balfour expressed the view that abstention from hostile action against their neighbours should be made a condition of their sending representatives to this meeting.

President Wilson agreed.

M. Clemenceau suggested that the manifesto to the Russian parties should be based solely on humanitarian grounds. They should say to the Russians, "You are threatened by famine; we are prompted by humanitarian feelings, we are making peace; we do not want people to die. We are prepared to see what can be done to remove the menace of starvation." He thought the Russians would at once prick up their ears, and be prepared to hear what the Allies had to say. They would add that food cannot be sent unless peace and order were re-established. It should, in fact, be made quite clear that the representatives of all parties would merely be brought together for purely humane reasons.

Mr. Lloyd George said that in this connection he wished to invite attention to a doubt expressed by certain of the delegates of the British Dominions, namely, whether there would be enough food and credit to go round, should an attempt be made to feed all Allied countries, and enemy countries, and Russia also. The export of so much food would inevitably have the effect of raising food prices in Allied countries, and so create discontent and Bolshevism. As regards grain, Russia had always been an exporting country, and there was evidence to show that plenty of food at present existed in the Ukraine.

President Wilson said that his information was that enough food existed in Russia, but either on account of its being hoarded or on account of difficulties of transportation, it could not be made available.

It was agreed that President Wilson should draft a proclamation, for consideration at the next meeting, inviting all organised parties in Russia to attend a meeting to be held at some selected place such as Salonika or Lemnos, in order to discuss with the representatives of the Allied and Associated Great Powers the means of restoring order and peace in Russia. Participation in the meeting should be conditional on a cessation of hostilities.